The Life of George Washington

The Life of George Washington

David Ramsay

WAKING LION PRESS

The views expressed in this book are the responsibility of the author and do not necessarily represent the position of the publisher. The reader alone is responsible for the use of any ideas or information provided by this book.

ISBN 978-1-4341-0263-8

Published by Waking Lion Press, an imprint of The Editorium

Any additions to original text (publisher's preface, editor's notes, etc.) © 2008 by The Editorium. All rights reserved. Printed in the United States of America.

Waking Lion Press™, the Waking Lion Press logo, and The Editorium™ are trademarks of The Editorium, LLC

The Editorium, LLC
West Valley City, UT 84128-3917
wakinglionpress.com
wakinglion@editorium.com

Contents

Foreword   ix

1 Of George Washington's birth, family, and education—Of his mission to the French commandant on the Ohio in 1753—His military operations as an officer of Virginia, from 1754 to 1758, and his subsequent employments to the commencement of the American Revolution.   1

2 Retrospect of the origin of the revolutionary war—Of George Washington as member of Congress, in 1774 and 1775—As Commander in Chief of the armies of the United Colonies in 1775 and 1776, and his operations near Boston, in these years.   13

3 The Campaign of 1776: Of the operations of General Washington in New-York and New-Jersey. The battle on Long Island. The retreat from York Island and through Jersey. The battles of Trenton and Princeton.   22

4 The Campaign of 1776: Of the operations of General Washington in New-Jersey and Pennsylvania, in the campaign of 1777. The battles of Brandywine and German-Town. Washington is advised by the Rev. Jacob Duche, to give up the contest. The distresses of the American army. Its winter quarters in Valley Forge. Gen. Washington is assailed by the clamours of discontented individuals and public bodies, and by the designs of a faction to supersede him in his office as commander in chief.   37

5 The Campaign of 1778: General Washington prepares for the campaign of 1778. Surprises the British, and defeats them at Monmouth. Arrests General Lee. Calms the irritation excited by the departure of the French fleet from Rhode Island to Boston. Dissuades from an invasion of Canada.   52

Contents

6 The Campaign of 1779: The distresses of the American army. Gen. Washington calms the uneasiness in the Jersey line. Finds great difficulty in supporting his troops and concentrating their force. Makes a disposition of them with a view to the security of West Point. Directs an expedition against the Six Nations of Indians, and for the reduction of Stony Point Paules Hook taken. A French fleet, expected to the northward, arrives on the coast of Georgia. Washington, unequal to offensive operations, retires into winter quarters. 63

7 The Campaign of 1780: Gen. Washington directs an expedition against Staten Island. Gives an opinion against risking an army for the defence of Charleston, S.C. Finds great difficulty in supporting his army. Kniphausen invades Jersey, but is prevented from injuring the American stores. Marquis de la Fayette arrives, and gives assurances that a French fleet and army might soon be expected on the American coast. Energetic measures of co-operation resolved upon, but so languidly executed, that Washington predicts the necessity of a more efficient system of national government. A French fleet and army arrives, and a combined operation against New-York is resolved upon, but the arrival of a superior British fleet, deranges the whole plan. 72

8 The Campaign of 1781: The Pennsylvania line mutinies. The Jersey troops follow their example, but are quelled by decisive measures. Gen. Washington commences a military journal, detailing the wants and distresses of his army. Is invited to the defence of his native state, Virginia, but declines. Reprimands the manager of his private estate for furnishing the enemy with supplies, to prevent the destruction of his property. Extinguishes the incipient flames of a civil war, respecting the independence of the state of Vermont. Plans a combined operation against the British, and deputes Lieut. Col. John Laurens to solicit the co-operation of the French. The combined forces of both nations rendezvous in the Chesapeak, and take lord Cornwallis and his army prisoners of war. Washington returns to the vicinity of New York, and urges the necessity of preparing for a new campaign. 82

Contents

9   1782 and 1783: Prospects of peace. Languor of the states. Discontents of the army. Gen. Washington prevents the adoption of rash measures. Some new levies in Pennsylvania mutiny, and are quelled. Washington recommends measures for the preservation of independence, peace, liberty, and happiness. Dismisses his army. Enters New-York. Takes leave of his officers. Settles his accounts. Repairs to Annapolis. Resigns his commission. Retires to Mount Vernon, and resumes his agricultural pursuits.   97

10 General Washington, on retiring from public life devotes himself to agricultural pursuits. Favours inland navigation. Declines offered emoluments from it. Urges an alteration of the fundamental rules of the society of the Cincinnati. Regrets the defects of the Federal system, and recommends a revisal of it. Is appointed a member of the continental convention for that purpose, which, after hesitation, he accepts. Is chosen President thereof. Is solicited to accept the Presidency of the United States. Writes sundry letters expressive of the conflict in his mind, between duty and inclination. Answers applicants for offices. His reluctance to enter on public life.   124

11 President Washington: Washington elected president. On his way to the seat of government at New-York, receives the most flattering marks of respect. Addresses Congress. The situation of the United States in their foreign and domestic relations, at the inauguration of Washington. Fills up offices solely with a view to the public good. Proposes a treaty to the Creek Indians, which is at first rejected. Col. Willet induces the heads of the nation 'to come New-York, to treat there. The North-Western Indians refuse a treaty, but after defeating Generals Harmar and Sinclair, they are defeated by Gen. Wayne. They then submit, and agree to treat. A new system is introduced for meliorating their condition.   139

Contents

12 President Washington: Gen. Washington attends to the foreign relations of the United States. Negotiates with Spain. Difficulties in the way. The free navigation of the Mississippi is granted by a treaty made with Major Pinckney. Negotiations with Britain. Difficulties in the way. War probable. Mr. Jay's mission. His treaty with Great-Britain. Opposition thereto. Is ratified. Washington refuses papers to House of Representatives. British posts in United States evacuated. Negotiations with France. Genet's arrival. Assumes illegal powers, in violation of the neutrality of the United States. Is flattered by the people, but opposed by the executive. Is recalled. Gen. Pinckney sent as public minister to adjust disputes with France. Is not received. Washington declines a re-election, and addresses the people. His last address to the national legislature. Recommends a navy, a military academy, and other public institutions. 152

13 Washington Retires: Washington rejoices at the prospect of retiring. Writes to the Secretary of State, denying the authenticity of letters said to be From him to J.P. Custis and Lund Washington, in 1776. Pays Respect to his successor, Mr. John Adams. Review of Washington's Administration. He retires to Mount Vernon. Resumes agricultural Pursuits. Hears with regret the aggression of the French republic. Corresponds on the subject of his taking the command of an army To oppose the French. Is appointed Lieutenant-General. His commission Is sent to him by the Secretary of War. His letter to President Adams on The receipt thereof. Directs the organization of the proposed army. Three Envoys Extraordinary sent to France, who adjust all disputes with Bonaparte, after the overthrow of the Directory. Gen. Washington dies. Is honoured by Congress, and by the citizens. His character 183

14 Reflections on Washington's life and death 193

Foreword

David Ramsay was a contemporary of George Washington. Ramsay was born in Pennsylvania seventeen years after Washington; as an adult he moved to Charleston, South Carolina, where he became a physician.

During the Revolutionary War years (1776–83), he served as a member of the South Carolina legislature. When the British threatened Charleston in 1780, he assisted the South Carolina militia as a field surgeon. Unfortunately, when the city was captured, Ramsay was caught as well, and he was held in a Florida prison for nearly a year.

After his release in a prisoner exchange in 1781, he was elected to the Congress of the Confederation (the official name of Congress under the Articles of Confederation), where he served from 1782 to 1783 and from 1785 to 1786. When John Hancock was absent from the meetings of the Congress in 1785–86, David Ramsay served as acting president of the Congress. Later he served in the South Carolina state senate (1801–15), including as president of the senate for many years.

In addition to his accomplishments in medicine (he had a large practice) and in politics, Ramsay became widely known as a historian. In 1785 he published a two-volume *History of the Revolution in South Carolina;* in 1789, a two-volume *History of the American Revolution;* and in 1809, a two-volume *History of South Carolina.* In 1788 he published a pamphlet arguing in favor of the ratification of the new Constitution, *An Address to the Freemen of Carolina.* He also published a three-volume *History of the United States,* which was published posthumously (1816–17). The present volume was published in 1807, less than a decade after the death of George Washington. Ramsay's books were generally received well both by reader and reviewers, and historians regard them as providing a helpful window into the times.

In his personal life, Ramsay experienced much sadness. In addition to his imprisonment by the British, his marriage to his first wife, Sabina Ellis, ended with her death after only sixteen months; his second wife, Frances Witherspoon, died in childbirth after they had been married only twenty-one months. Fortunately, his third marriage, to Martha Laurens, lasted some twenty-five years.

Ramsay's life ended tragically in May 1815, when he was shot in Charleston, South Carolina, by a mentally deranged man.

Prominent Connections

David Ramsay was well acquainted with some of the most prominent men of his time. His second father-in-law, John Witherspoon, was the president of the College of New Jersey (now Princeton University) and one of the signers of the Declaration of Independence. His third father-in-law, Henry Laurens, became a president of the Confederation Congress. A brother-in-law, Charles Pinckney, was a member of the Continental Congress, a delegate to the Constitutional Convention, governor of South Carolina, and eventually a member of the United States Congress.

David's older brother, Nathaniel, was an officer in the Revolutionary War, serving under George Washington. Later he served as a delegate to the Confederation Congress, representing New York.

Serving with David Ramsay in the two sessions of the Congress to which he was elected were such bright lights as

Oliver Ellsworth (participant in the Constitutional Convention and later chief justice of the Supreme Court),

Alexander Hamilton (officer in the Revolutionary War, participant in the Constitutional Convention, coauthor of the *Federalist Papers*, and the nation's first Secretary of the Treasury),

Thomas Mifflin (general during the Revolutionary War, a president of the Confederation Congress, participant in the Constitutional Convention, and governor of Pennsylvania),

James Monroe (later governor of Virginia, Secretary of State, Secretary of War, and President of the United States),

John Rutledge (signer of the Declaration of Independence, governor of South Carolina, participant in the Constitutional Convention, and chief justice of the Supreme Court),

James Wilson (signer of the Declaration of Independence, participant in the Constitutional Convention, and one of the first six justices of the Supreme Court),

Oliver Wolcott (signer of the Declaration of Independence, general in the Revolutionary War, and governor of Connecticut).

Also in those sessions of Congress were other men who were well known and much accomplished, including Elias Boudinot (a president of the Confederation Congress), Abraham Clark (signer of the Declaration of Independence), Thomas Fitzsimons (participant in the Constitutional Convention), Nathaniel Gorham (a president of the Confederation Congress and participant in the Constitutional Convention), William Samuel Johnson (participant in the Constitutional Convention and president of Columbia University), and Hugh Williamson (participant in the Constitutional Convention).

One of Ramsay's mentors was Benjamin Rush, a signer of the Declaration of Independence and delegate to the Continental Congress. Rush was on the faculty of the medical school at the College of Philadelphia, where Ramsay studied to be a doctor. When Ramsay graduated, Rush said that Ramsay was "far superior to any person we ever graduated at our college; his abilities are not only good, but great; his talents and knowledge are universal; I never saw so much strength of memory and imagination, united to so fine a judgment." (From Robert Y. Hayne, "Biographical Memoir of David Ramsay, M.D.," Analectic Magazine, 6 [1815]: 206.)

The Biography of George Washington

Not all biographies are created equal. Some George Washington biographies from the past fifty years have utilized careful research and the latest approaches of scholarship. Some have sought to look deep within Washington's psyche to try to understand his motivations. But a biography written by a contemporary is priceless.

David Ramsay walked the same roads in the same time period as George Washington did. Both partook of the same customs and both experienced life in generally the same way. Both heard the same debates at the same time. Both felt the same spirit of the times. Both were strong advocates of federalism, the mindset that for America to succeed, the colonies needed to view themselves as *one* country, rather than thirteen joined in loose confederation.

Further, David Ramsay had easy access to contemporary records, including the official records of the Continental Congress, and he likewise had access to interviews with prominent figures in the life of George Washington, particularly through correspondence. Although David knew many people who had personal dealings with George Washington (including his brother, Nathaniel), there appears to be no evidence that David Ramsay and George Washington ever met.

Foreword

This biography is not a particularly detailed or in-depth look at the Father of Our Country. But it does provide a wonderful overview of his life—as well as a feeling for the spirit of the man.

If you desire a biography told from the point of view of a man who was there, you probably could do no better than David Ramsay's *The Life of George Washington*.

JAY A. PARRY
Author, *The Real George Washington:
The True Story of America's Most Indispensable Man*

1

Of George Washington's birth, family, and education—Of his mission to the French commandant on the Ohio in 1753—His military operations as an officer of Virginia, from 1754 to 1758, and his subsequent employments to the commencement of the American Revolution.

The ancestors of George Washington were among the first settlers of the oldest British colony in America. He was the third in descent from John Washington, an English gentleman, who about the middle of the 17th century emigrated from the north of England, and settled in Westmoreland county, Virginia. In the place where he had fixed himself, his great grandson, the subject of the following history, was born on the 22d of February, 1732. His immediate ancestor was Augustine Washington, who died when his son George was only ten years old.

The education of the young orphan, or course, devolved on his mother, who added one to the many examples of virtuous matrons, who, devoting themselves to the care of their children, have trained them up to be distinguished citizens. In one instance her fears, combining with her affection, prevented a measure, which, if persevered in, would have given a direction to the talents and views of her son, very different form that which laid the foundation of his fame.

George Washington, when only fifteen years old, solicited and obtained the place of a midshipman in the British navy; but his ardent zeal to serve his country, then at war with France and Spain, was, on the interference of his mother, for the present suspended, and for ever diverted from the sea service. She lived to see him acquire higher honours than he ever could have obtained as a naval officer; nor did she depart this life till he was elevated to the first offices, both civil and military, in the gift of his country. She was, nevertheless, from the influence of long established habits, so far from being partial to the American revolution, that she often regretted the side her son had taken in the controversy between her king and her country.

In the minority of George Washington, the means of education in America were scanty; his was therefore very little extended beyond what is common, except in mathematics. Knowledge of this kind contributes more perhaps than any other to strengthen the mind. In his case it was doubly useful; for, in the early part of his life, it laid the foundation of his fortune, by qualifying him for the office of a practical surveyor, at a time when good land was of easy attainment; and its intimate connexion with the military art, enabled him at a later period to judge more correctly of the proper means of defending his country, when he was called upon to preside over its armies.

Of the first nineteen years of George Washington's life, little is known. His talents being more solid than showy, were not sufficiently developed for public notice, by the comparatively unimportant events of that early period. His contemporaries have generally reported, that in his youth he was grave, silent, and thoughtful; diligent and methodical in business, dignified in his appearance, and strictly honourable in all his deportment; but they have not been able to gratify the public curiosity with any striking anecdotes.

His patrimonial estate was small, but that little was managed with prudence and increased by industry. In the gayest period of his life, he was a stranger to dissipation and riot. That he had established a solid reputation, even in his juvenile years, may be fairly presumed from the following circumstances. At the age of nineteen he was appointed one of the adjutants general of Virginia, with the rank of major. When he was barely twenty-one, he was employed by the government of his native colony, in an enterprise which required the prudence of age as well as the vigour of youth.

The French, as the first European discoverers of the river Missisippi, claimed all that immense region whose waters run into that river. In pursuance of the claim, in the year 1753, they took possession of a tract of country supposed to be within the chartered limits of Virginia, and were proceeding to erect a chain of posts from the lakes of Canada to the river Ohio, in subserviency to their grand scheme of connecting Canada with Louisiana, and limiting the English colonies to the east of the Alleghany mountains.

Mr. Dinwiddie, then governor of Virginia, dispatched Washington with a letter to the French commandant on the Ohio, remonstrating against the prosecution of these designs, as hostile to the rights of his Britannic majesty. The young envoy was also instructed to penetrate the designs of

Birth, family, education, and employment

the French; to conciliate the affection of the native tribes; and to procure useful intelligence.

In the discharge of the trust, he set out on the 15th of November, from Will's Creek, then an extreme frontier settlement, and pursued his course through a vast extent of unexplored wilderness, amidst rains and snows and over rivers of very difficult passage, and among tribes of Indians, several of whom, from previous attentions of the French, were hostile to the English. When his horses were incompetent, he proceeded on foot with a gun in his hand and a pack on his back.

He observed everything with the eye of a soldier, and particularly designated the forks of the Monongahela and Alleghany river, (the spot where Fort Duquesne was afterwards built, and where Pittsburgh now stands) as an advantageous position for a fortress. Here he secured the affections of some neighbouring Indians, and engaged them to accompany him. With them; he ascended the Alleghany river and French Creek, to a fort on the river le Boeuf, one of its western branches. He there found Mons. Le Gardeur de St. Pierre, the commandant on the Ohio, and delivered to him Dinwiddie's letter; and receiving his answer, returned with it to Williamsburg on the 78th day after he had received his appointment.

The patience and firmness displayed on this occasion by Washington, (added to his judicious treatment of the Indians) both merited and obtained a large share of applause. A journal of the whole was published, and inspired the public with high ideas of the energies both of his body and mind.

The French were too intent on their favourite project of extending their empire in America, to be diverted from it by the remonstrances of a colonial governor. The answer brought by Washington was such as induced the assembly of Virginia to raise a regiment of 300 men, to defend their frontiers and maintain the right claimed in behalf of Great-Britain over the disputed territory. Of this Mr. Fry was appointed colonel, and George Washington, lieutenant-colonel. The latter advanced with two companies of this regiment early in April, as far as the Great Meadows, where he was informed by some friendly Indians, that the French were erecting fortifications in the fork between the Alleghany and Monongahela rivers; and also, that a detachment was on its march from that place towards the Great Meadows.

War had not been yet formally declared between France and England, but as neither was disposed to recede from their claims to the lands on the Ohio, it was deemed inevitable, and on the point of commencing. Several circumstances were supposed to indicate an hostile intention on the part of the advancing French detachment. Washington, under the

Birth, family, education, and employment

guidance of some friendly Indians, in a dark rainy night surprised their encampment, and, after firing once, rushed in and surrounded them. The commanding officer, Mr. Jumonville, was killed, one person escaped, and all the rest immediately surrendered.

Soon after this affair, Col. Fry died, and the command of the regiment devolved on Washington, who speedily collected the whole at the Great Meadows. Two independent companies of regulars, one from New York, and one from South Carolina, shortly after arrived at the same place. Col. Washington was now at the head of nearly 400 men.

A stockade, afterwards called Fort Necessity, was erected at the Great Meadows, in which a small force was left, and the main body advanced with a view of dislodging the French from Fort Duquesne, which they had recently erected, at the confluence of the Alleghany and Monongahela rivers. They had not proceeded more than thirteen miles, when they were informed by some friendly Indians, "that the French, as numerous as pigeons in the woods, were advancing in an hostile manner towards the English settlements, and also, that Fort Duquesne had been recently and strongly reinforced."

In this critical situation, a council of war unanimously recommended a retreat to the Great Meadows, which was effected without delay, and every exertion made to render Fort Necessity tenable. Before the works intended for that purpose were completed, Mons. de Villier, with a considerable force, attacked the fort. The assailants were covered by trees and high grass. The Americans received them with great resolution, and fought some within the stockade, and others in the surrounding ditch. Washington continued the whole day on the outside of the fort, and conducted the defense with the greatest coolness and intrepidity. The engagement lasted from ten in the morning till night, when the French commander demanded a parley, and offered terms of capitulation. His first and second proposals were rejected; and Washington would accept of none short of the following honourable ones, which were mutually agreed upon in the course of the night. "The fort to be surrendered on condition that the garrison should march out with the honours of war, and be permitted to retain their arms and baggage, and to march unmolested into the inhabited parts of Virginia."

The legislature of Virginia, impressed with a high sense of the bravery and good conduct of their troops, though compelled to surrender the fort, voted their thanks to Col. Washington and the officers under his command, and they also gave three hundred pistoles to be distributed among the soldiers engaged in this action, but made no arrangements for renewing offensive operations in the remainder of the year 1754. When the season for action was over, the regiment was reduced to independent companies, and Washington resigned his command.

The controversy about the Ohio lands, which began in Virginia, was taken up very seriously by Great-Britain, and two British regiments were sent to America to support the claims of his Britannic majesty. They arrived early in 1755, and were commanded by Gen. Braddock. That officer, being informed of the talents of George Washington, invited him to serve the campaign as a volunteer aid de camp. The invitation was cheerfully accepted, and Washington joined Gen. Braddock near Alexandria, and proceeded with him to Will's Creek, afterwards called Fort Cumberland. Here the army was detained till the 12th of June, waiting for waggons, horses, and provisions.

Washington had early recommended the use of pack horses, instead of waggons, for conveying the baggage of the army. The propriety of this advice soon became apparent, and a considerable change was made in conformity to it. The army had not advanced much more than ten miles from Fort Cumberland, when Washington was seized with a violent fever, but nevertheless continued with the army, being conveyed in a covered waggon, after he had refused to stay behind, though so much exhausted as to be unable to ride on horseback. He advised the general to leave his heavy artillery and baggage behind, and to advance rapidly to Fort Duquesne, with a select body of troops, a few necessary stores, and some pieces of light artillery.

Hopes were indulged that by this expeditious movement, Fort Duquesne might be reached in its present weak state, with a force sufficient to reduce it, before expected reinforcements should arrive. General Braddock approved the scheme, and submitted it to the consideration of a council held at the Little Meadows, which recommended that the commander in chief advance as rapidly as possible with 1200 select men, and that Col. Dunbar should remain behind with the remainder of the troops and the heavy baggage. This advanced corps commenced its march only 30 carriages, but did not proceed with the rapidity that was expected. They frequently halted to level the road, and to build bridges over inconsiderable brooks. They consumed four days in passing over the first nineteen miles from the Little Meadows. At this place, the physicians declared that Col.Washington's life would be endangered by advancing with the army. He was therefore ordered by Gen. Braddock stay behind with a small guard till Dunbar should arrive with the rear of the army. As soon as his strength would permit, he joined the advanced detachment, and immediately entered on the duties his office. On the next day, July 9th, a dreadful scene took place. When Braddock had crossed the Monongahela, and was only a few miles from Fort Duquesne, and was pressing forward without any apprehension danger, he was attacked in an open thick set with grass. An invisible enemy, consisting of French and Indians, commenced a heavy and well directed fire on his uncovered troops. The van fell back on the main body, and the whole was thrown into disorder. Marksmen levelled their pieces particularly at officers, and others on horseback. In a short time, Washington was the only aid de camp left alive and not wounded. On him, therefore, devolved the whole duty of carrying out the general's orders. He was of course obliged to be constantly in motion, traversing the field of battle on horseback in all directions. He had two horses shot under him, and four bullets passed through his coat, but he escaped unhurt, though every other officer on horseback was either killed or wounded.

Providence preserved him for further and greater services. Throughout the whole of the carnage and confusion of this fatal day, Washington displayed the greatest coolness and the most perfect self possession. Braddock was undismayed amidst a shower of bullets, and by his countenance and example, encouraged his men to stand their ground; but valour was useless, and discipline only offered surer marks to the destructive aim of unseen marksmen. Unacquainted with the Indian mode of fighting, Braddock neither advanced upon nor retreated from the assailants, but very injudiciously endeavored to form his broken troops on the ground where they were first attacked, and where they were exposed uncovered to the incessant galling fire of a sheltered enemy.

He had been cautioned of the danger to which he was exposed, and was advised to advance the provincials in front of his troops, to scour the woods and detect ambuscades, but he disregarded the salutary recommendation. The action lasted near three hours, in the course of which the general had three horses shot under him, and finally received a wound, of which he died in a few days in the camp of Dunbar, to which he had been brought by Col. Washington and others.

On the fall of Braddock, his troops gave way in all directions, and could not be rallied till they had crossed the Monongahela. The Indians, allured by plunder, did not pursue with vigour. The vanquished regulars soon fell back to Dunbar's camp, from which, after destroying such of their stores as could be spared they retired to Philadelphia.

The officers in the British regiments displayed the greatest bravery. Their whole number was 85 and 64 of them were killed or wounded. The common soldiers were so disconcerted by the unusual mode of attack, that they soon broke, and could not be rallied. The three Virginia companies in the engagement behaved very differently, and fought like

Birth, family, education, and employment

men till there were scarcely 30 men left alive in the whole. This reverse of fortune rather added to, than took from, the reputation of Washington. His countrymen extolled his conduct, and generally said and believed, that if he had been commander, the disasters of the day would have been avoided.

Intelligence of Braddock's defeat, and that Col. Dunbar had withdrawn all the regular forces from Virginia, arrived while the assembly of that colony was in session. Impressed with the necessity of protecting their exposed frontier settlements, they determined to raised a regiment of sixteen companies. The command of this was given to Washington. So great was the public confidence in the soundness of his judgment, that he was authorized to name the field officers. His commission also designated him as commander in chief of all the forces raised, or to be raised, in Virginia.

In execution of the duties of his new office, Washington, after giving the necessary orders for the recruiting service, visited the frontiers. He found many posts, but few soldiers. Of these the best disposition was made. While on his way to Williamsburg to arrange a plan of operations with the lieutenant-governor, he was overtaken by an express below Fredericksburg, with information that the back settlements were broken up by parties of French and Indians, who were murdering and capturing men, women, and children, burning their houses, and destroying their crops, and that the few troops stationed on the frontiers, unable to protect the country, had retreated to small stockade forts.

Washington altered his course from Williamsburg to Winchester, and endeavoured to collect a force for the defense of the country. But this was impossible. The in habitants, instead of assembling in arms and facing the invaders, fled before them, and extended the general panic. While the attention of individuals was engrossed by their families and private concerns, the general safety was neglected. The alarm became universal, and the utmost confusion prevailed. Before any adequate force was collected to repel the assailants, they had safely crossed the Alleghany mountains, after having done an immensity of mischief.

Irruptions of this kind were repeatedly made into the frontier settlements of Virginia, in the years 1756, 1757, and 1758. These generally consisted of a considerable number of French and Indians, who were detached from Fort Duquesne. It was their usual practice on their approaching the settlements, to divide into small parties, and avoiding the forts, to attack solitary families in the night, as well as the day. The savages, accustomed to live in the woods, found little difficulty in concealing themselves till their fatal blow was struck. Sundry unimportant skirmishes took place, with various result, but the number killed on both sides was inconsiderable, when compared with the mischief done, and the many who were put to death, otherwise than in battle.

The invaders could seldom be brought to a regular engagement. Honourable war was not in their contemplation. Plunder, devastation, and murder, were their objects, The assemblage of a respectable force to oppose them, was their signal for retreating. Irruptions of this kind were so frequent for three years following Braddock's defeat, that in Pennsylvania, the frontier settlers were driven back as far as Carlisle, and in Maryland, to Fredericktown, and in Virginia, to the Blue Ridge.

The distresses of the inhabitants exceeded all description. If they went into stockade forts, they suffered from the want of provisions—were often surrounded, and sometimes cut off. By fleeing, they abandoned the conveniences of home, and the means of support. If they continued on their farms, they lay down every night under apprehensions of being murdered before morning.

But this was not the worst. Captivity and torture were frequently their portion. To all these evils, women, aged persons, and children were equally liable with men in arms; for savages make no distinction. Extermination is their object. To Washington the inhabitants looked for that protection he had not the means of giving. In a letter to the governor, he observed, "the supplicating tears of the women, and moving petitions of the men, melt me with such deadly sorrow, that I solemnly declare, if I know my own mind, I could offer myself a willing sacrifice to the butchering enemy, provided that would contribute to the people's ease."

Virginia presented a frontier of three hundred and sixty miles, exposed to these incursions. Hard was the lot of Washington, to whom was intrusted the defense of these extensive settlements without means adequate to the purpose. The regiment voted by the assembly was never filled. Its actual number was oftener below than above 700 men. The militia afforded a very feeble aid, on which little reliance could be placed. They were slow in collecting, and when collected, soon began to hanker after home; and while in camp, could not submit to that discipline, without which an army is a mob.

The militia laws were very defective. Cowardice in time of action, and sleeping while on duty, though crimes of the most destructive nature, were very inadequately punished by the civil code under which they took the field. Desertion and mutiny, for some considerable time, subjected the offenders to nothing more than slight penalties.

Washington was incessant in his representations to the governor and to the assembly, that no reliance could be placed on the militia, under existing regulations, and that the inconsiderable number, enlisted for regular service, together with the plans proposed for the security of the frontiers, were altogether inadequate. He not only pointed out the defect of the systems which had been adopted, but submitted to the consideration of those in power, such measures as he thought best, and particularly recommended, in case offensive operations were not adopted, that twenty-two forts, extending in a line of three hundred and sixty miles, should be immediately erected and garrisoned by two thousand men, in constant pay and service; but on all occasions gave a decided preference to the reduction of Fort Duquesne, as the only radical remedy for the evils to which the frontier settlements were exposed.

Propositions to this effect were made and urged by him in 1756 and 1757, both to the government of Virginia, and the commanders in chief of the British forces in America; but a short-sighted policy in the first, and a preference given by the last to a vigorous prosecution of the war in the northern colonies, prevented their acceptance. To his inexpressible joy, the project obtained, in the year 1758 the complete approbation of Gen. Forbes, who was charged with the defense of the middle and southern colonies. This being resolved upon, the movements of the army were directed to that point. Part of the force destined for this expedition was at Philadelphia; part at Ray's Town; and part dispersed on the frontiers of Virginia.

To bring all together, was a work of time and difficulty. Washington urged the necessity of an early campaign; but such delays took place that he did not receive orders to assemble his regiment at Winchester, till the 24th of May; nor to proceed from thence to Fort Cumberland, till the 24th of June; nor to proceed to Ray's Town, till the 21st of September. The main body did not commence their march from Ray's Town, till the 2d of October, and it was as late as the 25th of November when they reached Fort Duquesne. These delays were extremely mortifying to Washington, and threatened to render the campaign abortive. He urged the necessity of expedition, and most pointedly remonstrated against one of the principal causes of delay. This was a resolution adopted by his superiours, for opening a new road for the army, in preference to that which was generally known by the name of Gen. Braddock's. Being overruled, he quietly submitted.

Instead of embarrassing measures he thought injudicious, the whole energies of himself and his regiment were exerted to make the most of those which his commanding officer preferred. The progress of the army was so slow that it did not reach Loyal Hannah till the 5th of November. Here it was determined in a council of war, "to be unadvisable to proceed any further that campaign." If this resolution had been adhered to, the only alternative would have been to winter an army of 8000 men in a cold inhospitable wilderness, remote from all friendly settlements, or to tread back their steps and wait for a more favourable season. In either case they would have suffered immensely. The propriety of the remonstrances made by Washington against the many delays which had taken place, now became obviously striking. The hopes of restoring peace to the frontier settlements by reducing Fort Duquesne, began to vanish. But contrary to all human appearances, success was now offered to their grasp at the very moment they had given up every hope of obtaining it.

Some prisoners were taken, who gave such information of the state of the garrison, as induced a reversal of the late determination, and encouraged the general to proceed. Washington was in front superintending the opening of the road for the accommodation of the troops. They advanced with slow and cautious steps until they reached Fort Duquesne. To their great surprise they found the fort evacuated, and that the garrison had retreated down the Ohio. The reasons for the abandonment of so advantageous a position, must be looked for elsewhere. The British had urged the war with so much vigour and success against the French to the northward of the Ohio, that no reinforcements could be spared to Fort Duquesne. The British fleet had captured a considerable part of the reinforcements designed by France for her colonies. The tide of fortune had begun to turn against the French in favour of the English. These weakened the influence of the former over the Indians, and caused them to withdraw from the support of the garrison. Under different circumstances, the success of the campaign would have been doubtful, perhaps impracticable. The benefits which resulted from the acquisition of Fort Duquesne, proved the soundness of Washington's judgment in so warmly urging, for three years, an expedition for its reduction. These were not confined to Virginia, but extended to Pennsylvania and Maryland.

While the French were in possession of that post, the Indians near the Ohio were entirely at their beck. This was their place of rendezvous, and from it they made frequent and ruinous incursions into these three colonies. They neither spared age nor sex, but killed or captivated indiscriminately all who came in their way. Fire and devastation—the scalping knife and tomahawk, marked their route. A complete revolution in the disposition of the Indians, resulted from the expulsion of the French.

Always prone to take part with the strongest, they deserted their ancient friends, and paid court to those who, by recent conquest, were now in possession of the country. A treaty of peace was soon after concluded with all the Indian tribes between the lakes and the Ohio.

Birth, family, education, and employment

Fort Duquesne henceforward assumed the name of Fort Pitt, received considerable repairs, and was garrisoned by 200 men from Washington's regiment. It became as useful in future to the English settlements, as it had been injurious while in the occupation of the French.

The campaign of 1758 ended the military career of Col. Washington, as a provincial officer. The great object on which his heart was set, the reduction of Fort Duquesne, being accomplished, he resigned his commission.

During the three preceding years in which he was charged with the defense of Virginia, none of those great events occurred which enliven and adorn the page of history; yet the duties he performed were extremely arduous. He established exact discipline in his regiment, though unaccustomed to restraint, and infused into them such a spirit as made them, when in action, fight like men, and die like soldiers.

The difficulties of defending such an extensive frontier, with so inadequate a force, would have chagrined almost any other man into a resignation of the command, but only excited in him greater importunity with the ruling powers, for the correction of errors. The plans he proposed, the systems he recommended for conducting the war, displayed an uncommon vigour of mind. He retired from the army with the thanks of his regiment, and the esteem not only of his countrymen, but of the officers of the British army; and what is particularly remarkable, with the undiminished confidence of the frontier settlers, to whom he was unable to extend that protection they expected from his hands. They were thoroughly convinced he had made the best possible use of his scanty means for the security of so extensive a frontier; and to the weight of his advice in recommending, and spirited co-operation in executing, they ascribed a large proportion of the merit of the late successful expedition against Fort Duquesne; an event from which they promised themselves an exemption from the calamities under which they had long laboured. As a reward of his gallant and patriotic services, he shortly after obtained the hand of Mrs. Custis, who, to a fine person and large fortune, added every accomplishment which contributes to the happiness of married life. Col. Washington, by the death of his elder brother Lawrence, had a few years before acquired an estate situated on the Potowmack, called Mount Vernon, in compliment to admiral Vernon, who, about the year 1741, commanded the British fleet in an expedition against Carthagena, in which expedition Mr. Lawrence Washington had been engaged.

To this delightful spot the late commander of the Virginia forces, released from the cares of a military life, and in possession of every thing that could make life agreeable, withdrew, and gave himself up to domestic pursuits. These were conducted with so much judgment, steadiness, and industry, as greatly to enlarge and improve his estate. To them he exclusively devoted himself for fifteen years, with the exception of serving in the house of burgesses of the colony of Virginia, and as a judge of the court of the county in which he resided. In these stations he acquitted himself with reputation, and acquired no inconsiderable knowledge in the science of civil government.

During this period, the clashing claims of Great-Britain and her colonies were frequently brought before the Virginia legislature. In every instance he took a decided part in the opposition made to the principle of taxation claimed by the parent state.

Had Great-Britain been wise, the history of George Washington would have ended here, with the addition that he died in the sixty-eighth year of his age, having sustained through life the character of a good man, an excellent farmer, a wise member of the legislature, and an impartial distributer of justice among his neighbours.

Very different was his destiny. From being the commander of the forces of his native colony, Virginia, he was advanced to the command of the armies of thirteen United Colonies, and successfully led them through a revolutionary war of eight years duration, which issued in their establishment as thirteen United States. The origin of these great events must be looked for across the Atlantic.

2

Retrospect of the origin of the American revolutionary war—Of George Washington as member of Congress, in 1774 and 1775—As Commander in Chief of the armies of the United Colonies in 1775 and 1776, and his operations near Boston, in these years.

Soon after the peace of Paris, 1763, a new system for governing the British colonies, was adopted. One abridgment of their accustomed liberties followed another in such rapid succession, that in the short space of twelve years they had nothing left they could call their own. The British parliament, in which they were unrepresented, and over which they had no control, not only claimed, but exercised the power of taxing them at pleasure, and of binding them in all cases whatsoever.

Claims so repugnant to the spirit of the British constitution, and which made such invidious distinctions between the subjects of the same king, residing on different sides of the Atlantic, excited a serious alarm among the colonists. Detached as they were from each other by local residence, and unconnected in their several legislatures, a sense of common danger pointed out to them the wisdom and propriety of forming a new representative body, composed of delegates from each colony, to take care of their common interests.

With very little previous concert, such a body was formed and met in Philadelphia, in September, 1774, and entered into the serious consideration of the grievances under which their constituents laboured. To this congress Virginia deputed seven of her most respectable citizens: Peyton Randolph, Richard Henry Lee, George Washington, Patrick Henry, Richard Bland, Benjamin Harrison, Edmund Pendleton; men who would have done honour to any age or country. The same were appointed in like manner to attend a second congress on the 10th of May, in the following year.

The historians of the American revolution will detail with pleasure and pride, the proceedings of this illustrious assembly: the firmness and precision with which they stated their grievances, and petitioned their sovereign to redress them; the eloquence with which they addressed the people of Great-Britain, the inhabitants of Canada, and their own constituents; the judicious measures they adopted for cementing union at home, and procuring friends abroad.

They will also inform the world of the unsuccessful termination of all plans proposed for preserving the union of the empire, and that Great-Britain, proceeding from one oppression to the another, threw the colonies out of her protection, made war upon them, and carried it on with a view to their subjugation. All these matters, together with the commencement of hostilities at Lexington, and the formation of an American army by the colony of Massachusetts, for defending themselves against a royal army in Boston, must be here passed over.

Our business is only with George Washington. The fame he had acquired as commander of the Virginia forces, together with his well known military talents, procured for him the distinguishing appellation of the Soldier of America. Those who, before the commencement of hostilities, looked forward to war as the probable consequence of the disputes between Great-Britain and her colonies, anticipated his appointment to the supreme command of the forces of his native country.

As long as he continued a member of Congress, he was chairman of every committee appointed by that body to make arrangements for defence. These duties in the Senate were soon superseded by more active employment in the field.

As soon as the Congress of the United Colonies had determined on making a common cause with Massachusetts, against which a British army had commenced hostilities, they appointed, by an unanimous vote, George Washington, commander in chief of all the forces raised or to be raised for the defence of the colonies.

His election was accompanied with no competition, and followed by no envy. The same general impulse on the public mind, which led the colonies to agree in many other particulars, pointed to him as the most proper person for presiding over the armies.

To the president of Congress announcing this appointment, General Washington replied in the following words:

"Mr. President,

"Though I am truly sensible of the high honour done me in this appointment, yet I feel great distress from a consciousness that my abilities and military experience may not be equal to the extensive and important trust. However, as the Congress desire it, I will enter upon the momentous duty, and exert every power I possess in their service, and for support of the glorious cause. I beg they will accept my most cordial thanks, for the distinguished testimony of their approbation.

"But lest some unlucky event should happen unfavorable to my reputation, I beg it may be remembered by every gentleman in the room, that I this day declare with the utmost sincerity, I do not think myself equal to the command I am honoured with.

"As to pay, Sir, I beg leave to assure the Congress that as no pecuniary consideration could have tempted me to accept this arduous employment, at the expense of my domestic ease and happiness, I do not wish to make any profit from it. I will keep an exact account of my expenses; those I doubt not they will discharge, and that is all I desire."

A special commission was made out for him, and at the same time an unanimous resolution was adopted by Congress, "that they would maintain and assist him, and adhere to him with their lives and fortunes, for the maintenance and preservation of American Liberty."

He immediately entered on the duties of his high station. After passing a few days in New-York, and making some arrangements with Gen. Schuyler, who commanded there, he proceeded to Cambridge, which was the head-quarters of the American army. On his way thither, he received from private persons and public bodies, the most flattering attention, and the strongest expressions of determination to support him.

He received an address from the Provincial Congress of New-York, in which, after expressing their approbation of his elevation to command, they say—"We have the fullest assurances, that whenever this important contest shall be decided by that fondest wish of each American soul, an accommodation with our mother country, you will cheerfully resign the important deposit committed into your hands, and re-assume the character of our worthiest citizen."

The General, after declaring his gratitude for the respect shown him, added—"Be assured that every exertion of my worthy colleagues and myself, will be extended to the re-establishment of peace and harmony between the mother country and these colonies. As to the fatal, but necessary operations of war, when we assumed the soldier we did not lay aside the citizen, and we shall most sincerely rejoice with you in that happy hour, when the re-establishment of American liberty, on the most firm and solid foundations, shall enable us to return to our private stations, in the bosom of a free, peaceful, and happy country."

A committee from the Massachusetts Congress received him at Springfield, about one hundred miles from Boston, and conducted him to the army. He was soon after addressed by the Congress of that colony in the most affectionate manner.

In his answer, he said—"Gentlemen, your kind congratulations on my appointment and arrival, demand my warmest acknowledgments, and will ever be retained in grateful remembrance. In exchanging the enjoyments of domestic life for the duties of my present honorable, but arduous station, I only emulate the virtue and public spirit of the whole province of Massachusetts, which, with a firmness and patriotism without example, has sacrificed all the comforts of social and political life in support of the rights of mankind, and the welfare of our common country. My highest ambition is to be the happy instrument of vindicating these rights, and to see this devoted province again restored to peace, liberty, and safety."

When Gen. Washington arrived at Cambridge, he was received with the joyful acclamations of the American army. At the head of his troops, he published a declaration previously drawn up by Congress, in the nature of a manifesto, setting forth the reasons for taking up arms. In this, after enumerating various grievances of the colonies, and vindicating them from a premeditated design of establishing independent states, it was added—

"In our own native land, in defence of the freedom which is our birthright, and which we ever enjoyed till the late violation of it; for the protection of our property, acquired solely by the industry of our forefathers and ourselves, against violence actually offered; we have taken up arms: We shall lay them down when hostilities shall cease on the part of the aggressors, and all danger of their being renewed shall be removed, and not before."

When Gen. Washington joined the American army, he found the British entrenched on Bunker's Hill, having also three floating batteries in Mystic River, and a twenty gun ship below the ferry between Boston and Charlestown. They had also a battery on Copse's Hill, and were strongly fortified on the Neck. The Americans were intrenched at Winter Hill, Prospect Hill, and Roxbury, communicating with one another by small posts over a distance of ten miles, nor could they be contracted without exposing the country to the incursions of the enemy.

The army put under the command of Washington amounted to 14,500 men. Several circumstances concurred to render this force very inadequate to active operations. Military stores were deficient in camp, and the whole in the country was inconsiderable. On the 4th of August, all the stock of powder in the American camp, and in the public magazines of the four New-England provinces, would have made very little more than nine rounds a man. In this destitute condition the army remained for a fortnight.

To the want of powder was added a very general want of bayonets, of clothes, of working tools, and a total want of engineers. Under all these embarrassments, the General observed, that "he had the materials of a good army; that the men were able-bodied, active, zealous in the cause, and of unquestionable courage."

He immediately instituted such arrangements as were calculated to increase their capacity for service. The army was distributed into brigades and divisions, and on his recommendation, general staff officers were appointed. Economy, union, and system, were introduced into every department.

As the troops came into service under the authority of distinct colonial governments, no uniformity existed among the regiments. In Massachusetts the men had chosen their officers, and (rank excepted) were in other respects, frequently their equals. To form one uniform mass of these discordant materials, and to subject freemen animated with the spirit of liberty, and collected for its defence, to the control of military discipline, required patience, forbearance, and a spirit of accommodation.

This delicate and arduous duty was undertaken by Gen. Washington, and discharged with great address. When he had made considerable progress in disciplining his army, the term for which enlistments had taken place was on the point of expiring. The troops from Connecticut and Rhode Island were only engaged to the first of December, 1775; and no part of the army longer than to the first of January, 1776.

The commander in chief made early and forcible representations to Congress on this subject, and urged them to adopt efficient measures for the formation of a new army. They deputed three of their members, Mr. Lynch, Dr. Franklin, and Mr. Harrison, to repair to camp, and, in conjunction with him and the chief magistrates of the New-England colonies, to confer on the most effectual mode of continuing, supporting, and regulating, a continental army. By them it was resolved to list 23,722 men, as far as practicable, from the troops before Boston, to serve till the last day of December, 1776, unless sooner discharged by Congress.

In the execution of this resolve, Washington called upon all officers and soldiers to make their election for retiring or continuing. Several of the inferior officers retired. Many of the men would not continue on any terms. Several refused, unless they were indulged with furloughs. Others, unless they were allowed to choose their officers. So many impediments obstructed the recruiting service, that it required great address to obviate them.

Washington made forcible appeals in general orders, to the pride and patriotism of both officers and men. He promised every indulgence compatible with safety, and every comfort that the state of the country authorized. In general orders of the 20th of October, he observed—

"The times, and the importance of the great cause we are engaging in, allow no room for hesitation and delay. When life, liberty, and property, are at stake; when our country is in danger of being a melancholy scene of bloodshed and desolation; when our towns are laid in ashes, innocent women and children driven from their peaceful habitations, exposed to the rigours of an inclement season, to depend perhaps on the hand of charity for support; when calamities like these are staring us in the face, and a brutal savage enemy threatens us and every thing we hold dear with destruction from foreign troops, it little becomes the character of a soldier to shrink from danger, and condition for new terms. It is the General's intention to indulge both officers and soldiers who compose the new army with furloughs for a reasonable time; but this must be done in such a manner as not to injure the service, or weaken the army too much at once."

In the instructions given to the recruiting officers, the General enjoined upon them "not to enlist any person suspected of being unfriendly to the liberties of America, or any abandoned vagabond, to whom all causes and countries are equal and alike indifferent."

Though great exertions had been made to procure recruits, yet the regiments were not filled. Several causes operated in producing this disinclination to the service. The sufferings of the army had been great. Fuel was very scarce. Clothes, and even provisions, had not been furnished them in sufficient quantities. The smallpox deterred many from entering; but the principal reason was a dislike to a military life. Much also of that enthusiasm which brought numbers to the field, on the commencement of hostilities, had abated.

The army of 1775 was wasting away by the expiration of the terms of service, and recruits for the new, entered slowly. The regiments which were entitled to their discharge on the 1st of December, were with great difficulty persuaded to stay ten days, when reinforcements of militia were expected to supply their place. From the eagerness of the old troops to go home, and the slowness of the new to enter service, it was difficult to keep up the blockade.

On the last day of the year, when the first were entirely disbanded, the last only amounted to 9650 men, and many of these were absent on furlough. At this time the royal army in Boston was about 8000. To assist the recruiting service, the General recommended to Congress to try the effects of a bounty, but this was not agreed to till late in January, 1776. In that and the following month the army was considerably increased.

The blockade of Boston was all this time kept up, and the enemy confined to the city, but this was far short of what the American people expected. Common fame represented the troops under the command of Washington to be nearly treble the royal army. This ample force was supposed to be furnished with every thing necessary for the most active operations. Their real numbers and deficient equipments were, for obvious reasons, carefully concealed.

The ardour and impatience of the public had long since counted on the expulsion of the British from Boston. Washington was equally ardent, but better informed and more prudent. He well knew the advantages that would result to the cause in which he was engaged from some brilliant stroke, nor was he insensible to insinuations by some that he was devoid of energy, and by others that he wished to prolong his own importance by continuing the war. He bore these murmurs with patience; but nevertheless, had his eyes directed to Boston, and wished for an opening to commence offensive operations.

The propriety of this measure was submitted to the consideration of repeated councils of war, who uniformly declared against it. A hope was nevertheless indulged that ice in the course of the winter, would be favourable to an assault. That this opportunity might not be lost, measures were adopted for procuring large reinforcements of militia to serve till the first of March, 1776. From 4 to 5000 men were accordingly procured.

Contrary to what is usual, the waters about Boston continued open till the middle of February. Councils of war were hitherto nearly unanimous against an assault. General Washington was less opposed to it than some others, but the want of ammunition for the artillery, together with the great probability of failure, induced him to decline the attempt. In lieu of it he formed a bold resolution to take a new position that would either compel the British General to come to an action, or to evacuate Boston.

The American army was now stronger than ever. Recruiting for the last two months had been unusually successful. The regular army exceeded 14,000 men, and the militia were about 6000. Washington, thus reinforced, determined to fortify the heights of Dorchester, from which he could annoy the ships in the harbour, and the army in the town.

To favour the execution of this plan, the town and lines of the enemy were bombarded on the 2nd, 3rd, and 4th of March. On the night of the 4th, Gen. Thomas, with a considerable detachment, took possession of the heights of Dorchester. By great exertions this party in the course of the night, nearly covered themselves from the shot of the enemy. The appearance of their works caused no little surprise in the British camp. These were every hour advancing so as to afford additional security to the Americans posted behind them.

The Admiral informed Gen. Howe, that if the Americans kept possession of these heights, he would not be able to keep one of the British ships in the harbour. The enemy were now brought to the alternative which Washington wished for. They must either risk an action without their lines, or abandon the place.

Gen. Howe preferred the former, and ordered 3000 men on this service. These were embarked, and fell down to the Castle with the intention of proceeding up the river to the attack, but were dispersed by a tremendous storm. Before they could be in readiness to proceed, the American works were advanced to such a state of security as to discourage any attempt against them.

Washington expecting an immediate assault on the new raised works at Dorchester, and judging that the best troops of the enemy would be ordered on that service, had prepared to attack the town of Boston at the same time——4000 men were ready for embarkation at the mouth of Cambridge river to proceed on this business, as soon as it was known that the British were gone out in force to their intended attack.

It was now resolved by the British to evacuate Boston as soon as possible. In a few days after, a flag came out of Boston with a paper signed by four select men, informing, "that they had applied to Gen. Robertson, who, on an application to Gen. Howe, was authorized to assure them, that he had no intention of burning the town, unless the troops under his command were molested during their embarkation, or at their departure, by the armed force without."

When this paper was presented to Gen. Washington, he replied, "that as it was an unauthenticated paper, and without an address, and not obligatory on Gen. Howe, he could take no notice of it; "but at the same time "intimated his good wishes for the security of the town."

Washington made arrangements for the security of his army, but did not advance his works nor embarrass the British army in their proposed evacuation. He wished to save Boston, and to gain time for the fortification of New-York, to which place he supposed the evacuating army was destined.

Under this impression, he detached a considerable part of his army to that place, and with the remainder took possession of Boston, as soon as the British troops had completed their embarkation. On entering the town, Washington was received with marks of approbation more flattering than the pomps of a triumph.

The inhabitants, released from the severities of a garrison life, and from the various indignities to which they were subjected, hailed him as their deliverer. Reciprocal congratulations between those who had been confined within the British lines, and those who were excluded from entering them, were exchanged with an ardour which cannot be described.

Gen. Washington was honoured by Congress with a vote of thanks. They also ordered a medal to be struck, with suitable devices to perpetuate the remembrance of the great event.

The Massachusetts Council, and House of Representatives complimented him in a joint address, in which they expressed their good wishes in the following words—"May you still go on approved by heaven, revered by all good men, and dreaded by those tyrants who claim their fellow men as their property." His answer was modest and proper.

3

The Campaign of 1776: Of the operations of General Washington in New-York and New-Jersey. The battle on Long Island. The retreat from York Island and through Jersey. The battles of Trenton and Princeton.

The evacuation of Boston varied the scene, but did not lessen the labours of Washington. Henceforward he had a much more formidable enemy to contend with. The royal army in Boston was, on a small scale, calculated to awe the inhabitants of Massachusetts into obedience, but the campaign of 1776 was opened in New-York with a force far exceeding any thing hitherto seen in America. Including the navy and army, it amounted to 55,000 men and was calculated on the idea of reducing the whole United Colonies.

The operations contemplated could be best carried on from the nearly central province of New-York, and the army could be supplied with provisions from the adjacent islands, and easily defended by the British navy. For these reasons, the evacuation of Boston, and the concentration of the royal forces at New-York, had been for some time resolved upon in England.

The reasons that induced the British to gain possession of New-York, weighed with Washington to prevent or delay it. He had therefore detached largely from his army before Boston, and sent Gen. Lee to take the command, and after providing for the security of Boston, proceeded soon after the evacuation thereof with the main army to New-York, and made every preparation in his power for its defence. Considerable time was allowed for this purpose; for Gen. Howe, instead of pushing directly for New-York, retired to Halifax with the forces withdrawn from Boston. He there waited for the promised reinforcements from England; but, impatient of delay, sailed without them for New-York, and took possession of Staten Island in the latter end of June.

He was soon followed by his brother, Admiral Howe, and their whole force was assembled about the middle of July, and in apparent readiness for opening the campaign. Before hostilities were commenced, the British General and Admiral, in their quality of civil commissioners for effecting a re-union between Great Britain and the Colonies, made an attempt at negotiation. To introduce this business, they sent a flag ashore with a letter addressed to George Washington, Esq. This he refused to receive, as not being addressed to him with the title due to his rank, and at the same time wrote to Congress, "That he would not, on any occasion, sacrifice essentials to punctilio, but in this instance, deemed it a duty to his country to insist on that respect which, in any other than a public view, he would willingly have waved."

Some time after, Adjutant General Patterson was sent by Gen. Howe with a letter addressed to George Washington, &c.&c.&c. On an interview, the Adjutant General, after expressing his high esteem for the person and character of the American General, and declaring that it was not intended to derogate from the respect due to his rank, expressed his hopes, that the et ceteras would remove the impediments to their correspondence. Gen. Washington replied, "That a letter directed to any person in a public character, should have some description of it, otherwise it would appear a mere private letter; that it was true the et ceteras implied every thing, but they also implied any thing, and that he should therefore decline the receiving any letter directed to him as a private person, when it related to his private station."

A long conference ensued, in which the Adjutant General observed that "the Commissioners were armed with great powers, and would be very happy in effecting an accommodation." He received for answer, "that from what appeared, their powers were only to grant pardons; that they who had committed no fault wanted no pardon."

On the arrival of Gen. Howe at Staten Island, the American army did not exceed 10,000 men, but by sundry reinforcements before the end of August, they amounted to 27,000. Of these a great part were militia, and one-fourth of the whole was sick. The diseases incident to new troops prevailed extensively, and were aggravated by a great deficiency in tents. These troops were so judiciously distributed on York Island, Long Island, Governor's Island, Paulus Hook, and on the Sound towards New Rochelle, East and West Chester, that the enemy were very cautious in determining when or where to commence offensive operations. Every probable point of debarkation was watched, and guarded with a force sufficient to embarrass, though very insufficient to prevent, a landing.

From the arrival of the British army at Staten Island, the Americans were in daily expectation of being attacked. General Washington was therefore strenuous in preparing his troops for action. He tried every expedient to kindle in their breasts the love of their country, an high toned indignation against its invaders. In general orders he addressed them as follows: "The time is now near at hand, which must probably determine whether Americans are to be freemen or slaves; whether they are to have any property they can call their own; whether their houses and farms are to be pillaged and destroyed, and themselves consigned to a state of wretchedness, from which no human efforts will deliver them. The fate of unborn millions will now depend, under God, on the conduct and courage of this army. Our cruel and unrelenting enemy, leaves us only the choice of a brave resistance, or the most abject submission.

"We have therefore to resolve to conquer or to die. Our own, our country's honor, calls upon us for a vigorous and manly exertion; and if we now shameful fail, we shall become infamous to the whole world. Let us then rely on the goodness of our cause, and the aid of the Supreme Being, in whose hands victory is, to animate and encourage us to great and noble actions. The eyes of all our countrymen are now upon us, and we shall have their blessings and praises, if happily we are the instruments of saving them from the tyranny mediated against them. Let us therefore animate and encourage each other, and show the whole world that a freeman contending for liberty on his own ground, is superior to any slavish mercenary on earth."

When the whole reinforcements of the enemy had arrived, Gen. Washington, in expectation of an immediate attack, again addressed his army, and called on them to remember that "liberty, property, life, and honour, were all at stake; that upon their courage and conduct, rested the hopes of their bleeding and insulted country; that their wives, children, and parents, expected safety from them only; and that they had every reason to believe that Heaven would crown with success so just a cause."

He further added—"The enemy will endeavor to intimidate by show and appearance, but remember they have been repulsed on various occasions by a few brave Americans. Their cause is bad—their men are conscious of it, and if opposed with firmness and coolness on their first onset, with our advantage of works, and knowledge of the ground, the victory is most assuredly ours. Every good soldier will be silent and attentive—wait for orders—and reserve his fire until he is sure of doing execution: of this the officers are to be particularly careful."

He then gave the most explicit orders that any soldier who should attempt to conceal himself, or retreat without orders, should instantly be shot down, as an example of the punishment of cowardice, and desired every officer to be particularly attentive to the conduct of his men, and report those who should distinguish themselves by brave and noble actions. These he solemnly promised to notice and reward.

On the 22d of August, the greatest part of the British troops landed on Long Island. Washington immediately made a farther effort to rouse his troops to deeds of valour. "The enemy," said he,"have landed, and the hour is fast approaching on which the honour and success of this army, and the safety of our bleeding country, depends. Remember, officers and soldiers, that you are freemen, fighting for the blessings of Liberty; that slavery will be your portion and that of your posterity, if you do not acquit yourselves like men. Remember how your courage has been despised and traduced by your cruel invaders, though they have found by dear experience at Boston, Charles-town, and other places, what a few brave men, contending in their own land, and in the best of causes, can do against hirelings and mercenaries. Be cool, but determined. Do not fire at a distance, but wait for orders from your officers."

He repeated his injunctions, "to shoot down any person who should misbehave in action," and his hope "that none so infamous would be found, but that, on the contrary, each for himself resolving to conquer or die, and trusting to the smiles of heaven on so just a cause, would behave with bravery and resolution."

His assurance of rewards to those who should distinguish themselves, were repeated; and he declared his confidence, that if the army would but emulate and imitate their brave countrymen in other parts of America, they would, by a glorious victory, save their country, and acquire to themselves immortal honour."

On the 5th day after their landing, the British attacked the Americans on Long Island, commanded by Gen. Sullivan. The variety of ground and the different parties employed in different places, both in the attack and defence, occasioned a succession of small engagements, pursuits, and slaughter, which lasted for many hours.

The Americans were defeated in all directions. The circumstances which eminently contributed to this, were the superior discipline of the assailants, and the want of early intelligence of their movements. There was not a single corps of Cavalry in the American army. The transmission of intelligence was of course always slow, and often impracticable. From the want of it, some of their detachments, while retreating before one portion of the enemy, were advancing towards another, of whose movements they were ignorant.

In the height of the engagement Washington passed over to Long Island, and with infinite regret saw the slaughter of his best troops, but had not the power to prevent it; for had he drawn his whole force to their support, he must have risked every thing on a single engagement. He adopted the wiser plan of evacuating the island, with all the forces he could bring off. In superintending this necessary, but difficult and dangerous movement, and the events of the preceding day, Washington was indefatigable. For forty-eight hours he never closed his eyes, and was almost constantly on horse-back. In less than thirteen hours, the field artillery, tents, baggage, and about 9000 men, were conveyed from Long Island to the city of New-York, over East River, and without the knowledge of the British, though not 600 yards distant. The darkness of the night and a heavy fog in the morning, together with a fair wind after midnight, favoured this retreat. It was completed without interruption some time after the dawning of the day.

The unsuccessful termination of the late action, led to consequences more seriously alarming to the Americans, than the loss of their men. Hitherto they had had such confidence in themselves, as engaged in the cause of liberty and their country, that it outweighed all their apprehensions from the exact discipline of the British troops; but now finding that many of them had been encircled in inextricable difficulties from the superior military skill of their adversaries, they went to the opposite extreme, and began to think but very indifferently of themselves and their leaders, when opposed to disciplined troops. As often as they saw the enemy approaching, they suspected a military maneuvre, from which they supposed nothing could save them but immediate flight. Apprehensions of this kind might naturally be expected from citizen soldiers, lately taken from agricultural pursuits, who expected to lay aside the military character at the end of the current year.

Washington, tremblingly alive to the state of his army, wrote to Congress on the sixth day after the defeat on Long Island, as follows: "Our situation is truly distressing. The check our detachment lately sustained has dispirited too great a proportion of our troops, and filled their minds with apprehension and despair. The militia, instead of calling forth their utmost efforts to a brave and manly opposition, in order to repair our losses, are dismayed, intractable, and impatient to return. Great numbers of them have gone off; in some instances, almost by whole regiments, in many by half ones, and by companies at a time. The circumstance of itself, independent of others, when fronted by a well appointed enemy, superior in number to our whole collected force, would be sufficiently disagreeable; but when it is added, that their example has infected

Campaign of 1776: New-York and New-Jersey

another part of the army; that their want of discipline and refusal of almost every kind of restraint and government, have rendered a like conduct but too common in the whole, and have produced an entire disregard of that order and subordination which is necessary for an army, our condition is still more alarming; and with the deepest concern I am obliged to confess my want of confidence in the generality of the troops.

"All these circumstances fully confirm the opinion I ever entertained, and which I more than once in my letters took the liberty of mentioning to Congress, that no dependence could be put in a militia, or other troops than those enlisted and embodied for a longer period than our regulations have hitherto prescribed. I am fully convinced that our liberties must of necessity be greatly hazarded, if not entirely lost, if their defence be left to any but a permanent army.

"Nor would the expense incident to the support of such a body of troops as would be competent to every exigency, far exceed that which is incurred by calling in daily succours and new enlistments, which, when effected, are not attended with any good consequences. Men who have been free and subject to no control, cannot be reduced to order in an instant; and the privileges and exemptions they claim, and will have, influence the conduct of others in such a manner, that the aid derived from them is nearly counterbalanced by the disorder, irregularity, and confusion they occasion."

In fourteen days after this serious remonstrance, Congress resolved to raise 88 battalions to serve during the war. Under these circumstances, to wear away the campaign with as little loss as possible, so as to gain time to raise a permanent army against the next year, was to the Americans an object of the greatest importance.

Gen. Washington, after much deliberation, determined on a war of posts. Recent events confirmed him in the policy of defending his country by retreating, when he could no longer stand his ground without risking his army. He well knew that by adopting it he would subject himself to the imputation of wanting energy and decision; but with him the love of country was paramount to all other considerations.

In conformity to these principles, the evacuation of New-York was about this time resolved upon, whensoever it could no longer be maintained without risking the army. Arrangements were accordingly made for a temporary defence, and an ultimate retreat when necessity required. The British, now in possession of Long Island, could at pleasure pass over to York Island or the main. Washington was apprehensive that they would land above him, cut off his retreat, and force him to a general action on York Island. He therefore moved his public stores to Dobbs' ferry, and stationed 12,000 men at the northern end of York Island. With the remainder he kept up the semblance of defending New-York, though he had determined to abandon it, rather than risk his army for its preservation.

While Washington was making arrangements to save his troops and stores by evacuating and retreating, the British commander was prosecuting his favourite scheme of forcing the Americans to a general action, or breaking the communication between their posts. With this view he landed about 4000 men at Kipp's Bay, three miles above New-York, under cover of five men of war. Works had been thrown up at this place, which were capable of being defended for some time, and troops were stationed in them for that purpose; but they fled with precipitation without waiting for the approach of the enemy. Two brigades were put in motion to support them. Gen. Washington rode to the scene of action, and to his great mortification met the whole party retreating. While he was exerting himself to rally them, on the appearance of a small corps of the enemy, they again broke, and ran off in disorder.

Such dastardly conduct raised a tempest in the usually tranquil mind of Gen. Washington. Having embarked in the American cause from the purest principles, he viewed with infinite concern this shameful behaviour, as threatening ruin to his country. He recollected the many declarations of Congress, of the army, and of the inhabitants, preferring liberty to life, and death to dishonour, and contrasted them with their present scandalous flight. His soul was harrowed up with apprehensions that his country would be conquered, her army disgraced, and her liberties destroyed. He anticipated, in imagination, that the Americans would appear to posterity in the light of high sounding boasters, who blustered when danger was at a distance, but shrunk at the shadow of opposition.

Extensive confiscations, and numerous attainders, presented themselves in full view to his agitated mind. He saw in imagination new formed states, with the means of defence in their hands, and the glorious prospects of liberty before them, levelled to the dust; and such constitutions imposed on them, as were likely to crush the vigor of the human mind; while the unsuccessful issue of the present struggle would, for ages to come, deter posterity from the bold design of asserting their rights. Impressed with these ideas, he hazarded his person for some for considerable time in rear of his own men, and in front of the enemy, with his horse's head towards the latter, as if in expectation that, by an honourable death, he might escape the infamy he dreaded from the dastardly conduct of troops on whom he could place no dependence. His aids, and the confidential friends around his person, by indirect violence, compelled him to retire. In consequences of their address and importunity, a life was saved for public service, which, otherwise, from a sense of honour and a gust of passion, seemed to be devoted to almost certain destruction.

The shameful events of this day, hastened the evacuation of New-York. This was effected with very little loss of men, but all the heavy artillery and a large portion of the baggage, provisions, military stores, and particularly the tents, were unavoidably left behind. The loss of the last mentioned article was severely felt in that season, when cold weather was rapidly approaching.

The British having got possession of the city of New York, advanced in front of it, and stretched their encampments across York Island; while their shipping defended their flanks. Washington had made his strongest post at Kingsbridge, as that preserved his communication with the country. In front of this, and near to the British, he had a strong detachment posted in an entrenched camp. This position of the two armies was particularly agreeable to him; for he wished to accustom his raw troops to face their enemies, hoping that by frequent skirmishes they would grow so familiar with the dangers incident to war, as to fear them less.

Opportunities of making the experiment soon occurred. On the day after the retreat from New-York, a skirmish took place between an advanced detachment of the British army and some American troops, commanded by Col. Knowlton, of Connecticut, and Major Leitch, of Virginia. Both these officers fell, bravely fighting at the head of their troops. The Captains with their men kept the ground, and fairly beat their adversaries from the field. This was the first advantage the army under the command of Washington had gained in the campaign. Its influence on the army was great. To increase its effects, the parole the next day was "Leitch," and the General gave public thanks to the troops engaged therein. He contrasted their conduct with the late shameful flight of the troops from the works on Kipp's Bay, and observed—"That the result proved what might be done, where officers and men exerted themselves;" and again called on all "so to act as not to disgrace the noble cause in which they were engaged."

General Howe continued to prosecute his scheme for cutting off Washington's communication with the eastern states, and enclosing him so as to compel a general engagement. With this view the royal army landed on Frog's Neck in West-Chester county, and soon after advanced to New Rochelle, and made sundry successive movements, all calculated to effect this purpose.

A few skirmishes took place, but a general action was carefully avoided by Washington, except in one case, in which he had such a manifest advantage from his position on hills near the White Plains, that Gen. Howe declined it. The project of getting in the rear of the American army was in like manner frustrated by frequent and judicious changes of its position. Gen. Howe failing in his first design, adopted a new plan of operations. His efforts were henceforward directed to an invasion of New Jersey. Washington, penetrating his designs, crossed the North River. He wrote to William Livingston, governor of New Jersey, urging him to put the militia of that State in the best state of preparation to defend their country, and also recommending the removal of stock and provisions from the sea coast.

About this time Fort Washington was taken by storm, and the garrison, consisting of more than 2000 men, with their commander, Col. Magaw, surrendered prisoners of war. This was the only post held by the Americans on York Island; and was exception to the general plan of evacuating and retreating. Hopes had been indulged that it might be defended, and, in conjunction with Fort Lee, on the opposite Jersey shore, made useful in embarrassing the passage of British vessels up and down the North River. This post having fallen, orders for the evacuation of Fort Lee were immediately given; But before the stores could be removed, Lord Cornwallis crossed the North River with 6000 men. Washington, retreating before him, took post along the Hackensack.

His situation there was nearly similar to that which he had abandoned; for he was liable to be enclosed between the Hackensack and the Pasaic rivers. He therefore, on the approach of the enemy, passed over to Newark. He stood his ground there for some days, as if determined on resistance; but being incapable of any effectual opposition, retreated to Brunswick, on the day Lord Cornwallis entered Newark.

At Brunswick Washington kept his troops in motion, and even advanced a small detachment, as if intending to engage the enemy. Nor did he quit this position till their advanced guards were in sight. Lord Stirling was left at Princeton with 1200 men, to watch the British; and Washington proceeded with the residue to Trenton. There he meant to make a stand.

Orders were previously given to collect and guard all the boats for 70 miles on the Delaware. The baggage and stores were also passed over. These being secured, Washington detached 1200 men to Princeton, to keep up the appearance of opposition, and soon followed with about 2000 militia men who had recently joined him. Before he reached Princeton, intelligence was received that Lord Cornwallis, strongly reinforced, was advancing from Brunswick in different directions, with the apparent design of getting in his rear. An immediate retreat over the Delaware became necessary. This was effected on the 8th of December.

Washington secured all his boats on the Pennsylvania side; broke down the bridges on roads leading to the opposite shores, and posted his troops at the different fording places. So keen was the pursuit, that as the rear guard of the retreating army embarked, the van of the enemy came in sight.

The British having driven the American army out of Jersey, posted themselves up and down the Delaware, and small parties passed and repassed from one to the other, without any interruption. They made some attempts to get boats, but failed. They also repaired some of the bridges that had been recently destroyed, and pushed forward a strong detachment to Bordenton. This was intended to increase their chances for crossing, and to embarrass Washington, who could not tell from which of their several positions they would make the attempt.

Gen. Putnam was in the meantime sent on to superintend the erection of lines of defence from the Schuylkill to the Delaware, for the security of Philadelphia. Small redoubts were hastily thrown up to guard the fording places; and Germantown was fixed upon as a place of rendezvous, in case the British should cross and drive the Americans from their extended encampments on the Delaware.

This retreat through the Jerseys was attended with almost every circumstance that could occasion embarrassment or depression. Washington was pressed with difficulties on all sides. In casting his eyes around, he could not promise himself adequate support from any quarter. His gloomy prospects were not brightened by any expectations, on the fulfillment of which he could depend. Distrusting, but not despairing, he asked Col. Reed—"Should we retreat to the back parts of Pennsylvania, will the Pennsylvanians support us?"

The Colonel answered—"If the lower counties are subdued and give up, the back counties will do the same."

Washington nobly replied—"We must retire to Augusta county, in Virginia. Numbers will be obliged to repair to us for safety, and we must try what we can do, in carrying on a predatory war; and if overpowered, we must cross the Alleghany mountains."

Gen. Washington had no cavalry but a small corps of badly mounted Connecticut militia, and was almost equally destitute of artillery, while conducting this retreat. It commenced in a few days after the reduction of Fort Washington, in which the flower of the American army were made prisoners of war. A great part of the retreating troops consisted of those who had garrisoned Fort Lee. These had been compelled to abandon their post so suddenly, that they left behind them their tents, blankets, and cooking utensils.

In this situation they retreated, badly armed, worse clad, and in many instances barefooted, in the cold months of November and December, through a desponding country, more disposed to seek safety by submission than resistance. Under all these disadvantages, they performed a march of about ninety miles, and had the address to prolong it to a space of nineteen days, that as much time as possible might be gained for expected reinforcements to arrive. As they retreated through the country, scarcely one of the inhabitants joined them; while numbers daily flocked to the British army, and took the benefit of a royal proclamation issued at this critical time, for pardoning all who, within sixty days, would return to the condition of British subjects.

The small force which began this retreat was daily lessening, by the expiration of the term of service for which they were engaged. This terminated in November with many, and in December with nearly two-thirds of the residue. No persuasions were availing to induce their continuance. They abandoned their General, when the advancing enemy was nearly in sight. The Pennsylvania militia was engaged to the first day of January, but they deserted in such numbers that it became necessary to place guards at the ferries to stop them.

Two regiments had been ordered from Ticonderoga to join Gen. Washington, but their term of service expired on the first of December. They refused to re-enlist, and went off, to a man. Gen. Lee, who commanded the eastern troops, was repeatedly ordered by Washington to cross the North River, and join the retreating army; but these orders were not obeyed. While at a distance both from his troops and the enemy, he was surpassed and taken prisoner by the British.

This begat suspicions, that. despairing of the success of the Americans, he had chosen to abandon their service. Though these apprehensions were without foundation, they produced the same mischievous effects on the minds of the people as if they were realities. About the same time Congress thought it expedient to leave Philadelphia and retire to Baltimore.

Under all these trying circumstances, Washington was undismayed. He did not despair of the public safety. With unconquerable firmness and the most perfect self-possession, he was always the same, and constantly showed himself to his army with a serene and undisturbed countenance. Nothing was omitted by him that could embarrass the enemy, or animate his army or country. He forcibly pointed out to Congress the defective

Campaign of 1776: New-York and New-Jersey

constitution of their army, without cavalry, without artillery and engineers; and enlarged upon the impolicy of short enlistments, and placing confidence in militia suddenly called out and frequently changed. He urged these matters with great warmth; but to prevent offence, added—"A character to lose—an estate to forfeit—the inestimable blessing of liberty at stake—and a life devoted, must be my excuse."

He also hinted at the propriety of enlarging his powers so as to enable him to act in cases of urgency, without application to Congress; but apologized for this liberty by declaring, "that he felt no lust of power, and wished with the greatest fervency for an opportunity of turning the sword into a ploughshare:" but added—"his feelings as an officer and a man had been such as to force him to say, that no person ever had a greater choice of difficulties to contend with than himself."

In this very dangerous crisis, Washington made every exertion to procure reinforcements to supply the place of those who were daily leaving him. He sent Generals Mifflin and Armstrong to rouse the citizens of Pennsylvania. Col. Reed was dispatched to Governor Livingston, to urge on him the necessity of calling out the Jersey militia. These exertions were in a great measure unavailing, except in and near the city of Philadelphia. Fifteen hundred of the citizens of that metropolis associated together, and marched to the aid of Washington. Though most of these were accustomed to the habits of a city life, they slept in tents, barns, and sometimes in the open air, during the cold months of December and January.

On the capture of Gen. Lee, the command of his army devolved on Gen. Sullivan, who, in obedience to the orders formerly given, joined Gen. Washington. About the same time an addition was made to his force by the arrival of a part of the northern army. The Americans now amounted to about 7000 men, though during the retreat through the Jerseys, they were seldom equal to half that number. The two armies were separated from each other by the river Delaware. The British, in the security of conquest, cantoned their troops in Burlington, Bordenton, Trenton, and other towns of New-Jersey, in daily expectation of being enabled to cross into Pennsylvania by means of ice, which is generally formed about that time.

On receiving information of their numbers and different cantonments, Washington observed—"Now is the time to clip their wings, when they are so spread." Yielding to his native spirit of enterprise which had hitherto been repressed, he formed the bold design of re-crossing the Delaware, and attacking the British posts on its eastern banks.

In the evening of Christmas day he made arrangements for passing over in three divisions; at M'Konkey's ferry, at Trenton, and at or near Bordentown. The troops which were to have crossed at the two last places exerted themselves to get over, but failed from the quantity of ice which obstructed their passage. The main body, about 2400 men, began to cross very early in the evening; but were so retarded by ice that it was nearly four o'clock in the morning before they were in a condition to take up their line of march on the Jersey side.

They were formed in two divisions. One was ordered to proceed on the lower or river road; the other on the upper or Pennington road. These having nearly the same distance to march, were ordered immediately on forcing the out guards, to push directly into Trenton, that they might charge the enemy before they had time to form. Though they marched different roads, yet they arrived within three minutes of each other. The out guards of the Hessian troops at Trenton soon fell back; but kept up a constant retreating fire. Their main body being hard pressed by the Americans, who had already got possession of half their artillery, attempted to file off by a road leading towards Princeton, but were checked by a body of troops thrown in their way. Finding they were surrounded, they laid down their arms.

The number that submitted was 23 officers and 886 men. Between 30 and 40 of the Hessians were killed and wounded. Col. Rahl was among the former, and seven of his officers among the latter. Captain Washington, of the Virginia troops, and five or six of the Americans, were wounded. Two were killed, and two or three were frozen to death. The detachment in Trenton consisted of the regiments of Rahl, Losberg, and Kniphausen, amounting in the whole to about 1500 men, and a troop of British light horse. All these were killed or captured, except about 600, who escaped by the road leading to Bordenton.

The British had a strong battalion of light infantry at Princeton, and a force yet remaining near the Delaware, superior to the American army. Washington, therefore, in the evening of the same day, thought it most prudent to cross into Pennsylvania with his prisoners. These being secured, he recrossed the Delaware, and took possession of Trenton. The detachments which had been distributed over New-Jersey previous to the capture of the Hessians, immediately after that event assembled at Princeton, and were joined by the army from Brunswick under Lord Cornwallis. From this position they came forward to Trenton in great force, hoping, by a vigorous onset, to repair the injury their cause had sustained by the late defeat.

Truly delicate was the situation of the feeble American army. To retreat was to hazard the city of Philadelphia, and to destroy every ray of hope which began to dawn from their late success. To risk an action with a superior force in front, and a river in rear, was dangerous in the extreme. To get round the advanced party of the British, and, by pushing forwards, to attack in their rear, was deemed preferable to either.

The British, on their advance from Princeton, attacked a body of Americans which were posted with four field pieces a little to the northward of Trenton, and compelled them to retreat. The pursuing British being checked at the bridge over Sanpink creek by some field pieces, fell back so far as to be out of their reach. The Americans were drawn up on the opposite side of the creek, and in that position remained till night, cannonading the enemy and receiving their fire.

In this critical hour, two armies, on which the success or failure of the American revolution materially depended, were crowded into the small village of Trenton, and only separated by a creek, in many places fordable.

The British, believing they had all the advantages they could wish for, and that they could use them when they pleased, discontinued all farther operations, and kept themselves in readiness to make the attack next morning. But the next morning presented a scene as brilliant on the one side, as it was unexpected on the other. Soon after it became dark, Washington ordered all his baggage to be silently removed, and having left guards for the purpose of deception, marched with his whole force by a circuitous route to Princeton. This maneuvre was determined upon in a council of war, from a conviction that it would avoid the appearance of a retreat, and at the same time the hazard of an action in a bad position, and that it was the most likely way to preserve the city of Philadelphia from falling into the hands of the British.

Washington also presumed, that, from an eagerness to efface the impressions made by the late capture of the Hessians at Trenton, the British commanders had pushed forward their principal force; and that the remainder in the rear at Princeton, was not more than equal to his own. The event more than verified this conjecture. The more effectually to disguise the departure of the Americans from Trenton, fires were lighted up in front of their camp. These not only gave the appearance of going to rest, but, as flame cannot be seen through, concealed from the British what was transacting behind them. In this relative position they were a pillar of fire to the one army, and the pillar of a cloud to the other.

Providence favoured this movement of the Americans. The weather had been for some time so warm and moist that the ground was soft, and the roads so deep as to be scarcely passable; but the wind suddenly changed to the northwest, and the ground in a short time was frozen so hard that when the Americans took up their line of march, they were no more retarded than if they had been upon a solid pavement.

Washington reached Princeton early in the morning, and would have completely surprised the British, had not a party which was on their way to Trenton descried his troops when they were about two miles distant, and sent back couriers to alarm their unsuspecting soldiers in their rear. These consisted of the 17th, the 40th, and 55th regiments of British infantry, and some of the royal artillery, with two field pieces, and three troops of light dragoons. The centre of the Americans, consisting of the Philadelphia militia, while on their line of march, was briskly charged by a party of the British, and gave way in disorder.

The moment was critical. Washington pushed forward, and placed himself between his own men and the British, with his horse's head fronting the latter. The Americans, encouraged by his example and exhortations, made a stand, and returned the British fire. The General, though between both parties, was providentially uninjured by either. A party of the British fled into the college, and were there attacked with field pieces, which were fired into it. The seat of the muses became for some time the scene of action.

The party which had taken refuge in the college, after receiving a few discharges from the American field pieces, came out and surrendered themselves prisoners of war. In the course of the engagement sixty of the British were killed, and a great number wounded, and about 300 of them taken prisoners. The rest made their escape, some by pushing on to Trenton; others by returning to Brunswick.

While they were fighting in Princeton, the British in Trenton were under arms, and on the point of making an assault on the evacuated camp of the Americans. With so much address had the movement to Princeton been conducted, that though from the critical situation of the two armies every ear may be supposed to have been open, and every watchfulness to have been employed, yet Washington moved completely off the ground with his whole force, stores, baggage, and artillery, unknown to and unsuspected by his adversaries. The British in Trenton were so entirely deceived, that when they heard the report of the artillery at Princeton, though it was in the depth of winter, they supposed it to be thunder.

The British, astonished at these bold movements of an enemy supposed to be vanquished, instantly fell back with their whole force, and abandoned every post they held to the southward of New-York, except Brunswick and Amboy.

4

The Campaign of 1776: Of the operations of General Washington in New-Jersey and Pennsylvania, in the campaign of 1777. The battles of Brandywine and German-Town. Washington is advised by the Rev. Jacob Duche, to give up the contest. The distresses of the American army. Its winter quarters in Valley Forge. Gen. Washington is assailed by the clamours of discontented individuals and public bodies, and by the designs of a faction to supersede him in his office as commander in chief.

The victories at Trenton and Princeton produced the most extensive effects, and had a decided influence on subsequent events. Philadelphia was saved for that winter. Jersey was recovered. The drooping spirits of the Americans were revived. The gloomy apprehensions which had lately prevailed, of their being engaged in a hopeless cause, yielded to a confidence in their General and their army, and in the ultimate success of their struggles for liberty and independence.

So strong an impulse was given to the recruiting service in every part of the United States, as gave good ground to hope that the commander in chief would be enabled to take the field in the spring with a permanent regular army, on the new terms of enlistment.

After the campaign had thus been carried into the month of January, Washington retired to Morristown, that he might afford shelter to his suffering army. His situation there was far from being eligible. His force for some considerable time was trifling, when compared with that of the British; but the enemy and his own countrymen believed the contrary. Their deception was cherished and artfully continued by the parade of a large army. Washington placed his officers in positions of difficult access, and they kept up a constant communication with each other. This secured them from insult and surprise. While they covered the country, they harassed the foraging parties of the British, and confined them to narrow limits.

The remainder of the winter season passed over in a light war of skirmishes. These were generally in favour of the Americans; but Washington's views were much more extensive. He hoped that his country, encouraged by the late successes at Trenton and Princeton, would have placed at his disposal a large and efficient army, equal to that of the enemy. To obtain it, he urged with great earnestness the advantage of being enabled to undertake decisive operations before reinforcements to the British army should arrive. Congress, at his instance, passed the requisite resolutions; but these could not be carried into effect without the aid of the state legislatures. The delays incident to this slow mode of doing business, added to the recollection of the suffering of the troops in the last campaign, retarded the recruiting service. Washington with infinite reluctance was obliged to give up his favourite project of an early active campaign.

In the advance of the spring, when recruits were obtained, a difficulty arose in assembling them from the different states in which they had been enlisted. As the British had possession of the ocean, they could at pleasure transfer the war to any maritime portion of the union. Each state, anxious for its particular safety, claimed protection from the common army of the whole. Had they been indulged, the feeble remnant under the immediate direction of the commander in chief, would have been unequal to any great enterprise. To these partial calls he opposed all his authority and influence, and his pointed representations made an impression in favour of primary objects. These were to prevent the British from getting possession of Philadelphia, or the Highlands on the Hudson. Both were of so nearly equal importance to their interest, that it was impossible to ascertain which should be preferred by Sir William Howe.

In this uncertainty, Washington made such an arrangement of his troops as would enable him to oppose either. The northern troops were divided between Ticonderoga and Peekskill; while those from Jersey and the south were encamped at Middlebrook, near the Rariton. The American force collected at this strong and defencible encampment, was nominally between nine and ten thousand men; but the effective rank and file was about six thousand.

A majority of these were raw recruits; and a considerable number of such as had been enlisted in the middle states were foreigners or servants. To encourage the desertion of troops so slightly attached to the American cause, Gen. Howe offered a reward to every soldier who would come over to his army, and an additional compensation to such as would bring their arms with them. To counteract these propositions, Washington recommended to Congress to give full pardon to all Americans who would relinquish the British service.

The campaign opened early in June on the part of the British, who advanced towards Philadelphia as far as Somerset county, in New-Jersey; but they soon fell back to New-Brunswick. After this retreat, Sir William Howe endeavored to provoke Washington to an engagement, and left no manoeuvre untried that was calculated to induce him to quit his position. At one time he appeared as if he intended to push on, without regarding the army opposed to him. At another, he accurately examined the situation of the American encampment; hoping that some unguarded part may be found on which an attack might be made that would open the way to a general engagement.

All these hopes were frustrated. Washington knew the full value of his situation. He had too much penetration to lose it from the circumvention of military manoeuvres, and too much temper to be provoked to a dereliction of it. He was well apprised it was not the interest of his country to commit its fortune to a single action.

Sir William Howe suddenly relinquished his position in front of the Americans, and retired with his whole force to Amboy. The apparently retreating British were pursued by a considerable detachment of the American army, and Washington advanced from Middlebrook to Quibbletown, to be near at hand for the support of his advanced parties. The British General immediately marched his army back from Amboy, with great expedition, hoping to bring on a general action on equal ground; but he was disappointed. Washington fell back, and posted his army in such an advantageous situation as compensated for the inferiority of his numbers.

Sir William Howe was now fully convinced of the impossibility of compelling a general engagement on equal terms, and also satisfied that it would be too hazardous to attempt passing the Delaware while the country was in arms, and the main American army in full force in his rear. He therefore returned to Amboy, and thence passed over to Staten Island, resolving to prosecute the objects of the campaign by an embarkation of his whole force at New-York.

During the period of these movements, the real designs of Gen. Howe were involved in obscurity. Though the season for military operations was advanced as far as the month of July, yet his determinate object could not be ascertained. Nothing on his part had hitherto taken place, but alternately advancing and retreating.

Campaign of 1776: New-Jersey and Pennsylvania

Washington's embarrassment on this account was increased by intelligence which arrived, that Burgoyne was advancing in great force towards New-York from Canada. Apprehending that Sir William Howe would ultimately move up the North River, and that his movements which looked southwardly were feints, the American chief detached a brigade to reinforce the northern division of his army.

Successive advices of the advance of Burgoyne favoured the idea that a junction of the two royal armies, near Albany, was intended. Some movements were therefore made by Washington towards Peekskill, and on the other side towards Trenton, while the main army was encamped near the Clove, in readiness to march either to the south or north, as the movements of Sir William Howe might require.

After the British had left Sandy Hook, they looked into the Delaware, and suddenly again put out to sea, and were not heard of for near three weeks, except that once or twice they had been seen near the coast steering southwardly. Charlestown, in South Carolina, was supposed to be their object at one time; at another, Philadelphia by the way of Chesapeak; at another, the Highlands of New-York, to co-operate with Burgoyne.

The perplexing uncertainty concerning the destination of the enemy which embarrassed the movements of Washington, was not away before the middle of August, when certain accounts were received that the British had taken possession of the Chesapeak, and landed as near to Philadelphia as was practicable. While the object of the campaign was doubtful, every disposition was made to defend all the supposed probable points of attack except Charlestown. This being at the distance of seven or eight hundred miles, could not be assisted by an army marching over land, in time to oppose the enemy conveyed thither by water.

While this idea prevailed, arrangements were made to employ the American army either against the enemy advancing from Albany, or against the British posts in New-York, with the hope of making reparation for the expected loss of Charlestown. As soon as the arrival of the British in the Chesapeak was known, Washington ordered the different divisions of his army to unite in the neighbourhood of Philadelphia, towards the head of Elk; and the militia of Pennsylvania, Maryland, and the northern counties of Virginia, to take the field.

He had previously written very pressing letters to the Governors of the eastern states, and to the Generals in the western parts of these states, to strengthen the northern army opposed to Burgoyne; and even weakened himself by detaching some of his best troops, particularly Morgan's riflemen, on that important service. In the spirit of true patriotism, he

Campaign of 1776: New-Jersey and Pennsylvania

diminished his own chances of acquiring fame, that the common cause might be most effectually promoted by the best disposition of the forces under his command, for simultaneous opposition to both Howe and Burgoyne.

Washington passed his army with every appearance of confidence through the city of Philadelphia, with a view of making some impression on the disaffected of that city, and afterwards proceeded towards the head of Elk. About the same time he directed Gen. Smallwood, with the militia of Maryland and Delaware, and come continental troops, to hang on the rear of the enemy. As a substitute for Morgan's riflemen, Gen. Maxwell was furnished with a corps of light infantry, amounting to one thousand men, and directed to annoy the British on their march through the country. These troops were afterwards reinforced with Gen. Wayne's division. Though the militia did not turn out with that alacrity which might have been expected from the energetic calls of Washington, yet a respectable force was assembled, which imposed on Sir William Howe a necessity of proceeding with caution.

The royal army set out from the eastern heads of the Chesapeak on the third of September, with a spirit which promised to compensate for the various delays which had hitherto wasted the campaign. They advanced with great circumspection and boldness till they were within two miles of the American army, which was then posted in the vicinity of New Port.

Washington soon changed his ground, and took post on the high ground near Chadd's Ford, on the Brandywine creek, with an intention of disputing the passage. It was the wish, but by no means the interest, of the Americans, to try their strength in an engagement. Their regular troops were not only inferior in discipline, but in numbers, to the royal army. The opinion of the inhabitants, though founded on no circumstances more substantial than their wishes, imposed a species of necessity on the American General to keep his army in front of the enemy, and to risk an action for the security of Philadelphia. Instead of this, had he taken the ridge of high mountains on his right, the British might have respected his numbers, and probably would have followed him up the country.

In this manner the campaign might have been wasted away in a manner fatal to the invaders; but the bulk of the American people were so impatient of delays, and had such an overweening conceit of the numbers and prowess of their army, that they could not comprehend the wisdom and policy of manoeuvres to shun a general engagement.

On this occasion necessity dictated that a sacrifice should be made on the altar of public opinion. A general action was therefore hazarded.

This took place at Chadd's Ford, on the Brandywine, a small stream which empties itself into Christiana creek, near its conflux with the river Delaware.

The royal army advanced at day break in two columns, commanded by Lieutenant General Kniphausen and Lord Cornwallis. They first took the direct road to Chadd's Ford, and made a show of passing it, in front of the main body of the Americans. At the same time the other column moved up on the west side of the Brandywine to its fork, and crossed both its branches, and then marched down on the east side thereof, with the view of turning the right wing of their adversaries.

This they effected, and compelled them to retreat with great loss. Gen. Kniphausen amused the Americans with the appearance of crossing the Ford, but did not attempt it until Lord Cornwallis, having crossed above and moved down on the opposite side, had commenced his attack. Kniphausen then crossed the Ford and attacked the troops posted for its defence. These, after a severe conflict, were compelled to give way. The retreat of the Americans soon became general, and was continued to Chester. Their loss was about nine hundred, and considerably exceeded that of the British.

The final issue of battles often depends on small circumstances, which human prudence cannot control. One of these occurred here, and prevented Gen. Washington from executing a bold design, to effect which his troops were actually in motion. This was to cross the Brandywine, and attack Kniphausen, while Gen. Sullivan and Lord Stirling should keep Earl Cornwallis in check. In the most critical moment Washington received intelligence which he was obliged to credit, that the column of Lord Cornwallis had been only making a feint, and was returning to join Kniphausen. This prevented the execution of a plan, which, if carried into effect, would probably have given a different turn to the events of the day.

Washington made every exertion to repair the loss which had been sustained. The battle of Brandywine was represented as not being decisive. Congress and the people wished to hazard a second engagement, for the security of Philadelphia. Howe sought for it, and Washington did not decline it. He therefore advanced as far as the Warren tavern, on the Lancaster road, with an intention of meeting his adversary. Near that place both armies were on the point of engaging with their whole force; but were prevented by a most violent storm of rain, which continued for a whole day and night. When the rain ceased, the Americans found that their ammunition was entirely ruined. They therefore withdrew to a place of safety.

Campaign of 1776: New-Jersey and Pennsylvania

Before a proper supply was procured, the British marched from their position near the White Horse tavern, down towards the Swedes Ford. The Americans again took post in their front, but the British, instead of urging an action, began to march up towards Reading. To save the stores which had been deposited in that place, Washington took a new position, and left the British in undisturbed possession of the roads which lead to Philadelphia. His troops were worn down with a succession of severe duties. There were in his army above a thousand men who were barefooted, and who had performed all their late movements in that condition.

Though Washington had failed in his object of saving Philadelphia, yet he retained the confidence of Congress and the States. With an army inferior in numbers, discipline, and equipments, he delayed the British army thirty days in advancing sixty miles through an open country, without fortifications, and the waters of which were every where fordable. Though defeated in one general action, he kept together his undisciplined and unprovided army, and in less than a week offered battle to his successful adversary. When this was prevented by a storm of rain which ruined his ammunition, while many of his soldiers were without bayonets, he extricated them from the most imminent danger, and maintained a respectable standing.

Instead of immediately retiring into winter quarters, he approached the enemy and encamped on the Skippack road. The British army took their stand in Philadelphia and Germantown, shortly after the battle of Brandywine. FFrom these positions, especially the last, considerable detachments were sent to Chester and the vicinity, to favour an attempt to open the navigation of the river Delaware, which had been obstructed with great ingenuity and industry by the Americans.

About the same time the American army received a reinforcement of two thousand five hundred men, which increased its effective force to eleven thousand.

General Washington conceived that the present moment furnished a fair opportunity for enterprise. He therefore resolved to attack the British in Germantown. Their line of encampment crossed that village at right angles; the left wing extending on the west to the Schuylkill. That wing was covered in front and flank by the German chasseurs. A battalion of light infantry, and the queen's American rangers, were in front of the right. The 40th regiment, with another battalion of infantry, was posted at the head of the village.

The Americans moved from their encampment on the Skippack road in the evening of the 3d of October, with the intention of surprising their

Campaign of 1776: New-Jersey and Pennsylvania

adversaries early next morning, and to attack both wings in front and rear at the same time, so as to prevent the several parts from supporting each other. The divisions of Greene and Stevens, flanked by M'Dougal's brigade, were to enter by the lime kiln road. The militia of Maryland and Jersey, under Generals Smallwood and Furman, were to march by the old York road, and to fall upon the rear of their right.

Lord Stirling, with Nashe's and Maxwell's brigade, were to form a corps de reserve. The Americans began their attack about sunrise, on the 40th regiment and a battalion of light infantry. These being obliged to retreat, were pursued into the village. On their retreat, Lieut. Col. Musgrove, with six companies, took post in Mr. Chew's strong stone house, which lay in front of the Americans. From an adherence to the military maxim of never leaving a fort possessed by an enemy in the rear, it was resolved to attack the party in the house.

In the mean time Gen. Greene got up with his column, and attacked the right wing. Col. Mathews routed a party of the British opposed to him, killed several, and took 110 prisoners; but, from the darkness of the day, lost sight of the brigade to which he belonged, and having separated from it, was taken prisoner, with his whole regiment; and the prisoners which he had previously taken were released. A number of the troops in Greene's division were stopped by the halt of the party before Chew's house. Near one half of the American army remained for some time at that place inactive.

In the mean time Gen. Grey led on three battalions of the third brigade, and attacked with vigour. A sharp contest followed. Two British regiments attacked at the same time on the opposite side of the town. General Grant moved up the 49th regiment to the aid of those who were engaged with Greene's column.

The morning was foggy. This, by concealing the true situation of the parties, occasioned mistakes, and made so much caution necessary as to give the British time to recover from the effects of their first surprise. From these causes the early promising appearances on the part of the assailants were speedily reversed.

The Americans left the field hastily, and all efforts to rally them were ineffectual. Washington was obliged to relinquish the victory he had thought within his grasp, and to turn his whole attention to the security of his army. A retreat about 20 miles to Perkioming was made, with the loss of only one piece of artillery. In the engagement the loss of the Americans, including the wounded and four hundred prisoners, was about 1100. A considerable part of this was occasioned by the 40th regiment, which, from the doors and windows of Mr. Chew's large stone house, kept up a constant fire on their uncovered adversaries.

The plan of the battle of Germantown was judicious, and its commencement well conducted; but to ensure its successful execution, a steady cooperation of the several divisions of the assailants was necessary. The numerous enclosures to be passed, and the thickness of the fog, rendered this impossible; especially by troops who were imperfectly disciplined, and without the advantages of experience.

Congress voted their unanimous thanks "to General Washington for his wise and well concerted attack, and to the officers and soldiers of the army, for their brave exertions on that occasion;" and added—"They were well satisfied that the best designs and boldest efforts may sometimes fail by unforeseen incidents."

In the latter part of the campaign of 1777, in proportion as the loss of Philadelphia became more probable, Washington took every precaution eventually to diminish its value to the enemy. Orders were given for moving the military stores and the vessels at the wharves of that city higher up the Delaware. From the time that the British got possession, every aid consistent with greater objects was given to the forts constructed on the Delaware for opposing the British in their attempts to open the navigation of that river. Troops were stationed on both sides of the Delaware to prevent the inhabitants from going with their provisions to the market of Philadelphia, and to destroy small foraging parties sent out to obtain supplies for the royal army. These arrangements being made, Washington advanced towards Philadelphia.

His objects were to enfeeble the royal army in their operations against the forts on the Delaware; to attack them if circumstances favoured, and prevent their receiving supplies from the country. The British shortly after evacuated Germantown; concentered their force at Philadelphia, and directed their principal attention to the opening the navigation of the Delaware. This employed them for more than six weeks; and after a great display of gallantry on both sides, was finally accomplished.

In this discouraging state of public affairs, a long letter was addressed by the reverend Jacob Duche, late chaplain of Congress, and a clergyman of the first rank, for character, piety, and eloquence, to Gen. Washington; the purport of which was, to persuade him that farther resistance to Great-Britain was hopeless, and would only increase the calamities of their common country; and under this impression to urge him to make the best terms he could with the British commander, and to give up the contest.

Such a letter, at such a time, in unison with the known sentiments of many desponding citizens, from a person whose character and connexions placed him above all suspicion of treachery, and whose attachment to his native country, America, was unquestionable, could not have failed to make an impression on minds of a feeble texture; but from Washington, who never despaired of his country, the laboured epistle of the honest, but timid divine, received no farther notice than a verbal message to the writer thereof, "That if the contents of his letter had been known, it should have been returned unopened."

While Sir William Howe was succeeding in every enterprise in Philadelphia, intelligence arrived that Gen. Burgoyne and his whole army had surrendered prisoners of war to the Americans. Washington soon after received a considerable reinforcement from the northern army, which had accomplished this great event. With this increased force he took a position at and near Whitemarsh.

The royal army having succeeded in removing the obstructions in the river Delaware, were ready for new enterprises. Sir William Howe marched out of Philadelphia, with almost his whole force, expecting to bring on a general engagement. The next morning he appeared on Chesnut hill, in front of, and about three miles distant from the right wing of the Americans. On the day following the British changed their ground, and moved to the right. Two days after they moved still farther to the right, and made every appearance of an intention to attack the American encampment. Some skirmishes took place, and a general action was hourly expected; but instead thereof, on the morning of the next day, after various marches and countermarches, the British filed off from their right by two or three different routes, in full march for Philadelphia.

While the two armies were manoeuvering, in constant expectation of an immediate engagement, Washington rode through every brigade of his army, and with a firm steady countenance gave orders in person how to receive the enemy, and particularly urged on his troops to place their chief dependence on the bayonet.

His position, in a military point of view, was admirable. He was so sensible of the advantages of it, that the manoeuvres of Sir William Howe for some days could not allure him from it. In consequence of the reinforcement lately received, he had not in any preceding period of the campaign been in an equal condition for a general engagement. Though he ardently wished to be attacked, yet he would not relinquish a position from which he hoped for reparation for the adversities of the campaign. He could not believe that Gen. Howe, with a victorious army,

Campaign of 1776: New-Jersey and Pennsylvania

and that lately reinforced with 4000 men from New-York, should come out of Philadelphia only to return thither again.

He therefore presumed, that to avoid the disgrace of such a movement, the British commander would, from a sense of military honour, be compelled to attack him, though under great disadvantages. When he found him cautious of engaging, and inclined to his left, a daring design was formed, which would have been executed had the British either continued in their position, or moved a little farther to the left of the American army. This was to have (been) attempted in the night to surprise Philadelphia.

Three days after the retreat of the British, Washington communicated in general orders, his intention of retiring into winter quarters. He expressed to his army his approbation of their past conduct; gave an encouraging statement of the prospects of their country; exhorted them to bear the hardships inseparable from their situation, and endeavored to convince their judgments that that these were necessary for the public good, and unavoidable from the distressed situation of the new formed states.

The same care to cut off all communication between the enemy and the country was continued, and the same means employed to secure that object. Gen. Smallwood was detached to Wilmington to guard the Delaware. Col. Morgan, who had lately returned from the victorious northern army, was placed on the lines on the west side of the Schuylkill; and Gen. Armstrong near the old camp at the Whitemarsh, with a respectable force under the command of each, to prevent the country people from carrying provisions to the market in Philadelphia.

Valley Forge, about twenty-five miles distant from Philadelphia, was fixed upon for the winter quarters of the Americans. This position was preferred to distant and more comfortable villages, as being calculated to give the most extensive security to the country. The American army might have been tracked by the blood of their feet in marching without shoes or stockings, over the hard frozen ground between Whitemarsh and the Valley Forge. Under these circumstances they had to sit down in a wood in the latter end of December, and to build huts for their accommodation.

To a want of cloathing was added a want of provisions. For some days there was little less than a famine in the camp. Washington was compelled to make seizures for the support of his army. Congress had authorized him so to do; but he wished the civil authority to manage the delicate business of impressment, and regretted the measure as subversive of discipline, and calculated to raise in the soldiers a disposition to licentiousness and plunder. To suffer his army to starve or disband, or to feed them by force, were the only alternatives offered to his choice.

Though he exercised these extraordinary powers with equal reluctance and discretion, his lenity was virtually censured by Congress, "as proceeding from a delicacy in exerting military authority on the citizens, which, in their opinion, might prove prejudicial to the general liberties of America;" at the same time his rigour was condemned by those from whom provisions were forcibly taken. The sound judgment and upright principles of the commander in chief gave a decided preference to the mode of supplying his army by fair contract, but the necessities thereof proceeding from bad management in the commissary department—the depreciation of the Congress bills of credit—the selfishness of the farmers in preferring British metallic to American paper money, together with the eagerness of Congress to starve the British army in Philadelphia, compelled him to extort supplies for his army at the point of the bayonet. In obedience to Congress, he issued a proclamation, "calling on the farmers within seventy miles of headquarters to thresh out one half of their grain by the first of February, and the residue by the first of March, under the penalty of having the whole seized as straw."

Great were the difficulties Washington had to contend with for feeding and cloathing his army; but they were not the only ones which at this time pressed on him. The states of Pennsylvania and New-Jersey were importunate with him to cover them from the incursions of the enemy. In both there were many discontented individuals, who, regretting their past losses and present danger from the vicinity of a conquering army, were so far misled by their feelings as to suppose it to be the fault of Gen. Washington, that the inferior destitute army under his immediate command had not been as successful as the superior well supported northern army under Gen. Gates.

The legislature of Pennsylvania, probably sore from the loss of their capital, on hearing that Washington was about to retire into winter quarters, presented a remonstrance to Congress on that subject, in which their dissatisfaction with the General was far from being concealed. A copy of this being sent to him, he addressed Congress in terms very different from his usual style.

He stated, "that though every thing in his power had been done for supporting his army, yet their inactivity, arising from their manifold wants, was charged to his account; that the army seldom had provisions for two days in advance; that few of his men had more than one shirt, many only a moiety of one, and some none at all; that soap, vinegar, and such like articles, though allowed by Congress, had not been seen in camp for several weeks; that by a field return 2898 of his army were unfit for duty, because they were barefooted, and otherwise naked; that his whole effective force in camp amounted to no more than 8200 men fit for duty; that notwithstanding these complicated wants, the remonstrance of the Pennsylvania legislature reprobated the measure of his going into winter quarters, as if its authors thought the soldiers were made of stocks or stones, and as if they conceived it easily practicable for an inferior army, circumstanced as his was, to confine a superior one, well appointed and every way provided for a winter's campaign, within the city of Philadelphia, and to cover all the circumjacent country from their depredation."

He assured the complainers, "that it was much easier to draw up remonstrances in a comfortable room by a good fire-side, than to occupy a cold bleak hill, and sleep under frost and snow, without clothes or blankets."

To the other vexations which crowded on Gen. Washington at the close of the campaign of 1777, was added one of a peculiar nature. Though he was conscious he had never solicited, and that it was neither from motives of interest nor of ambition he had accepted the command of the army, and that he had with clean hands and a pure heart, to the utmost of his power, steadily pursued what his best judgment informed him was for the interest of his country; yet he received certain information that a cabal, consisting of some members of Congress, and a few General Officers of the army, was plotting to supersede him in his command.

The scheme was to obtain the sanction of some of the state legislatures to instruct their delegates to move in Congress for an inquiry into the causes of the failures of the campaigns of 1776 and 1777, with the hope that some intemperate resolutions passed by them would either lead to the removal of the General, or would his military feelings so as to induce his resignation. Anonymous papers containing high charges against him, and urging the necessity of putting some more energetic officer at the head of the army, were sent to Henry Laurens, President of Congress, Patrick Henry, Governor of Virginia, and others. These were forwarded to Gen. Washington.

In his reply to Mr. Laurens, he wrote as follows:

"I cannot sufficiently express the obligation I feel towards you for your friendship and politeness, upon an occasion in which I am so deeply interested. I was not unapprized that a malignant faction had been for some time forming to my prejudice, which, conscious as I am of having ever done all in my power to answer the important purposes of the trust reposed in me, could not but give me some pain on a personal account;

but my chief concern arises from an apprehension of the dangerous consequences which intestine dissentions may prove to the common cause.

"As I have no other view than to promote the public good, and am unambitious of honours not founded in the approbation of my country, I would not desire in the least degree to suppress a free spirit of inquiry into any part of my conduct, that even faction itself may deem reprehensible.

"The anonymous paper handed you exhibits many serious charges, and it is my wish that it may be submitted to Congress. This I am the more inclined to, as the suppression or concealment may possibly involve you in embarrassments hereafter, since it is uncertain how many, or who may be privy to the contents.

"My enemies take an ungenerous advantage of me. They know the delicacy of my situation, and that motives of policy deprive me of the defence I might otherwise make against their insidious attacks. They know I cannot combat insinuations, however injurious, without disclosing secrets it is of the utmost moment to conceal. But why should I expect to be exempt from censure, the unfailing lot of an elevated station? Merit and talents, which I cannot pretend to rival, have ever been subject to it; my heart tells me it has been my unremitted aim to do the best which circumstances would permit; yet I may have been very often mistaken in my judgment of the means, and may, in many instances, deserve the imputation of error."

About the same time it was reported that Washington had determined to resign his command. On this occasion he wrote to a gentleman in New-England as follows:

"I can assure you that no person ever heard me drop an expression that had a tendency to resignation. The same principles that led me to embark in the opposition to the arbitrary claims of Great-Britain, operate with additional force at this day; nor is it my desire to withdraw my service while they are considered of importance in the present contest: but to report a design of this kind is among the arts which those who are endeavoring to effect a change, are practising to bring it to pass.

"I have said, and I still do say, that there is not an officer in the United States that would return to the sweets of domestic life with more heart-felt joy than I should. But I would have this declaration accompanied by these sentiments, that while the public are satisfied with my endeavors, I mean not to shrink from the cause; but the moment her voice, not that of faction, calls upon me to resign, I shall do it with as much pleasure as ever the weary traveller retired to rest."

These machinations did not abate the ardour of Washington in the common cause. His patriotism was too solid to be shaken either by envy or ingratitude. Nor was the smallest effect produced in diminishing his well earned reputation. Zeal the most active, and services the most beneficial, and at the same time disinterested, had rivetted him in the affections of his country and army.

Even the victorious troops under General Gates, though comparisons highly flattering to their vanity had been made between them and the army in Pennsylvania, clung to Washington as their political saviour. The resentment of the people was generally excited against those who were supposed to be engaged in or friendly to the scheme of appointing a new commander in chief over the American army.

5

The Campaign of 1778: General Washington prepares for the campaign of 1778. Surprises the British, and defeats them at Monmouth. Arrests General Lee. Calms the irritation excited by the departure of the French fleet from Rhode Island to Boston. Dissuades from an invasion of Canada.

Washington devoted the short respite from field duty which followed the encampment of the army at Valley Forge, to prepare for an early and active campaign in the year 1778. He laboured to impress on Congress the necessity of having in the field a regular army, at least equal to that of the enemy. He transmitted to the individual states a return of the troops they had severally furnished for the continental army. While this exhibited to each its deficiency, it gave the General an opportunity to urge on them respectively the necessity of completing their quotas.

Congress deputed a committee of their body to reside in camp, and, in concert with Gen. Washington, to investigate the state of the army, and to report such reforms as might be deemed expedient. This committee, known by the name of "the committee of arrangement," repaired to Valley Forge, in January, 1778.

Washington laid before them a statement, in which a comprehensive view of the army was taken, and in which he minutely pointed out what he deemed necessary for the correction of existing abuses, and for the advancement of the service. He recommended "as essentially necessary, that in addition to present compensation, provision should be made by half pay, and a pensionary establishment for the future support of the officers, so as to render their commissions valuable."

He pointed out "the insufficiency of their pay (especially in its present state of depreciation) for their decent subsistence; the sacrifices they had already made, and the unreasonableness of expecting that they would continue patiently to bear such an over proportion of the common calamities growing out of the necessary war, in which all were equally interested; the many resignations that had already taken place, and the probability that more would follow, to the great injury of the service; the impossibility of keeping up a strict discipline among officers whose commissions, in a pecuniary view, were so far from being worth holding, that they were the means of impoverishing them."

These, and other weighty considerations, were accompanied with a declaration by Gen. Washington, "that he neither could nor would receive the smallest benefit from the proposed establishment, and that he had no other inducement in urging it, but a full conviction of its utility and propriety."

In the same statement the commander in chief explained to the committee of Congress the defects in the quarter-masters, and other departments connected with the support and comfort of the army; and also urged the necessity of each state completing its quota by draughts from the militia. The statement concludes with these impressive words—"Upon the whole, gentlemen, I doubt not you are fully impressed with the defects of our present military system, and with the necessity of speedy and decisive measures to place it on a satisfactory footing. The disagreeable picture I have given you of the wants and sufferings of the army, and the discontents reigning among the officers, is a just representation of evils equally melancholy and important; and unless effectual remedies be applied without loss of time, the most alarming and ruinous consequences are to be apprehended."

The committee were fully impressed with the correctness of the observations made by the commander in chief, and grounded their report upon them. A general concurrence of sentiment took place. Congress passed resolutions, but with sundry limitations, in favour of half pay to their officers for seven years after the war; and gave their sanction to the other measures suggested by Washington, and recommended by their committee. But, from the delays incidental to large bodies, either deliberating upon or executing public business, much time necessarily elapsed before the army received the benefits of the proposed reforms; and in the mean time their distresses approached to such a height as threatened their immediate dissolution.

Respect for their commander attached both officers and soldiers so strongly to his person, as enabled him to keep them together under privations almost too much for human nature to bear. Their effective force throughout the winter was little more than 5000 men, though their numbers on paper exceeded 17,000. It was well for them that the British made no attempt to disturb them while in this destitute condition. In that case the Americans could not have kept their camp for want of provisions; nor could they have retreated from it without the certain loss of some thousands who were barefooted and otherwise almost naked. Neither could they have risked an action with any probable hope of success, or without hazarding the most serious consequences.

The historians of the American revolution will detail the particulars of a treaty entered into about this time between France and the United States, and also that thereupon the government of Great Britain offered terms to the Americans equal to all they had asked anterior to their declaration of Independence. The first certain intelligence of these offers was received by Gen. Washington in a letter from Major General Tryon, the British Governor of New-York, enclosing the conciliatory proposals, and recommending "that they should be circulated by Gen. Washington among the officers and privates of his army."

Instead of complying with this extraordinary request, he forwarded the whole to Congress. The offers of Great-Britain, which, if made in due time, would have prevented the dismemberment of the empire, were promptly rejected. The day after their rejection a resolution formerly recommended by Washington was adopted by Congress, in which they urged upon the different states "to pardon, under certain limitations, such of their misguided citizens as had levied war against the United States."

Copies of this were struck off in English and German, and Gen. Washington was directed to take measures for circulating them among the American levies in the British army. He immediately enclosed them in a letter to Tryon, in which he acknowledged the receipt of his late letter covering the British conciliatory bills, and requesting their circulation in the American army; and in the way of retort requested the instrumentality of Tryon in making the resolves of Congress known to the Americans in the British army, on whom they were intended to operate.

About this time Sir William Howe resigned the command of the British army, and returned to Great-Britain. His successor, Sir Henry Clinton, had scarcely entered on the duties of his office, when he received orders to evacuate Philadelphia. This was deemed expedient from an apprehension that it would be a dangerous position in case a French fleet, as was expected, should arrive in the Delaware to co-operate with the Americans.

The design of evacuating Philadelphia was soon discovered by Washington; but the object or course of the enemy could not be precisely ascertained. Their preparations equally denoted an expedition to the south; an embarkation of their whole army for New-York; or a march to that city through New-Jersey.

In the two first cases Washington had not the means of annoyance; but as the probability of the last daily increased, he directed his chief attention to that point. Gen. Maxwell, with the Jersey brigade, was ordered over the Delaware to take post about Mount Holly, and to co-operate with Gen. Dickinson at the head of the Jersey militia, in obstructing the progress of the royal army till time should be gained for Washington to overtake them.

The British crossed the Delaware to Gloucester Point, on the 18th of June, 1778: the Americans in four days after, at Corryel's ferry. The General officers of the latter, on being asked what line of conduct they deemed most advisable, had previously, and with one consent, agreed to attempt nothing till the evacuation of Philadelphia was completed; but after the Delaware was crossed, there was a diversity of sentiment respecting the measures proper to be pursued.

Gen. Lee, who, having been exchanged, joined the army, was of opinion that the United States, in consequence of their late foreign connexions, were secure of their independence, unless their army was defeated; and that under such circumstances it would be criminal to hazard an action, unless they had some decided action. Though the numbers in both armies were nearly equal, and about 10,000 effective men in each, he attributed so much to the superiority of British discipline, as made him apprehensive of the issue of an engagement on equal ground. The sentiments were sanctioned by the voice of a great majority of the general officers.

Washington was nevertheless strongly inclined to risk an action. Though cautious, he was enterprising, and could not readily believe that the chances of war were so much against him as to threaten consequences of the alarming magnitude which had been announced. There was a general concurrence in a proposal for strengthening the corps on the left flank of the enemy with 1500 men, to improve any partial advantages that might offer, and that the main body should preserve a relative position for acting as circumstances might require.

When Sir Henry Clinton had advanced to Allen-town, he determined, instead of keeping the direct course towards Staten-Island, to draw towards the sea coast, and to push on towards Sandy Hook. Washington, on receiving intelligence that Sir Henry was proceeding in that direction towards Monmouth court-house, dispatched 1000 men under Gen. Wayne, and sent the Marquis de la Fayette to take command of the whole, with orders to seize the first fair opportunity of attacking the enemy's

Campaign of 1778: Preparation

rear. The command of this advanced corps was offered to Gen. Lee, but he declined it.

The whole army followed at a proper distance for supporting the advanced corps, and reached Cranberry the next morning. Sir Henry Clinton, sensible of the approach of the Americans, placed his grenadiers, light-infantry, and chasseurs, in his rear, and his baggage in his front. Washington increased his advanced corps with two brigades, and sent Gen. Lee, who now wished for the command, to take charge of the whole, and followed with the main army to give it support.

On the next morning orders were sent to Lee to move on and attack, unless there should be powerful reasons to the contrary. When Washington had marched about five miles to support the advanced corps, he found the whole of it retreating by Lee's orders, and without having made any opposition of consequence.

Washington rode up to Lee and proposed certain questions. Lee answered with warmth, and unsuitable language. The commander in chief ordered Col. Stewart's, and <u>Lieut. Col. Ramsay's</u> battalions, to form on a piece of ground which he judged suitable for giving a check to the advancing enemy. Lee was then asked if he would command on that ground, to which he consented, and was ordered to take proper measures for checking the enemy; to which he replied, "your orders shall be obeyed, and I will not be the first to leave the field."

Washington then rode to the main army, which was formed with the utmost expedition. A warm cannonade immediately commenced between the British and American artillery, and a heavy firing between the advanced troops of the British army and the two battalions which Washington had halted. These stood their ground till they were intermixed with a part of the British army. Gen. Lee continued till the last on the field of battle, and brought off the rear of the retreating troops.

The check the British received gave time to make a disposition of the left wing and second line of the American army, in the wood and on the eminence to which Lee was retreating. On this some cannon were placed by lord Stirling, who commanded the left wing, which, with the co-operation of some parties of infantry, effectually stopped the advance of the British in that quarter. Gen. Greene took a very advantageous position on the right of lord Stirling. The British attempted to turn the left flank of the Americans, but were repulsed. They also made a movement to the right, with as little success; for Greene, with artillery, disappointed their design. Wayne advanced with a body of troops, and kept up so severe and well directed a fire, that the British were soon compelled to give way. They retired, and took the position which Lee had before occupied.

Campaign of 1778: Preparation

Washington resolved to attack them, and ordered Gen. Poor to move round upon their right, and Gen. Woodford to their left; but they could not get within reach before it was dark. These remained on the ground which they had been directed to occupy, during the night, with an intention of attacking early next morning; and the main body lay on their arms in the field to be ready for supporting them.

Gen. Washington, after a day of great activity and much personal danger, reposed among his troops on his cloak under a tree, in hopes of renewing the action the next day. But theses hopes were frustrated.

The British marched away in the night in such silence, that Gen. Poor, though he lay very near them, knew nothing of their departure. They left behind them four officers and about forty privates, all so badly wounded that they could not be removed. Their other wounded were carried off. The British pursued their march without farther interruption, and soon reached the neighbourhood of Sandy Hook, without the loss of either their covering party or baggage.

The American General declined all farther pursuit of the royal army, and soon after drew off his troops to the borders of the North river. The loss of the Americans in killed and wounded was about 250. The loss of the royal army, inclusive of prisoners, was about 350.

On the ninth day after this action, Congress unanimously resolved, "that their thanks be given to Gen. Washington for the activity with which he marched from the camp at Valley Forge in pursuit of the enemy; for his distinguished exertions in forming the line of battle; and for his great good conduct in leading on the attack, and gaining the important victory of Monmouth, over the British grand army, under the command of Gen. Sir Henry Clinton, in their march from Philadelphia to New-York."

It is probable that Washington intended to take no further notice of Lee's conduct in the day of action, but the latter could not brook the expressions used by the former at their first meeting, and wrote him two passionate letters. This occasioned his being arrested, and brought to trial. The charges exhibited against him were,

1st. For disobedience of orders in not attacking the enemy on the 28th of June, agreeable to repeated instructions.

2dly. For misbehaviour before the enemy on the same day, by making an unnecessary, disorderly, and shameful retreat.

3dly. For disrespect to the commander in chief in two letters.

After a tedious hearing before a court martial, of which lord Stirling was president, Lee was found guilty, and sentenced to be suspended from any command in the armies of the United States for the term of one year; but the second charge was softened by the court, which only found him

Campaign of 1778: Preparation

guilty of misbehaviour before the enemy, and, in some few instances, a disorderly retreat.

Soon after the battle of Monmouth the American army took post at the White Plains, and remained there, and in the vicinity, till autumn was far advanced, and then retired to Middlebrook in New-Jersey. During this period, nothing of more importance occurred than skirmishes, in which Gen. Washington was not particularly engaged. He was nevertheless fully employed. His mild conciliatory manners, and the most perfect subjection of his passions to reason, together with the soundness of his judgment, enabled him to serve his country with equal effect, though with less splendor than is usually attached to military exploits.

The French fleet, the expectation of which had induced the evacuation of Philadelphia, arrived too late for attacking the British in the Delaware. It was also deemed unadvisable to attempt New-York; but the British posts on Rhode-Island were judged proper objects of a conjunct expedition with the sea and land forces of France and America. This being resolved upon, Gen. Sullivan was appointed to conduct the operations of the Americans.

When the preparations for commencing the attack were nearly completed, a British fleet appeared in sight. D'Estaing, who commanded the French fleet, put out to sea to engage them; but a storm came on which crippled both fleets to such an extent, as induced the one to go to New-York, and the other to Boston, for the purpose of being repaired. While the fleets were out of sight, Sullivan had commenced the siege, and flattered himself that a few days co-operation of the returned French ships could not fail of crowning him with success.

The determination of D'Estaing to retire to Boston instead of co-operating in the siege, excited the greatest alarm in Sullivan's army. By this dereliction of the original plan, the harbours of Rhode-Island were left free and open for reinforcements to the British, which might be easily poured in from their head-quarters in New-York. Instead of anticipated conquests, Sullivan had reason to fear for the safety of his army.

Irritated at the departure of D'Estaing, he expressed in general orders to his army, "his hope that the event would prove America able to procure that, by her own arms, which her allies refused to assist in obtaining." These expressions were considered as imputing to D'Estaing and the French nation a disinclination to promote the interests of the United States.

When entreaties failed of persuading D'Estaing to return to the siege, a paper was drawn up and signed by the principal officers of the Americans, and sent to him, in which they protested against his taking the fleet to Boston, "as derogatory to the honour of France; contrary to the intentions of his most Christian Majesty, and the interest of his nation; destructive to the welfare of the United States, and highly injurious to the alliance between the two nations." So much discontent prevailed, that serious apprehensions were entertained that the means of repairing the French fleet would not be readily obtained.

Washington foresaw the evils likely to result from the general and mutual irritation which prevailed, and exerted all his influence to calm the minds of both parties. He had a powerful co-adjutor in the Marquis de la Fayette, who was deservedly dear to the Americans as to the French. His first duties were due to his king and country; but he loved America, and was so devoted to the commander in chief of its armies, as to enter into his views, and second his softening conciliatory measures, with truly filial affection.

Washington also wrote to Gen. Heath, who commanded at Boston, and to Sullivan and Greene, who commanded at Rhode-Island. In his letter to Gen. Heath, he stated his fears "that the departure of the French fleet from Rhode-Island, at so critical a moment, would not only weaken the confidence of the people in their new allies, but produce such prejudice and resentment as might prevent their giving the fleet, in its present distress, such zealous and effectual assistance as was demanded by the exigence of affairs, and the true interests of America;" and added, "that it would be sound policy to combat these effects, and to give the best construction of what had happened; and at the same time to make strenuous exertions for putting the French fleet as soon as possible, in a condition to defend itself, and be useful."

He also observed as follows—"The departure of the fleet from Rhode-Island, is not yet publicly announced here; but when it is, I intend to ascribe it to necessity produced by the damage received in the late storm. This it appears to me is the idea which ought to be generally propagated. As I doubt not the force of these reasons will strike you equally with myself, I would recommend to you to use your utmost influence to palliate and soften matters, and to induce those whose business it is to provide succours of every kind for the fleet, to employ their utmost zeal and activity in doing it. It is our duty to make the best of our misfortunes, and not suffer passion to interfere with our interest and the public good."

In a letter to Gen. Sullivan, he observed—"The disagreement between the army under your command and the fleet, has given me very singular uneasiness. The continent at large is concerned in our cordiality, and it should be kept up by all possible means consistent with our honour and policy. First impressions are generally longest retained, and will serve to fix in a great degree our national character with the French. In our conduct towards them, we should remember, that they are a people old in war, very strict in military etiquette, and apt to take fire when others seem scarcely warmed. Permit me to recommend in the most particular manner, the cultivation of harmony and good agreement, and your endeavors to destroy that ill-humour which may have found its way among the officers. It is of the utmost importance too that the soldiers and the people should know nothing of this misunderstanding; or if it has reached them, that means may be used to stop its progress, and prevent its effects."

In a letter to Gen. Greene, he observed—"I have not now time to take notice of the several arguments which were made use of, for and against the Count's quitting the harbour of Newport, and sailing for Boston. Right or wrong, it will probably disappoint our sanguine expectations of success, and, which I deem a still worse consequence, I fear it will sow the seeds of dissention and distrust between us and our new allies, unless the most prudent measures be taken to suppress the feuds and jealousies that have already arisen. I depend much on your temper and influence to conciliate that animosity which subsists between the American and French officers in our service. I be g you will take every measure to keep the protest entered into by the General Officers from being made public.

"Congress, sensible of the ill consequences that will flow from our differences being known to the world, have passed a resolve to that purpose. Upon the whole, my dear sir, you can conceive my meaning better than I can express it; and I therefore fully depend on your exerting yourself to heal all private animosities between our principal officers and the French, and to prevent all illiberal expressions and reflections that may fall from the army at large."

Washington also improved the first opportunity of recommencing his correspondence with count D'Estaing, in a letter to him, which, without noticing the disagreements that had taken place, was well calculated to soothe every angry sensation which might have rankled in his mind. In the course of a short correspondence, the irritation which threatened serious mischiefs entirely gave way to returning good humour and cordiality.

In another case about the same time the correct judgment of Washington proved serviceable to his country. In the last months of the year 1778, when the most active part of the campaign was over, Congress decided on a magnificent plan for the conquest of Canada. This was to attempted in 1779 by land and water, on the side of the United States, and by a fleet and army from France. The plan was proposed, considered, and agreed to, before Washington was informed of it. He was then desired to write to Dr. Franklin, the American minister at Paris, to interest him in securing the propose co-operation of France.

In reply to the communications of Congress, he observed—"The earnest desire I have strictly to comply in every instance with the views and instructions of Congress, cannot but make me feel the greatest uneasiness which I find myself in circumstances of hesitation or doubt, with respect to their directions; but the perfect confidence I have in the justice and candour of that honourable body, emboldens me to communicate without reserve the difficulties which occur in the execution of their present order; and the indulgence I have experienced on every former occasion induces me to imagine that the liberty I now take will not meet with disapprobation.

I have attentively taken up the report of the committee respecting the proposed expedition into Canada. I have considered it in several lights, and sincerely regret that I should feel myself under any embarrassment in carrying it into execution. Still I remain of opinion, from a general review of things, and the state of our resources, that no extensive system of co-operation with the French for the complete emancipation of Canada, can be positively decided on for the ensuing year. To propose a plan of perfect co-operation with a foreign power, without a moral certainty in our supplies; and to have that plan actually ratified with the court of Versailles, might be attended, in case of failure in the conditions on our part, with very fatal effects.

"If I should seem unwilling to transmit the plan as prepared by Congress, with my observations, it is because I find myself under a necessity (in order to give our minister sufficient ground to found an application on,) to propose something more than a vague and indecisive plan, which, even in the event of a total evacuation of the states by the enemy, may be rendered impracticable in the execution by a variety of insurmountable obstacles; or if I retain my present sentiments, and act consistently, I must point out the difficulties, as they appear to me, which must embarrass his negociations, and may disappoint the views of Congress.

"But proceeding on the idea of the enemy's leaving these states before the active part of the ensuing campaign, I should fear to hazard a mistake as to the precise aim and extent of the views of Congress. The conduct I am to observe in writing to our minister at the court of France, does not appear sufficiently delineated. Were I to undertake it, I should be much afraid of erring through misconception. In this dilemma, I would esteem it a particular favour to be excused from writing at all on the subject, especially as it is the part of candour in me to acknowledge that I do not see my way clear enough to point out such a plan for co-operation, as I conceive to be consistent with the ideas of Congress, and as will be sufficiently explanatory with respect to time and circumstances to give efficacy to the measure.

"But if Congress still think it necessary for me to proceed in the business, I must request their more definitive and explicit instructions, and that they will permit me previous to transmitting the intended dispatches, to submit them to their determination.

"I could wish to lay before Congress more minutely the state of the army, the condition of our supplies, and the requisites necessary for carrying into execution an undertaking that may involve the most serious events. If Congress think this can be done more satisfactorily in a personal conference, I hope to have the army in such a situation before I can receive their answer as to afford me an opportunity of giving my attendance."

The personal interview requested in this letter was agreed to by Congress, and a committee appointed by them to confer with him. The result was that the proposed expedition against Canada was given up by those who, after repeated deliberation, had resolved upon it.

6

The Campaign of 1779: The distresses of the American army. Gen. Washington calms the uneasiness in the Jersey line. Finds great difficulty in supporting his troops and concentrating their force. Makes a disposition of them with a view to the security of West Point. Directs an expedition against the Six Nations of Indians, and for the reduction of Stony Point Paules Hook taken. A French fleet, expected to the northward, arrives on the coast of Georgia. Washington, unequal to offensive operations, retires into winter quarters.

The years 1779 and 1780 passed away in the northern states without any of those great military exploits which enliven the pages of history; but they were years of anxiety and distress, which called for all the passive valour, the sound practical judgment, and the conciliatory address, for which Gen. Washington was so eminently distinguished. The states, yielding to the pleasing delusion that their alliance with France placed their independence beyond the reach of accident, and that Great-Britain, despairing of success, would speedily abandon the contest, relaxed in their preparations for a vigorous prosecution of the war.

To these ungrounded hopes Washington opposed the whole weight of his influence. In his correspondence with Congress, the Governors of particular states, and other influential individuals, he pointed out the fallacy of the prevailing opinion that peace was near at hand; and the necessity for raising, equipping, and supporting, a force sufficient for active operations.

He particularly urged that the annual arrangements for the army should be made so early that the recruits for the year should assemble at head-quarters on the first of January; but such was the torpor of the public mind that. notwithstanding these representations, it was as late as the 23rd of January, 1779, when Congress passed resolutions authorizing the commander in chief to re-enlist the army; and as late as the 9th of the following March, that the requisitions were made on the several states for their quotas. The military establishment for 1780 was later; for it was not agreed upon till the 9th of February; nor were the men required before the first of April. Thus, when armies ought to have been in the field, nothing more was done than a grant of the requisite authority for raising them.

The depreciation of the current paper money had advanced so rapidly as to render the daily pay of an officer unequal to his support. This produced serious discontents in the army. An order was given in May, 1779, for the Jersey brigade to march by regiments to join the western army. In answer to this order a letter was received from Gen. Maxwell, stating that the officers of the first regiment had delivered to their Colonel a remonstrance, addressed to the legislature of New-Jersey, in which they declared, that unless their former complaints on the deficiency of pay obtained immediate attention, they were to be considered at the end of three days as having resigned their commission; and on that contingency they requested the legislature to appoint other officers in their stead.

General Washington, who was strongly attached to the army, and knew their virtue, their sufferings, and also the justice of their complaints, immediately comprehended the ruinous consequences likely to result from the measures they had adopted. After serious deliberation, he wrote a letter to Gen. Maxwell, to be laid before the officers. In the double capacity of their friend and their commander, he made a forcible address both to their pride and their patriotism.

"There is nothing," he observed, "which has happened in the course of the war, which has given me so much pain as the remonstrance you mention from the officers of the first Jersey regiment. I cannot but consider it a hasty and imprudent step, which, on more cool consideration, they will themselves condemn. I am very sensible of the inconveniences under which the officers of the army labour, and I hope they do me the justice to believe, that my endeavors to procure them relief are incessant.

"There is more difficulty, however, in satisfying their wishes, than perhaps they are aware of. Our resources have been hitherto very limited. The situation of our money is no small embarrassment, for which, though there are remedies, they cannot be the work of a moment. Government is not insensible of the merits and sacrifices of the officers, nor unwilling to make a compensation; but it is a truth of which a very little observation must convince us, that it is very much straitened in the means.

"Great allowances ought to be made on this account, for any delay and seeming backwardness which may appear. Some of the states, indeed, have done as generously as was in their power; and if others have been less expeditious, it ought to be ascribed to some peculiar cause, which a little time, aided by example, will remove. The patience and perseverance of the army have been, under every disadvantage, such as do them the highest honour at home and abroad, and have inspired me with an unlimited confidence in their virtue, which has consoled me almost every perplexity and reverse of fortune, to which our affairs, in a struggle of this nature, were necessarily exposed.

"Now that we have made so great a progress to the attainment of the end we have in view, so that we cannot fail, without a most shameful desertion of our own interests, any thing like a change of conduct would imply a very unhappy change of principles, and a forgetfulness as well of what we owe to ourselves as to our country.

"Did I suppose it possible this should be the case, even in a single regiment of the army. But this I believe to be impossible. Any corps that was about to set an example of the kind, would weigh well the consequences; and no officer of common discernment and sensibility would hazard them. If they should stand alone in it, independent of other consequences, what would be their feelings on reflecting that they had held themselves out to the world in a point of light inferior to the rest of the army? Or, if their example should be followed, and become general, how could they console themselves for having been the foremost in bringing ruin and disgrace upon their country? They would remember that the army would share a double portion of the general infamy and distress; and that the character of an American officer would become as despicable as it is now glorious.

"I confess that the appearances in the present instance are disagreeable; but I am convinced they seem to mean more than they really do. The Jersey officers have not been outdone by any others, in the qualities either of citizens or soldiers; and I am confident no part of them would seriously intend any thing that would be a stain on their former reputation. The gentlemen cannot be in earnest; they have only reasoned wrong about the means of attaining a good end, and, on consideration, I hope and flatter myself they will renounce what must appear improper.

"At the opening of a campaign, when under marching orders for an important service, their own honour, duty to the public, and to themselves, and a regard to military propriety, will not suffer them to persist in a measure which would be a violation of them all. It will even wound their delicacy coolly to reflect, that they have hazarded a step which has an air of dictating terms to their country, by taking advantage of the necessity of the moment.

"The declaration they have made to the state, at so critical a time, that 'unless they obtain relief in the short period of three days, they must be considered out of the service,' has very much that aspect; and the seeming relaxation of continuing until the state can have a reasonable time to provide other officers, will be thought only a superficial veil. I am now to request that you will convey my sentiments to the gentlemen concerned, and endeavor to make them sensible of their error. The service for which the regiment was intended, will not admit of delay. It must at all events march on Monday morning, in the first place to this camp, and further directions will be given when it arrives. I am sure I shall not be mistaken in expecting a prompt and cheerful obedience."

The officers did not explicitly recede from their claims, but were brought round so far as to continue in service. In an address to Gen. Washington, they declared, "their unhappiness that any step of theirs should give him pain; but alleged in justification of themselves, "that repeated memorials had been presented to their legislature, which had been neglected;" and added—"We have lost all confidence in that body. Reason and experience forbid that we should have any. Few of us have private fortunes; many have families who already are suffering every thing that can be received from an ungrateful country.

"Are we then to suffer all the inconveniences, fatigues and dangers, of a military life, while our wives and our children are perishing for want of common necessaries at home; and that without the most distant prospect of reward, for our pay is now only nominal? We are sensible that your excellency cannot wish or desire this from us.

"We are sorry that you should imagine we meant to disobey orders. It was, and still is, our determination to march with our regiment, and to do the duty of officers, until the legislature should have a reasonable time to appoint others; but no longer.

"We beg leave to assure your Excellency, that we have the highest sense of your ability and virtues; that executing your orders has ever given us pleasure; that we love the service, and we love our country; but when that country is so lost to virtue and to justice as to forget to support its servants, it then becomes their duty to retire from its service."

The ground adopted by the officers for their justification, was such as interdicted a resort to stern measures; at the same time a compliance with their demands was impossible. In this embarrassing situation, Washington took no other notice of their letter than to declare to the officers, through Gen. Maxwell, "that while they continued to do their duty, he should only regret the part they had taken." The legislature of New-Jersey, roused by these events, made some partial provision for their troops. The officers withdrew their remonstrance, and continued to do their duty.

The consequences likely to result from the measures adopted by the Jersey officers being parried by the good sense and prudence of Gen. Washington, he improved the event when communicated to Congress, by urging on them the absolute necessity of some general and adequate provision for the officers of their army; and observed, "that the distresses in some corps are so great, that officers have solicited even to be supplied with the clothing destined for the common soldiery, coarse and unsuitable as it was. I had not power to comply with the request.

"The patience of men animated by a sense of duty and honour, will support them to a certain point, beyond which it will not go. I doubt not Congress will be sensible of the danger of an extreme in this respect, and will pardon my anxiety to obviate it."

The members of Congress were of different opinions respecting their military arrangements. While some were in unison with the General for a permanent national army, well equipped and well supported, others were apprehensive of danger to their future liberties from such establishments, and gave preference to enlistments for short periods, not exceeding a year. These also were partial to state systems, and occasional calls to the militia, instead of a numerous regular force, at the disposal of Congress or the commander in chief. From the various aspect of public affairs, and the frequent change of members composing the national legislature, sometimes one party predominated, and sometimes another. On the whole, the support received by Washington was far short of what economy, as well as sound policy, required.

The American army in these years was not only deficient in clothing, but in food. The seasons both in 1779 and 1780, were unfavourable to the crops. The labours of the farmers had often been interrupted by calls for militia duty. The current paper money was so depreciated as to be deemed no equivalent for the productions of the soil. So great were the necessities of the American army, that Gen. Washington was obliged to call on the magistrates of the adjacent counties for specified quantities of provisions, to be supplied in a given number of days.

At other times he was compelled to send out detachments of his troops to take provisions at the point of the bayonet from the citizens. This expedient at length failed, for the country in the vicinity of the army afforded no further supplies. These impressments were not only injurious to the morals and discipline of the army, but tended to alienate the affections of the people.

Much of the support which the American General had previously experienced from the inhabitants, proceeded from the difference of treatment they received from their own army, compared with what they suffered from the British. The General, whom the inhabitants hitherto regarded as their protector, had now no alternative but to disband his troops, or to support them by force. The army looked to him for provisions; the inhabitants for protection of their property. To supply the one and not offend the other, seemed little less than an impossibility.

To preserve order and subordination in an army of free republicans, even when well fed, paid, and clothed, would have been a work of difficulty; but to retain them in service and restrain them with discipline, when destitute not only of the comforts, but often of the necessaries of life, required address and abilities of such magnitude as are rarely found in human nature. In this choice of difficulties, Gen. Washington not only kept his army together, but conducted with so much discretion as to command the approbation both of the army and of the citizens.

Nothing of decisive importance could be attempted with an army so badly provided, and so deficient in numbers. It did not exceed 13,000 men, while the British, strongly fortified in New-York and Rhode-Island, amounted to 16 or 17,000. These were supported by a powerful fleet, which, by commanding the coasts and the rivers, furnished easy means for concentrating their force in any given point before the Americans could march to the same.

This disparity was particularly striking in the movements of the two armies in the vicinity of the Hudson. Divisions of both were frequently posted on each side of that noble river. While the British could cross directly over and unite their forces in any enterprise, the Americans could not safely effect a correspondent junction, unless they took a considerable circuit to avoid the British shipping.

To preserve West-Point and its dependencies, was a primary object with Washington. To secure these he was obliged to refuse the pressing applications from the neighbouring states for large detachments from the continental army for their local defence. Early in the year, Sir Henry Clinton made some movements up the North river, which indicated an intention of attacking the posts in the Highlands; but in proportion as these were threatened, Washington concentrated his force for their defence. This was done so effectually, that no serious direct attempt was made upon them.

Clinton, hoping to allure the Americans from these fortresses, sent detachments to burn and lay waste the towns on the coast of Connecticut. This was done extensively. Norwalk, Fairfield, and New-London, were

Campaign of 1779: Distresses of the American army

destroyed. Washington, adhering to the principle of sacrificing small objects to secure great ones, gave no more aid to the suffering inhabitants than was compatible with the security of West-Point.

Though the force under his immediate command throughout the campaign of 1779, was unequal to any great undertaking, yet his active mind sought for and embraced such opportunities for offensive operations, as might be attempted without hazarding too much.

The principal expedition of this kind, was directed against the Six Nations of Indians, who inhabited the fertile country between the western settlements of New-York and Pennsylvania, and the lakes of Canada. These, from their vicinity and intercourse with the white people, had attained a degree of civilization exceeding what was usual among savages. To them, many refugee tories had fled, and directed them to the settlements, which they laid waster, and at the same time massacred the inhabitants.

In the early period of Washington's life, while the commander of the Virginia troops, he had ample experience of the futility of forts for defence against Indians, and of the superior advantage of carrying offensive operations into their towns and settlements. An invasion of the country of the Six Nations being resolved upon, the commander in chief bestowed much thought on the best mode of conducting it.

The instructions he gave to Gen. Sullivan, who was appointed to this service, were very particular, and much more severe than was usual, but not more so than retaliation justified, or policy recommended. Sullivan, with a considerable force, penetrated into the country of the Indians in three directions, laid wasted their crops, and burnt their towns. His success was decisive, and in a great measure secured the future peace of the frontier settlements. The late residence of the savages was rendered so far uninhabitable, that they were reduced to the necessity of seeking an asylum in the more remote western country.

While the British were laying waste Connecticut, Washington, after reconnoitring the ground in person, planned an expedition against Stony Point, a commanding hill projecting far into the Hudson, on the top of which a fort had been erected, which was garrisoned with about 600 men. One of the motives for assaulting this work, was the hope that, if successful, it might induce the detachment which had invaded Connecticut, to desist from their devastations, and to return to the defence of their own outposts. The enterprise was assigned to Gen. Wayne, who completely succeeded in reducing the fort and capturing its garrison.

Campaign of 1779: Distresses of the American army

Sir Henry Clinton, on receiving intelligence of Wayne's success, relinquished his views on Connecticut, and made a forced march to Dobb's ferry, twenty-six miles above New-York.

The reduction of Stony Point was speedily followed by the surprise of the British garrison at Paules Hook. This was first conceived and planned by Major Henry Lee. On being submitted to Gen. Washington, he favoured the enterprise, but withheld his full assent, till he was satisfied of the practicability of a retreat, of which serious doubts were entertained. Lee, with 300 men, entered the fort about three o'clock in the morning, and with very inconsiderable loss, took 159 prisoners, and brought them off in safety from the vicinity of large bodies of the enemy.

The reasons already mentioned, for avoiding all hazardous offensive operations, were strongly enforced by a well founded expectation that a French fleet would appear on the coast, in the course of the year 1779. Policy required that the American army should be reserved for a co-operation with their allies. The fleet, as expected, did arrive, but in the vicinity of Georgia.

The French troops, in conjunction with the southern army commanded by Gen. Lincoln, made an unsuccessful attempt on the British post in Savannah. This town had been reduced in December 1778, by Col. Campbell, who had proceeded so far as to re-establish British authority in the state of Georgia. Soon after the defeat of the combined forces before Savannah, and the departure of the French fleet from the coast, Sir Henry Clinton proceeded with the principal part of his army to Charleston, and confined his views in New-York to defensive operations.

The campaign of 1779 terminated in the northern states as has been related, without any great events on either side. Washington defeated all the projects of the British for getting possession of the Highlands. The indians were scourged, and a few brilliant strokes kept the public mind from despondence. The Americans went into winter quarters when the month of December was far advanced. These were chosen for the convenience of wood, water, and provisions, and with an eye to the protection of the country.

To this end, the army was thrown into two grand divisions. The northern was put under the command of Gen. Heath, and stationed with a view to the security of West-Point, its dependencies, and the adjacent country. The other retired to Morris-town in New-Jersey. In this situation, which was well calculated to secure the country to the southward of New-York, Washington, with the principal division of his army, took their station for the winter.

Campaign of 1779: Distresses of the American army

The season following their retirement, was uncommonly severe. The British in New-York and Staten-Island no longer enjoyed the security which their insular situation usually afforded. The former suffered from the want of fuel, and other supplies from the country. To add to their difficulties, Washington so disposed his troops as to give the greatest possible obstruction to the communication between the British garrison, and such of the inhabitants without their lines as were disposed to supply their wants. This brought on a partisan war, in which individuals were killed, but without any national effect.

Had Washington been supported as he desired, the weakness of the British army, in consequence of their large detachments to the southward, in conjunction with the severity of the winter, would have given him an opportunity for indulging his native spirit of enterprise.

But he durst not attempt anything on a grand scale, for his army was not only inferior in number to that opposed to him, but so destitute of cloathing as to be unequal to a winter campaign.

7

The Campaign of 1780: Gen. Washington directs an expedition against Staten Island. Gives an opinion against risking an army for the defence of Charleston, S.C. Finds great difficulty in supporting his army. Kniphausen invades Jersey, but is prevented from injuring the American stores. Marquis de la Fayette arrives, and gives assurances that a French fleet and army might soon be expected on the American coast. Energetic measures of co-operation resolved upon, but so languidly executed, that Washington predicts the necessity of a more efficient system of national government. A French fleet and army arrives, and a combined operation against New-York is resolved upon, but the arrival of a superior British fleet, deranges the whole plan.

The military establishment for the year 1780 was nominally 35,000; but these were not voted till the 9th of February, and were not required to be in camp before the first of April following. Notwithstanding these embarrassments, the active mind of Washington looked round for an opportunity of deriving some advantage from the present exposed situation of his adversary. From recent intelligence, he supposed that an attack on about 1,200 British, posted on Staten Island, might be advantageously made, especially in its present state of union with the continent, by an unbroken body of frozen ice.

    The prospect of success depended on the chance of a surprise; and if this failed, of reducing the enemy, though retired within their fortifications, before reinforcements could arrive from New-York. The vigilance of the commanding officer prevented the first; the latter could not be depended on; for, contrary to the first received intelligence, the communication between the island and the city, though difficult, was practicable. The works were too strong for an assault, and relief too near to admit the delays of a siege.

Campaign of 1780: Expedition against Staten Island

Lord Stirling, with 2,500 men, entered the island on the night of the 14th of January. An alarm was instantly and generally communicated to the posts, and a boat dispatched to New-York to communicate intelligence, and to solicit aid. The Americans, after some slight skirmishes, seeing no prospect of success, and apprehensive that a reinforcement from New-York might endanger their safety, very soon commenced their retreat. This was effected without any considerable loss; but from the intenseness of the cold, and deficiency of warm cloathing, several were frost bitten.

Soon after this event, the siege of Charleston commenced, and was so vigorously carried on by Sir Henry Clinton, as to effect the surrender of that place on the 12th of May, 1780. Gen. Washington, at the distance of more than eight hundred miles, could have no personal agency in defending that most important southern part. What was in his power was done, for he weakened himself by detaching from the army under his own immediate command, the troops of North-Carolina, the new levies of Virginia, and the remnants of the southern cavalry.

Though he had never been in Charleston, and was without any personal knowledge of its harbour, yet he gave an opinion respecting it, which evinced the soundness of his practical judgment. In every other case, the defence of towns had been abandoned, so far as to risk no armies for that purpose; but in South-Carolina, Gen. Lincoln, for reasons that were satisfactory to his superiors, adopted a different line of conduct.

Four continental frigates were ordered to the defence of Charleston, and stationed within its bar; and a considerable state marine force cooperated with them. This new mode of defence was the more readily adopted, on the generally received idea, that this marine force could be so disposed of within the bar, as to make effectual opposition to the British ships attempting to cross it. In the course of the siege this was found to be impracticable, and all ideas of disputing the passage of the bar were given up.

This state of things being communicated by Lieut. Col. John Laurens to Gen. Washington, the General replied—"The impracticability of defending the bar, I fear, amounts to the loss of the town and the garrison. At this distance, it is impossible to judge for you. I have the greatest confidence in Gen. Lincoln's prudence; but it really appears to me, that the propriety of attempting to defend the town, depended on the probability of defending the bar, and that when this ceased, the attempt ought to have been relinquished. In this, however, I suspend a definitive judgment; and wish you to consider what I say as confidential."

The event corresponded with the General's predictions. The British vessels, after crossing the bar without opposition, passed the forts and took such a station in Cooper river, as, in conjunction with the land forces, made the evacuation of the town by the Americans impossible, and finally produced the surrender of their whole southern army.

When intelligence of this catastrophe reached the northern states, the American army was in the greatest distress. This had often been represented to Congress, and was particularly stated to Gen. Schuyler in a letter from Gen. Washington, in the following words: "Since the date of my last, we have had the virtue and patience of the army put to the severest trial. Sometimes it has been five or six days together without bread; at other times as many days without meat; and once or twice two or three days without either.

"I hardly thought it possible, at one period, that we should be able to keep it together, nor could it have been done, but for the exertions of the magistrates in the several counties of this state, on whom I was obliged to call; expose our situation to them; and, in plain terms, declare that we were reduced to the alternative of disbanding or catering for ourselves, unless the inhabitants would afford us their aid.

"I allotted to each county a certain proportion of flour or grain, and a certain number of cattle, to be delivered on certain days; and, for the honour of the magistrates, and the good disposition of the people, I must add, that my requisitions were punctually complied with, and in many counties exceeded. Nothing but this great exertion could have saved the army from dissolution or starving, as we were bereft of every hope from the commissaries.

"At one time the soldiers ate every kind of horse food but hay. Buckwheat, common wheat, rye and Indian corn, composed the meal which made their bread. As an army, they bore it with most heroic patience; but sufferings like these, accompanied by the want of clothes, blankets, &c. will produce frequent desertion in all armies; and so it happened with us, though it did not excite a single mutiny."

The paper money with which the troops were paid, was in a state of depreciation daily increasing. The distresses from this source, though felt in 1778, and still more so in 1779, did not arrive to the highest pitch till the year 1780. Under the pressure of sufferings from this cause, the officers of the Jersey line addressed a memorial to their state legislature, setting forth "that four months pay of a private, would not procure for his family a single bushel of wheat; that the pay of a colonel would not purchase oats for his horse; that a common labourer or express rider, received four times as much as an American officer."

Campaign of 1780: Expedition against Staten Island

They urged that "unless a speedy and ample remedy was provided, the total dissolution of their line was inevitable." In addition to the insufficiency of their pay and support, other causes of discontent prevailed. The original idea of a continental army to be raised, paid, subsisted, and regulated, upon an equal and uniform principle, had been in a great measure exchanged for state establishments. This mischievous measure partly originated from necessity; for state credit was not quite so much depreciated as continental.

Congress not possessing the means of supporting their army, devolved the business on the component parts of the confederacy. Some states, from their internal ability and local advantages, furnished their troops not only with cloathing, but with many conveniences. Others supplied them with some necessaries, but on a more contracted scale. A few, from their particular situation, could do little, or nothing at all.

The officers and men in the routine of duty mixed daily, and compared circumstances. Those who fared worse than others, were dissatisfied with a service which made such injurious distinctions. From causes of this kind, superadded to a complication of wants and sufferings, a disposition to mutiny began to show itself in the American army.

Very few of the officers were rich. To make an appearance suitable to their station, required an expenditure of the little all which most of them possessed. The supplies from the public were so inadequate as to compel frequent resignations. The officers of whole lines announced their determination to quit the service. The personal influence of Gen. Washington was exerted with the officers in preventing their adoption of such ruinous measures, and with the states to remove the causes which led to them.

Soon after the surrender of the whole southern army, and at the moment the northern was in the greatest distress for the necessaries of life, Gen. Kniphausen passed from New-York into New-Jersey with 5,000 men. These were soon reinforced with a detachment of the victorious troops returned with Sir Henry Clinton from South-Carolina. It is difficult to tell what was the precise object of this expedition. Perhaps the royal commanders hoped to get possession of Morristown, and destroy the American stores. Perhaps they flattered themselves that the inhabitants, dispirited by the recent fall of Charleston, would submit without resistance; and that the soldiers would desert to the royal standard.

Sundry movements took place on both sides, and also smart skirmishes, but without any decisive effects. At one time Washington conjectured that the destruction of his stores was the object of the enemy; at another, that the whole was a feint to draw off his attention, while they pushed up the North river from New-York, to attack West Point.

The American army was stationed with a view to both objects. The security of the stores was attended to, and such a position taken, as would compel the British to fight under great disadvantages, if they risked a general action to get at them. The American General Howe, who commanded at the Highlands, was ordered to concentrate his force for the security of West Point; and Washington, with the principal division of his army, took such a middle position, as enabled him either to fall back to defend his stores, or to advance for the defence of West Point, as circumstance might require.

The first months of the year were spent in these desultory operations. The disasters to the south produced no disposition in the north to give up the contest; but the tardiness of the Congress and of the states; the weakness of government, and the depreciation of the money, deprived Washington of all means of attempting any thing beyond defensive operations.

In this state of languor Marquis de la Fayette arrived from France, with assurances that a French fleet and army might soon be expected on the coast. This roused the Americans from that lethargy into which they seemed to be sinking. Requisitions on the states for men and money, were urged with uncommon earnestness. Washington, in his extensive correspondence throughout the United States, endeavored to stimulate the public mind to such exertions as the approaching crisis required.

In addition to arguments formerly used, he endeavoured on this occasion, by a temperate view of European politics, to convince his countrymen of the real danger of their independence, if they neglected to improve the advantages they might obtain by a great and manly effort, in conjunction with the succours expected from France.

The resolutions of Congress for this purpose were slowly executed. The quotas assigned to the several states were by their respective legislatures apportioned on the several counties and towns. These divisions were again subdivided into classes, and each class was called upon to furnish a man. This predominance of state systems over those which were national, was foreseen and lamented by the commander in chief.

In a letter to a member of the national legislature he observed, "that unless Congress speaks in a more decisive tone; unless they are vested with powers by the several states competent to the great purposes of the war, or assume them as a matter of right, and they and the states respectively act with more energy than hitherto they have done; our cause is lost.

"We can no longer drudge on in the old way. By illtiming the adoption of measures; by delays in the execution of them, or by unwarrantable jealousies, we incur enormous expenses, and derive no benefit. One state will comply with a requisition from Congress; another neglects to do it; a third executes it by halves; and all differ in the manner, the matter, or so much in point of time, that we are always working up hill; and while such a system as the present one, or rather want of one, prevails, we ever shall be unable to apply our strength or resources to any advantage.

"This, my dear sir, is plain language to a member of Congress; but it is the language of truth and friendship. It is the result of long thinking, close application, and strict observation. I see one head gradually changing into thirteen; and, instead of looking up to Congress as the supreme controlling power of the United States, considering themselves as dependent on their respective states. In a word, I see the power of Congress declining too fast for the consequence and respect which are due to them as the great representative body of America, and am fearful of the consequences."

From the embarrassments which cramped the operations of Washington, a partial temporary relief was obtained from private sources. When Congress could neither command money nor credit for the subsistence of their army, the citizens of Philadelphia formed an association to procure a supply of necessary articles for their suffering soldiers. The sum of 300,000 dollars was subscribed in a few days, and converted into a bank, the principal design of which was to purchase provisions for the troops in the most prompt and efficacious manner. The advantages of this institution were great, and particularly enhanced by the critical time in which it was instituted.

The Ladies of Philadelphia, about the same time, subscribed large donations for the immediate relief of the suffering soldiers. These supplies, though liberal, were far short of a sufficiency for the army. So late as the 20th of June, Gen. Washington informed Congress that he still laboured under the painful and humiliating embarrassment of having no shirts to deliver to the troops, many of whom were absolutely destitute of that necessary article; nor were they much better supplied with summer overalls.

"For the troops to be without cloathing at any time," he added, "is highly injurious to the service, and distressing to our feelings; but the want will be more peculiarly mortifying when they come to act with those of our allies. If it be possible, I have no doubt immediate measures will be taken to relieve their distress.

Campaign of 1780: Expedition against Staten Island

"It is also most sincerely to be wished that there could be some supplies of cloathing furnished to the officers. There are a great many whose condition is miserable. This is, in some instances, the case with whole lines. It would be well for their own sakes, and for the public good, if they could be furnished. They will not be able, when our friends come to co-operate with us, to go on a common routine of duty; and if they should, they must from their appearance be held in low estimation."

The complicated arrangements for raising and supporting the American army, which was voted for the campaign, were so tardily executed that when the summer was far advanced, Washington was uninformed of the force on which he might rely; and of course could not fix on any certain plan of operations for the combined armies. In a letter to Congress he expressed his embarrassment in the following words—

"The season is come when we have every reason to expect the arrival of the fleet; and yet for want of this point of primary consequence, it is impossible for me to form a system of co-operation. I have no basis to act upon, and of course were this generous succour of our ally to arrive, I should find my self in the most awkward, embarrassing, and painful situation. The General and the Admiral, as soon as they approach our coast, will require of me a plan of the measures to be pursued, and there ought of right to be one prepared; but circumstanced as I am, I cannot even give them conjectures.

"From these considerations I yesterday suggested to the committee the indispensable necessity of their writing again to the states, urging them to give immediate and precise information of the measures they have taken, and of the result. The interest of the states—the honour and reputation of our councils—the justice and gratitude due to our allies—all require that I should without delay be enabled to ascertain and inform them what we can or cannot undertake.

"There is a point which ought now to be determined, on the success of which all our future operations may depend; on which, for want of knowing our prospects, I can make no decision. For fear of involving the fleet and army of our allies in circumstances which would expose them, if not seconded by us, to material inconvenience and hazard, I shall be compelled to suspend it, and the delay may be fatal to our hopes."

In this state of uncertainty, Washington meditated by night and day on the various contingencies which were probable. He revolved the possible situations in which the contending armies might be placed, and endeavoured to prepare for every plan of combined operations which future contingent events might render adviseable.

Campaign of 1780: Expedition against Staten Island

On the 10th of July the expected French fleet and army appeared on the coast of Rhode-Island. The former consisted of seven sail of the line, five frigates, and five smaller vessels. The latter of 6,000 men. The Chevalier Terney and Count Rochambeau, who commanded the fleet and army, immediately transmitted to Gen. Washington an account of their arrival, of their strength, their expectations, and orders.

At that time not more than one thousand men had joined the American army. A commander of no more than common firmness, would have resigned his commission in disgust, for not being supported by his country. Very different was the line of conduct adopted by Washington. Trusting that the promised support would be forwarded with all possible dispatch, he sent on to the French commanders by the Marquis de la Fayette, definite proposals for commencing the siege of New-York.

Of this he gave information to Congress in a letter, in the following words: "Pressed on all sides by a choice of difficulties, in a moment which required decision, I have adopted that line of conduct which comported with the dignity and faith of Congress, the reputation of these states, and the honour of our arms. I have sent on definitive proposals of co-operation to the French General and Admiral. Neither the period of the season, nor a regard to decency, would permit delay.

"The die is cast; and it remains with the states either to fulfill their engagements, preserve their credit, and support their independence, or to involve us in disgrace and defeat. Notwithstanding the failures pointed out by the committee, I shall proceed on the supposition that they will ultimately consult own interest and honour, and not suffer us to fail for the want of means, which it is evidently in their power to afford.

"What has been done, and is doing by some of the states, confirms the opinion I have entertained, of sufficient resources in the country. Of the disposition of the people to submit to any arrangement for bringing them forth, I see no reasonable ground to doubt. If we fail for want of proper exertions in any of the governments, I trust the responsibility will fall where it ought, and that I shall stand justified to Congress, my country, and the world."

The fifth of the next month, August, was named as the day when the French troops should embark, and the American army assemble in Morrisania, for the purpose of commencing their combined operations.

Very soon after the arrival of the French fleet, Admiral Greaves reinforced the British naval force in the harbour of New-York, with six ships of the line. Hitherto the French had a naval superiority. Without it, all prospect of success in the proposed attack on New-York was visionary; but

Campaign of 1780: Expedition against Staten Island

this being suddenly and unexpectedly reversed, the plan for combined operations became eventual.

The British Admiral having now the superiority, proceeded to Rhode-Island to attack the French in that quarter. He soon discovered that the French were perfectly secure from any attack by sea. Sir Henry Clinton, who had returned in the preceding month with his victorious troops from Charleston, embarked about 8,000 of his best men, and proceeded as far as Huntingdon Bay, on Long-Island, with the apparent design of concurring with the British fleet in attacking the French force at Rhode-Island.

When this movement took place, Washington set his army in motion, and proceeded to Peekskill. Had Sir Henry Clinton prosecuted what appeared to be his design, Washington intended to have attacked New-York in his absence. Preparations were made for this purpose, but Sir Henry Clinton instantly turned about from Huntingdon Bay towards New-York.

In the mean time, the French fleet and army being blocked up at Rhode-Island, were incapacitated from co-operating with the Americans. Hopes were nevertheless indulged, that by the arrival of another fleet of his Most Christian Majesty, then in the West-Indies, under the command of Count de Guichen, the superiority would be so much in favour of the allies, as to enable them to prosecute their original intention of attacking New-York. When the expectations of the Americans were raised to the highest pitch, and when they were in great forwardness of preparation to act in concert with their allies, intelligence arrived that Count de Guichen had sailed for France. This disappointment was extremely mortifying.

Washington still adhered to his purpose of attacking New-York at some future more favourable period. On this subject he corresponded with the French commanders, and had a personal interview with them on the twenty-first of September, at Hartford. The arrival of Admiral Rodney on the American coast, a short time after, with eleven ships of the line, disconcerted for that season, all the plans of the allies.

Washington felt with infinite regret, a succession of abortive projects throughout the campaign of 1780. In that year, and not before, he had indulged the hope of happily terminating the war. In a letter to a friend, he wrote as follows:

"We are now drawing to a close an inactive campaign, the beginning of which appeared pregnant with events of a very favourable complexion. I hoped, but I hoped in vain, that a prospect was opening which would enable me to fix a period to my military pursuits, and restore me to domestic life. The favourable disposition of Spain; the promised succour

Campaign of 1780: Expedition against Staten Island

from France; the combined force in the West-Indies; the declaration of Russia, (acceded to by other powers of Europe, humiliating the naval pride and power of Great-Britain;) the superiority of France and Spain by sea, in Europe; the Irish claims, and English disturbances, formed in the aggregate an opinion in my breast, (which is not very susceptible of peaceful dreams,) that the hour of deliverance was not far distant: for that, however unwilling Great-Britain might be to yield the point, it would not be in her power to continue the contest.

"But alas! these prospects, flattering as they were, have proved delusory; and I see nothing before us but accumulating distress. We have been half of our time without provisions, and are likely to continue so. We have no magazines, nor money to form them. We have lived upon expedients until we can live no longer.

"In a word, the history of the war is a history of false hopes and temporary devices, instead of system and economy. It is in vain, however, to look back; nor is it our business to do so.

"Our case is not desperate, if virtue exists in the people, and there is wisdom among our rulers. But, to suppose that this great revolution can be accomplished by a temporary army; that this army will be subsisted by state supplies; and that taxation alone is adequate to our wants, is, in my opinion, absurd."

8

The Campaign of 1781: The Pennsylvania line mutinies. The Jersey troops follow their example, but are quelled by decisive measures. Gen. Washington commences a military journal, detailing the wants and distresses of his army. Is invited to the defence of his native state, Virginia, but declines. Reprimands the manager of his private estate for furnishing the enemy with supplies, to prevent the destruction of his property. Extinguishes the incipient flames of a civil war, respecting the independence of the state of Vermont. Plans a combined operation against the British, and deputes Lieut. Col. John Laurens to solicit the co-operation of the French. The combined forces of both nations rendezvous in the Chesapeak, and take lord Cornwallis and his army prisoners of war. Washington returns to the vicinity of New York, and urges the necessity of preparing for a new campaign.

The year 1780 ended in the northern states with disappointment, and the year 1781 commenced with mutiny.

In the night of the first of January about 1,300 of the Pennsylvania line paraded under arms in their encampment, near Morristown, avowing a determination to march to the seat of Congress, and obtain a redress of their grievances, without which they would serve no longer.

The exertions of Gen. Wayne and the other officers to quell the mutiny, were in vain. The whole body marched off with six field-pieces towards Princeton. They stated their demands in writing; which were, a discharge to all who had served three years, an immediate payment of all that was due to them, and that future pay should be made in real money to all who remained in the service. Their officers, a committee of Congress, and a deputation from the executive council of Pennsylvania, endeavoured to effect an accommodation; but the mutineers resolutely refused all terms, of which a redress of their grievances was not the foundation.

To their demands as founded in justice, the civil authority of Pennsylvania substantially yielded. Intelligence of this mutiny was communicated to Gen. Washington at New-Windsor, before any accommodation had taken place. Though he had long been accustomed to decide in hazardous and difficult situations, yet it was no easy matter in this delicate crisis, to determine on the most proper course to be pursued. His personal influence had several times extinguished rising mutinies.

The first scheme that presented itself was, to repair to the camp of the mutineers, and try to recall them to a sense of their duty; but on mature reflection this was declined. He well knew that their claims were founded in justice, but he could not reconcile himself to wound the discipline of his army, by yielding to their demands while they were in open revolt with arms in their hands. He viewed the subject in all its relations, and was well apprised that the principal grounds of discontent were not peculiar to the Pennsylvania line, but common to all his troops.

If force was requisite, he had none to spare without hazarding West-Point. If concessions were unavoidable, they had better be made by any person other than the commander in chief. After that due deliberation which he always gave to matters of importance, he determined against a personal interference, and to leave the whole to the civil authorities, which had already taken it up; but at the same time prepared for those measures which would become necessary, if no accommodation took place. This resolution was communicated to Gen. Wayne, with a caution to regard the situation of the other lines of the army in any concessions which might be made, and with a recommendation to draw the mutineers over the Delaware, with a view to increase the difficulty of communicating with the enemy in New-York.

The dangerous policy of yielding even to the just demands of soldiers with arms in their hands, soon became apparent. The success of the Pennsylvania line induced a part of that of New-Jersey to hope for similar advantages, from similar conduct. A part of the Jersey brigade rose in arms, and making the same claims which had been yielded to the Pennsylvanians, marched to Chatham. Washington, who was far from being pleased with the issue of the mutiny in the Pennsylvania line, determined by strong measures to stop the progress of a spirit which was hostile to all his hopes. Gen. Howe, with a detachment of the eastern troops, was immediately ordered to march against the mutineers, and instructed to make no terms with them while they were in a state of resistance; and on their surrender to seize a few of the most active leaders, and to execute them immediately in the presence of their associates. These orders were obeyed: two of the ringleaders were shot, and the survivors returned to their duty.

Though Washington adopted these decisive measures, yet no man was more sensible of the merits and sufferings of his army, and none more active and zealous in procuring them justice. He improved the late events, by writing circular letters to the states, urging them to prevent all future causes of discontent by fulfilling their engagements with their respective lines.

Some good effects were produced, but only temporary, and far short of the well founded claims of the army. Their wants with respect to provisions were only partially supplied, and by expedients, from short time to another. The most usual was ordering an officer to seize on provisions wherever found. This differed from robbing only in its being done by authority for the public service, and in the officer being always directed to give the proprietor a certificate of the quantity and quality of what was taken from him. At first, some reliance was placed on these certificates, as vouchers to support a future demand on the United States; but they soon became so common as to be of little value. Recourse was so frequently had to coercion, both legislative and military, that the people not only lost confidence in public credit, but became impatient under all exertions of authority for forcing their property from them.

About this time Gen. Washington was obliged to apply 9,000 dollars sent by the state of Massachusetts, for the payment of her troops, to the use of the quarter-master's department, to enable him to transport provisions from the adjacent states. Before he consented to adopt this expedient, he had consumed every ounce of provision which had been kept as a reserve in the garrison of West-Point, and had strained impress by military force to so great an extent, that there was reason to apprehend the inhabitants, irritated by such frequent calls, would proceed to dangerous insurrections. Fort Schuyler, West-Point and the posts up the North river, were on the point of being abandoned by their starving garrisons.

At this period there was little or no circulating medium, either in the form of paper or specie, and in the neighbourhood of the American army, there was a real want of necessary provisions. The deficiency of the former occasioned many inconveniences, but the insufficiency of the latter had well nigh dissolved the army, and laid the country in every direction open to British excursions.

On the first of May, 1781, Gen. Washington commenced a military journal. The following statement is extracted from it:

"I begin at this epoch a concise journal of military transactions, &c. I lament not having attempted it from the commencement of the war, in aid of my memory; and wish the multiplicity of matter which continually surrounds me, and the embarrassed state of affairs, which is momentarily calling the attention to perplexities of one kind or another, may not defeat altogether, or so interrupt my present intention and plan, as to render it of little avail.

"To have the clearer understanding of the entries which may follow, it would be proper to recite in detail, our wants and our prospects; but this alone would be a work of much time and great magnitude. It may suffice to give the sum of them, which I shall do in few words: viz.

"Instead of having magazines filled with provisions, we have a scanty pittance scattered here and there in the distant states.

Instead of having our arsenals well supplied with military stores, they are poorly provided, and the workmen all leaving them. Instead of having the various articles of field equipage in readiness, the Quarter-master-general is but now applying to the several states to provide these things for their troops respectively.

"Instead of having a regular system of transportation established upon credit, or funds in the Quarter-master's hands to defray the contingent expenses thereof, we have neither the one nor the other; and all that business, or a great part of it, being done by impressment, we are daily and hourly oppressing the people, souring their tempers, and alienating their affections.

"Instead of having the regiments completed agreeable to the requisitions of Congress, scarce any state in the union has at this hour one eighth part of its quota in the field, and there is little prospect of ever getting more than half. In a word, instead of having any thing in readiness to take the field, we have nothing; and, instead of having the prospect of a glorious offensive campaign before us, we have a bewildered and gloomy prospect of a defensive one; unless we should receive a powerful aid of ships, troops, and money, from our generous allies, and these at present are too contingent to build upon."

While the Americans were suffering the complicated calamities which introduced the year 1781, their adversaries were carrying on the most extensive plan of operations against them which had ever been attempted. It had often been objected to the British commanders, that they had not conducted the war in the manner most likely to effect the subjugation of the revolted provinces. Military critics found fault with them for keeping a large army idle at New-York, which, they said, if properly applied, would have been sufficient to make successful impressions at

Campaign of 1781: Pennsylvania line mutinies

one and the same time, on several of the states. The British seem to have calculated the campaign of 1781, with a view to make an experiment of the comparative merit of this mode of conducting military operations. The war raged in that year not only in the vicinity of the British headquarters at New-York, but in Georgia, South-Carolina, North-Carolina, and in Virginia.

In this extensive warfare, Washington could have no immediate agency in the southern department. His advice in corresponding with the officers commanding in Virginia, the Carolinas, and Georgia, was freely and beneficially given; and as large detachments sent to their aid as could be spared consistently with the security of West-Point. In conducting the war, his invariable maxim was, to suffer the devastation of property, rather than hazard great and essential objects for its preservation.

While the war raged in Virginia, the Governor thereof, its representatives in Congress, and other influential citizens, urged his return to the defence of his native state. But, considering America as his country, and the general safety as his object, he deemed it of more importance to remain on the Hudson: there he was not only securing the most important post in the United States, but concerting a grand plan of combined operations, which, as shall soon be related, not only delivered Virginia, but all the states, from the calamities of the war.

In Washington's disregard of property when in competition with national objects, he was in no respect partial to his own. While the British were in the Potowmac, they sent a flag on shore to Mount Vernon, (his private estate) requiring a supply of fresh provisions. Refusals of such demands were often followed by burning the houses and other property near the river. To prevent this catastrophe, the person intrusted with the management of the estate, went on board with the flag, and carrying a supply of provisions, requested that the buildings and improvements might be spared.

For this he received a severe reprimand in a letter to him, in which the General observed—"That it would have been a less painful circumstance to me to have heard, that, in consequence of your non-compliance with the request of the British, they had burnt my house, and laid my plantation in ruins. You ought to have considered yourself as my representative, and should have reflected on the bad example of communicating with the enemy, and making a voluntary offer of refreshment to them, with a view to prevent a conflagration."

To the other difficulties with which Washington had to contend in the preceding years of the war, a new one was about this time added. While the whole force at his disposal was unequal to the defence of the country against the common enemy, a civil war was on the point of breaking out among his fellow citizens. The claims of the inhabitants of Vermont to be a separate independent state, and of the state of New-York, to their country, as within its chartered limits, together with open offers from the Royal Commanders to establish and defend them as a British province, produced a serious crisis, which called for the interference of the American chief.

This was the more necessary, as the governments of New-York and of Vermont were both resolved on exercising a jurisdiction over the same people and the same territory. Congress, wishing to compromise the controversy on middle ground, resolved, in August, 1781, to accede to the independence of Vermont on certain conditions, and within certain specified limits, which they supposed would satisfy both parties.

Contrary to their expectations, this mediatorial act of the national legislature was rejected by Vermont, and yet was so disagreeable to the legislature of New-York as to draw from them a spirited protest against it. Vermont complained that Congress interfered in their internal police; New-York viewed the resolve as a virtual dismemberment of their state, which was a constituent part of the confederacy.

Washington, anxious for the peace of the union, sent a message to Chittenden, Governor of Vermont, desiring to know "what were the real designs, views, and intentions, of the people of Vermont; whether they would be satisfied with the independence proposed by Congress, or had it seriously in contemplation to join with the enemy, and become a British province."

The Governor returned an unequivocal answer—"that there were no people on the continent more attached to the cause of America than the people of Vermont; but they were fully determined not to be put under the government of New-York; that they would oppose this by force of arms, and would join with the British in Canada rather than to submit to that government."

While both states were dissatisfied with Congress, and their animosities, from increasing violence and irritation, became daily more alarming, Washington, aware of the extremes to which all parties were tending, returned an answer to Gov. Chittenden, in which were these expressions.

"It is not my business, neither do I think it necessary now to discuss the origin of the right of a number of inhabitants to that tract of country formerly distinguished by the name of the New-Hampshire grants, and now known by that of Vermont. I will take it for granted that their right was good, because Congress by their resolve of the 7th of August, imply it, and by that of the 21st are willing fully to confirm it, provided the new state is confined to certain prescribed bounds. It appears therefore to me, that the dispute of boundary is the only one that exists; and that being removed, all other difficulties would be removed also, and the matter terminated to the satisfaction of all parties. You have nothing to do but withdraw your jurisdiction to the confines of your old limits, and obtain an acknowledgment of independence and sovereignty, under the resolve of the 21st of August, for so much territory as does not interfere with the ancient established bounds of New-York, New Hampshire, and Massachusetts.

"In my private opinion, while it behooves the delegates to do ample justice to a body of people sufficiently respectable by their numbers, and entitled by other claims to be admitted into that confederation, it becomes them also to attend to the interests of their constituents, and see that under the appearance of justice to one, they do not materially injure the rights of others. I am apt to think this is the prevailing opinion of Congress."

The impartiality, moderation, and good sense, of this letter, together with a full conviction of the disinterested patriotism of the writer, brought round a revolution in the minds of the legislature of Vermont; and they accepted the propositions of Congress, thought they had rejected them four months before. A truce among the contending parties followed, and the storm blew over. Thus the personal influence of one man, derived from his pre-eminent virtues and meritorious services, extinguished the sparks of civil discord at the time they were kindling into flame.

Though in conducting the American war, Gen. Washington often acted on the Fabian system, by evacuating, retreating, and avoiding decisive engagements; yet this was much more the result of necessity than of choice. His uniform opinion was in favour of energetic offensive operations, as the most effectual means of bringing the war to a termination. On this principle he planned attacks in almost every year on some or other of the British armies or strong posts in the United States. He endeavoured, from year to year, to stimulate the public mind to some great operation; but was never properly supported.

In the years 1778. 1779, and 1780, the projected combined operations with the French, as has been related, entirely miscarried. The idea of ending the war by some decisive military exploit, continually occupied his active mind. To ensure success, a naval superiority on the coast, and a loan of money, were indispensably necessary. The last was particularly so in the year 1781; for the resources of the United States were then so reduced, as to be unequal to the support of their army, or even to the transportation of it to any distant scene of action.

Campaign of 1781: Pennsylvania line mutinies

To obtain these necessary aids, it was determined to send an envoy extraordinary to the court of Versailles. Lieut. Col. John Laurens was selected for this purpose. He was in every respect qualified for the important mission. In addition to the most engaging personal address, his connexion with the commander in chief, as one of his aids, gave him an opportunity of being intimately acquainted with the military capacities and weaknesses of his country. These were also particularly detailed in the form of a letter to him from Gen. Washington. This was written when the Pennsylvania line was in open revolt.

Among other interesting matters it stated—"That the efforts already made by the United States exceeded the natural ability of the country; and that any revenue they were capable of making would leave a large surplus to be supplied by credit; that experience had proved the impossibility of a paper system without funds, and that domestic loans could not be effected, because there were few men of monied capital in the United States; that from necessity recourse had been had to military impressments for supporting the army, which, if continued longer, or urged farther, would probably disgust the people, and bring round a revolution of public sentiment.

"That the relief procured by these violent means was so inadequate, that the patience of the army was exhausted, and their discontents had broke out in serious and alarming mutinies; that the relief necessary was not within the power of the United States; and that from a view of all circumstances, a loan of money was absolutely necessary for reviving public credit, and giving vigour to future operations."

It was further stated—"that next to a loan of money, a French naval superiority in the American seas was of so much consequence, that without it nothing decisive could be undertaken against the British, who were in the greatest force on and near the coasts."

The future capacities of the United States to repay any loan that might be made, were particularly stated; and that "there was still a fund of resource and inclination in the country equal to great exertions, provided a liberal supply of money would furnish the means of stopping the progress of disgust which resulted from the unpopular mode of supplying the army by requisition and impressment."

Such interesting statements, sanctioned by the American chief, and enforced by the address of Col. Laurens, directly from the scene of action, and the influence of Dr. Franklin, who, for the five preceding years, had been minister plenipotentiary from the United States to the court of Versailles, produced the desired effect. His Most Christian Majesty gave his American allies a subsidy of six millions of livres, and became their security for ten million more, borrowed for their use in the United Netherlands. A naval co-operation was promised, and a conjunct expedition against their common foes projected.

The American war was now so far involved in the consequences of naval operations, that a superior French fleet seemed to be the hinge on which it was likely soon to take a favourable turn. The British army being parcelled in the different sea-ports of the United States, any division of it, blocked up by a French fleet, could not long resist the superior combined force which might be brought to operate against it. The Marquis de Castries, who directed the marine of France with great precision, calculated the naval force which the British could concenter on the coast of the United States, and disposed his own in such a manner as ensured him a superiority.

In conformity to these principles, and in subserviency to the design of the campaign, M. de Grasse sailed in March, 1781, from Brest, with twenty-five sail of the line, several thousand land forces, and a large convoy amounting to more than two hundred ships. A small part of this force was destined for the East-Indies' but M. de Grasse with the greater part sailed for Martinique.

The British fleet then in the West-Indies had been previously weakened by the departure of a squadron for the protection of the ships which were employed in carrying to England the booty which had been taken at St. Eustatius. The British Admirals Hood and Drake were detached to intercept the outward bound French fleet, commanded by M. de Grasse; but a junction between his force and eight ships of the line, and one of 50 guns, which were previously at Martinique and St. Domingo, was nevertheless effected. By this combination of fresh ships from Europe, with the French fleet previously in the West-Indies, they had a decided superiority.

M. de Grasse having finished his business in the West-Indies, sailed in the beginning of August with a prodigious convoy. After seeing this out of danger, he directed his course for the Chesapeak, and arrived there on the thirtieth of the same month. Five days before his arrival in the Chesapeak, the French fleet in Rhode Island sailed for the same place. These fleets, notwithstanding their original distance from the scene of action, and from each other, coincided in their operations in an extraordinary manner, far beyond the reach of military calculation. They all tended to one object, and at one and the same time; and that object was neither known nor suspected by the British, till the proper season for counteraction was elapsed.

This coincidence of favourable circumstances extended to the marches of the American and French land forces. The plan of operations had been so well digested, and was so faithfully executed by the different commanders, that Gen. Washington and Count Rochambeau had passed the British head-quarters in New-York, and were considerably advanced in their way to Yorktown, before Count de Grasse had reached the American coast. This was effected in the following manner: Mons. de Barras, appointed to the commander of the French squadron at New-Port, arrived at Boston with dispatches for Count de Rochambeau.

An interview soon after took place at Weathersfield, between Generals Washington, Knox, and du Portail, on the part of the Americans, and Count de Rochambeau and the Chevalier Chastelleux, on the part of the French. At this interview an eventual plan of the whole campaign was fixed. This was to lay siege to New-York, in concert with a French fleet, which was to arrive on the coast in the month of August. It was agreed that the French troops should march towards the North river. Letters were addressed by Gen. Washington to the executive officers of New Hampshire, Massachusetts, Connecticut, and New-Jersey, requiring them to fill up their battalions, and to have their quotas of 6,200 militia in readiness within a week of the time they might be called for.

Conformably to these outlines of the campaign, the French troops marched from Rhode-Island in June, and early in the following month joined the American army. At the same time Washington marched his army from their winter encampment near Peekskill to the vicinity of Kingsbridge. Gen. Lincoln fell down the North river with a detachment in boats, and took possession of the ground where Fort Independence formerly stood. An attack was made upon him, but was soon discontinued.

The British about this time retired with almost the whole of their force to York Island. Washington hoped to be able to commence operations against New-York about the middle, or at farthest the latter end of July. Flat bottomed boats sufficient to transport 5,000 men were built near Albany, and brought down the North river to the neighbourhood of the American army before New-York. Ovens were erected opposite to Staten Island for the use of the French troops. Every movement introductory to the commencement of the siege was made.

To the great mortification of Washington, he found himself on the 2d of August, to be only a few hundreds stronger than he was on the day his army first moved from their winter quarters. To have fixed on a plan of operations with a foreign officer at the head of a respectable force; to have brought that force from a considerable distance in confident expectation of reinforcements sufficiently large to commence effective operations against the common enemy; and at the same time to have engagements in behalf of the states violated in direct opposition to their own interest, and in a manner derogatory to his personal honour, was enough to have excited storms and tempests in any mind less calm than that of Gen. Washington.

He bore this hard trial with his usual magnanimity, and contended himself with repeating his requisitions to the states; and at the same time urging them by every tie to enable him to fulfill engagements entered into on their account with the commander of the French troops.

That tardiness which at other times had brought the Americans near the brink of ruin, was now the accidental cause of real service. Had they sent forward their recruits for the regular army, and their quotas of militia, as was expected, the siege of New-York would have commenced in the latter end of July, or early in August.

While the season was wasting away in expectation of these reinforcements, lord Cornwallis, as has been mentioned, fixed himself near the Capes of Virginia. His situation there; the arrival of a reinforcement of 3,000 Germans from Europe to New-York; the superior strength of their garrison; the failure of the states in filling up their battalions and embodying their militia; and especially recent intelligence from Count de Grasse, that his destination was fixed to the Chesapeak, concurred about the middle of August to make a total change of the plan of the campaign.

The appearance of an intention to attack New-York was, nevertheless, kept up. While this deception was played off, the allied army crossed the North river, and passed on by the way of Philadelphia through the intermediate country to Yorktown. An attempt to reduce the British force in Virginia promised success with more expedition, and to secure an object of nearly equal importance as the reduction of New-York.

While the attack of New-York was in serious contemplation, a letter from Gen. Washington, detailing the particulars of the intended operations of the campaign, being intercepted, fell into the hands of Sir Henry Clinton. After the plan was changed, the royal commander was so much under the impression of the intelligence contained in the intercepted letter, that he believed every movement towards Virginia to be a feint calculated to draw off his attention from the defence of New-York. Under the influence of this opinion, he bent his whole force to strengthen that post; and suffered the American and French armies to pass him without molestation.

When the best opportunity of striking at them was elapsed, then for the first time he was brought to believe, that the allies had fixed on Virginia for the theatre of their combined operations. As truth may be made to answer the purposes of deception, so no feint of attacking New-York could have been more successful than the real intention.

In the latter end of August, the American army began their march to Virginia from the neighbourhood of New-York. Washington had advanced as far as Chester, before he received the news of the arrival of the fleet commanded by M. de Grasse. The French troops marched at the same time, and for the same place. Gen. Washington and Count Rochambeau with Generals Chastelleux, du Portail, and Knox, proceeded to visit Count de Grasse on board his ship, the Ville de Paris, and agreed on a plan of operations.

The Count afterwards wrote to Washington, that in case a British fleet appeared, "he conceived that he ought to go out and meet them at sea, instead of risking an engagement in a confined situation." This alarmed the General. He sent the Marquis de la Fayette with a letter to dissuade him from the dangerous measure. This letter, and the persuasions of the Marquis, had the desired effect.

The combined forces proceeded on their way to Yorktown, partly by land, and partly down the Chesapeak. The whole together, with a body of Virginia militia, under the command of Gen. Nelson, rendezvoused at Williamsburg, on the 25th of September, and in five days after moved down to the investiture of Yorktown.

The French fleet at the same time moved to the mouth of York river, and took a position which was calculated to prevent lord Cornwallis either from retreating, or receiving succour by water. Previously to the march from Williamsburg to Yorktown, Washington gave out in general orders as follows:—"If the enemy should be tempted to meet the army on its march, the General particularly enjoins the troops to place their principal reliance on the bayonet, that they may prove the vanity of the boast, which the British make of their particular prowess, in deciding battles with that weapon."

The works erected for the security of Yorktown on the right, were redoubts and batteries, with a line of stockade in the rear. A marshy ravine lay in front of the right, over which was placed a large redoubt. The morass extended along the centre, which was defended by a line of stockade, and by batteries. On the left of the centre was a hornwork with a ditch, a row of fraize, and an abbatis. Two redoubts were advanced before the left. The combined forces advanced, and took possession of the ground from which the British had retired.

About this time the legion cavalry and mounted infantry passed over the river to Gloucester. Gen. de Choisy invested the British post on that side so fully, as to cut off all communication between it and the country. In the mean time the royal army was straining every nerve to strengthen their works, and their artillery was constantly employed in impeding the operations of the combined army.

On the ninth and tenth of October, the Americans and French opened their batteries. They kept up a brisk and well directed fire from heavy cannon, from mortars, and howitzers. The shells of the besiegers reached the ships in the harbour; the Charon of 44 guns, and a transport ship, were burned. The besiegers commenced their second parallel two hundred yards from the works of the besieged. Two redoubts which were advanced on the left of the British, greatly impeded the progress of the combined armies. It was therefore proposed to carry them by storm. To excite a spirit of emulation, the reduction of the one was committed to the French, of the other to the Americans. The assailants marched to the assault with unloaded arms; having passed the abbatis and palisades, they attacked on all sides, and carried the redoubt in a few minutes, with the loss of eight men killed, and twenty-eight wounded.

The French were equally successful on their part. They carried the redoubt assigned to them with rapidity, but lost a considerable number of men. These two redoubts were included in the second parallel, and facilitated the subsequent operations of the besiegers.

By this time the batteries of the besiegers were covered with nearly a hundred pieces of heavy ordnance, and the works of the besieged were so damaged that they could scarcely show a single gun. Lord Cornwallis had now no hope left, but from offering terms of capitulation, or attempting an escape. He determined on the latter. This, though less practicable than when first proposed, was not altogether hopeless.

Boats were prepared to receive the troops in the night, and to transport them to Gloucester point. After one whole embarkation had crossed, a violent storm of wind and rain dispersed the boats, and frustrated the whole scheme. The royal army, thus weakened by division, was exposed to increased danger. Orders were sent to those who had passed, to recross the river to Yorktown.

With the failure of this scheme, the last hope of the British army expired. Longer resistance could answer no good purpose, and might occasion the loss of many valuable lives. Lord Cornwallis therefore wrote a letter to Gen. Washington, requesting a cessation of arms for twenty-four hours; and that commissioners might be appointed to digest terms of capitulation.

This was agreed to, and in consequence thereof, the posts of New-York and Gloucester were surrendered on certain stipulations; the principal of which were as follows:

—"The troops to be prisoners of war to Congress, and the naval force to France:—"The officers to retain their side arms and private property of every kind, but every thing obviously belonging to the inhabitants of the United States, to be subject to be reclaimed:—"The soldiers to be kept in Virginia, Maryland, and Pennsylvania, and to be supplied with the same rations as are allowed to soldiers in the service of Congress:—"A proportion of the officers to march into the country with the prisoners, the rest to be allowed to proceed on parole to Europe, to New-York, or to any other American maritime post in possession of the British."

The honour of marching out with colours flying, which had been refused to Gen. Lincoln on his giving up Charleston, was now refused to Earl Cornwallis; and Gen. Lincoln was appointed to receive the submission of the royal army at Yorktown, precisely in the same way his own had been conducted about eighteen months before.

The regular troops of America and France, employed in this siege, consisted of about 5,500 of the former, and 7,000 of the latter, and they were assisted by about 4,000 militia. On the part of the combined army, about three hundred were killed or wounded. On the part of the British about five hundred and seventy were taken in the redoubts, which were carried by assault on the 14th of October. The troops of every kind that surrendered prisoners of war, exceeded 7,000 men; but so great was the number of sick and wounded, that there were only 3,800 capable of bearing arms.

Congress honoured Gen. Washington, Count de Rochambeau, Count de Grasse, and the officers of the different corps, and the men under them, with thanks for their services in the reduction of lord Cornwallis. The whole project was conceived with profound wisdom, and the incidents of it had been combined with singular propriety. It is not therefore wonderful, that from the remarkable coincidence in all its parts, it was crowned with unvaried success.

General Washington, on the day after the surrender, ordered "that those who were under arrest, should be pardoned and set at liberty." His orders closed as follows—"Divine service shall be performed tomorrow in the different brigades and divisions. The commander in chief recommends that all the troops that are not upon duty, do assist at it with a serious deportment, and that sensibility of heart which the recollection of the surprising and particular interposition of providence in our favour claims." The interesting event of captivating a second royal army, produced strong emotions, which broke out in all the variety of ways in which the most rapturous joy usually displays itself.

After the capture of lord Cornwallis, Washington, with the greatest part of his army, returned to the vicinity of New-York. In the preceding six years he had been accustomed to look forward and to provide for all possible events. In the habit of struggling with difficulties, his courage at all times grew with the dangers which surrounded him. In the most disastrous situations he was far removed from despair. On the other hand, those fortunate events which induced many to believe that the revolution was accomplished, never operated on him so far as to relax his exertions or precautions.

In a letter to Gen. Greene he observed, "I shall endeavour to stimulate Congress to the best improvement of our late success, by taking the most vigorous and effectual measures to be ready for an early and decisive campaign the next year. My greatest fear is that, viewing this stroke in a point of light which may too much magnify its importance, they may think our work too nearly closed, and fall into a state of languor and relaxation. To prevent this error, I shall employ every means in my power; and if unhappily we sink into this fatal mistake, no part of the blame shall be mine."

9

1782 and 1783: Prospects of peace. Languor of the states. Discontents of the army. Gen. Washington prevents the adoption of rash measures. Some new levies in Pennsylvania mutiny, and are quelled. Washington recommends measures for the preservation of independence, peace, liberty, and happiness. Dismisses his army. Enters New-York. Takes leave of his officers. Settles his accounts. Repairs to Annapolis. Resigns his commission. Retires to Mount Vernon, and resumes his agricultural pursuits.

The military establishment for 1782 was passed with unusual celerity shortly after the surrender of lord Cornwallis; but no exertions of America alone could do more than confine the British to the sea coast. To dislodge them from their strong holds in New-York and Charleston, occupied the unceasing attention of Washington.

While he was concerting plans for farther combined operations with the French, and at the same time endeavouring by circular letters to rouse his countrymen to spirited measures, intelligence arrived that sundry motions for discontinuing the American war had been debated in the British Parliament, and nearly carried. Fearing that this would relax the exertions of the states, he added in his circular letters to their respective Governors—

"I have perused these debates with great attention and care, with a view, if possible, to penetrate their real design; and upon the most mature deliberation I can bestow, I am obliged to declare it as my candid opinion, that the measure in all its views, so far as it respects America, is merely delusory, having no serious intention to admit our independence upon its true principles; but is calculated to produce a change of ministers to quiet the minds of their own people, and reconcile them to a continuance of the war; while it is meant to amuse this country with a false sense of peace, to draw us from our connexion with France, and to lull us into a

1782 and 1783: Prospects of peace

state of security and inactivity; which taking place, the ministry will be left to prosecute the war in other parts of the world with greater vigour and effect.

"Your excellency will permit me on this occasion to observe, that even if the nation and parliament are really in earnest to obtain peace with America, it will undoubtedly be wisdom in us to meet them with great caution and circumspection, and by all means to keep our arms firm in our hands; and instead of relaxing one iota in our exertions, rather to spring forward with redoubled vigour, that we may take the advantage of every favourable opportunity, until our wishes are fully obtained. No nation yet suffered in treaty by preparing (even in the moment of negociations) most vigorously for the field."

Early in May, Sir Guy Carleton, who had succeeded Sir Henry Clinton as commander in chief of the British forces in America, arrived in New-York, and announced in successive communications, the increasing probability of a speedy peace, and his disapprobation of farther hostilities, which, he observed, "could only tend to multiply the miseries of individuals, without a possible advantage to either nation."

The cautious temper of Washington gradually yielded to increasing evidence that the British were seriously inclined to terminate the war; but in proportion as this opinion prevailed, the exertions of the states relaxed. No more than 80,000 dollars had been received from all of them, when the month of August was far advanced. Every expenditure yielded to the subsistence of the army. A sufficiency of money could scarcely be obtained for that indispensably necessary purpose. To pay the troops was impossible.

Washington, whose sagacity anticipated events, foresaw with concern the probable consequences likely to result from the tardiness of the states to comply with the requisitions of Congress. These had been ample. Eight millions of dollars had been called for, to be paid in four equal quarterly instalments, for the service of the year 1782.

In a confidential letter to the Secretary of War, Washington observed—"I cannot help fearing the result of reducing the army, where I see such a number of men, goaded by a thousand stings of reflection on the past, and of anticipation on the future, about to be turned into the world, soured by penury, and what they call the ingratitude of the public; involved in debts without one farthing of money to carry them home, after having spent the flower of their days, and many of them their patrimonies, in establishing the freedom and independence of their country, and having suffered every thing which human nature is capable is enduring on this side of death. I repeat it, when I reflect on these irritable circumstances,

1782 and 1783: Prospects of peace

I cannot avoid apprehending that a train of evils will follow, of a very serious and distressing nature.

"I wish not to heighten the shades of the picture so far as the real life would justify me in doing, or I would give anecdotes of patriotism and distress, which have scarcely ever been paralleled, never surpassed, in the history of mankind. But you may rely upon it; the patience and long sufferance of this army are almost exhausted, and there never was so great a spirit of discontent as at this instant. While in the field, it may be kept from breaking out into acts of outrage; but when we retire into winter quarters (unless the storm be previously dissipated), I cannot be at ease respecting the consequences. It is high time for a peace."

These apprehensions were well founded. To watch the discontents of his troops, the American chief continued in camp after they had retired into winter quarters, though there was no prospect of any military operation which might require his presence. Soon after their retirement, the officers presented a petition to Congress respecting their pay, and deputed a committee of their body to solicit their interests while under consideration.

Nothing had been decided on the claims of the army, when intelligence (in March, 1783) arrived that preliminary and eventual articles of peace between the United States and Great-Britain had been signed on the 30th of the preceding November, in which the independence of the United States was amply recognized. In the general joy excited by this event, the army partook; but one unpleasant idea mingled itself with their exultations. They suspected that as justice had not been done to them while their services were indispensable, they would be less likely to obtain it when they ceased to be necessary.

Their fears on this account were increased by a letter which about the same time was received from their committee in Philadelphia, announcing that the objects which they had solicited from Congress had not yet been obtained. Smarting as they were under past sufferings, and present wants, their exasperation became violent and almost universal.

While they were brooding over their gloomy prospects, and provoked at the apparent neglect with which they had been treated, an anonymous paper was circulated, proposing a meeting of the General and Field Officers on the next day. The avowed object of this meeting was to consider the late letter from their committee with Congress, and what measures should be adopted to obtain that redress of grievances which they seemed to have solicited in vain. On the same day the following address was privately circulated:

1782 and 1783: Prospects of peace

"TO THE OFFICERS OF THE ARMY.

"Gentlemen,

"A FELLOW-SOLDIER, whose interest and affections bind him strongly to you; whose past sufferings have been as great, and whose future fortune may be as desperate as yours—would beg leave to address you. Age has its claims, and rank is not without its pretensions to advise; but though unsupported by both, he flatters himself that the plain language of sincerity and experience, will neither be unheard nor unregarded. Like many of you, he loved private life, and left it with regret. He left it, determined to retire from the field with the necessity that called him to it, and not till then; not till the enemies of his country, the slaves of power, and the hirelings of injustice, were compelled to abandon their schemes, and acknowledge America as terrible in arms as she had been humble in remonstrance.

"With this object in view, he has long shared in your toils, and mingled in your dangers; he has felt the cold hand of poverty without a murmur, and has seen the insolence of wealth without a sigh. But, too much under the direction of his wishes, and sometimes weal enough to mistake desire for opinion, he has, till lately, very lately, believed in the justice of his country. He hoped, that as the clouds of adversity scattered, and as the sun-shine of peace and better fortune broke in upon us, the coldness and severity of government would relax, and that, more than justice, that gratitude would blaze forth upon those hands which had upheld her in the darkest stages of her passage, from impending servitude to acknowledged independence.

"But faith has its limits, as well as temper; and there are points beyond which neither can be stretched, without sinking into cowardice, or plunging into credulity. This, my friends, I conceive to be your situation. Hurried to the very verge of both, another step would ruin you forever. To be tame and unprovoked when injuries press hard upon you, is more than weakness; but to look up for kinder usage, without one manly effort of your own, would fix your character, and show the world how richly you deserve those chains you broke. To guard against this evil, let us take a review of the ground upon which we now stand, and from thence carry our thoughts forward for a moment, into the unexplored field of expedient.

"After a pursuit of seven long years, the object for which we set out is at length brought within our reach!—Yes, my friends, that suffering courage of yours, was active once—it has conducted the United States of America through a doubtful and a bloody war! It has placed her in the chair of independency, and peace again returns to bless—whom? A country willing to redress your wrongs, cherish your worth, and reward your services; a country courting your return to private life, with tears of gratitude, and smiles of admiration; longing to divide with you that independency which your gallantry has given, and those riches which your wounds have preserved? Is this the case? Or is it rather, a country that tramples upon your rights, disdains your cries, and insults your distresses? Have you not, more than once, suggested your wishes, and made known your wants to Congress? Wants and wishes which gratitude and policy should have anticipated, rather than evaded. And have you not lately, in the meek language of entreating memorial, begged from their justice, what you would no longer expect from their favour? How have you been answered? Let the letter which you are called to consider to-morrow, make reply.

"If this, then, be your treatment, while the swords you wear are necessary for the defence of America, what have you to expect from peace, when your voice shall sink, and your strength dissipate by division?

"When these very swords, the instruments and companions of your glory, shall be taken from your sides, and no remaining mark of military distinction left, but your wants, infirmities, and scars! can you then consent to be the only sufferers by this revolution, and retiring from the field, grow old in poverty, wretchedness, and contempt? Can you consent to wade through the vile mire of dependency, and owe the miserable remnant of that life to charity, which has hitherto been spent in honour?—if you can, go—and carry with you the jest of tories, and the scorn of whigs—the ridicule, and what is worse, the pity of the world! Go, starve, and be forgotten!

"But if your spirit should revolt at this; if you have sense enough to discover, and spirit enough to oppose tyranny, under whatever garb it may assume; whether it be the plain coat of republicanism, or the splendid robe of royalty; if you have yet learned to discriminate between a people and a cause, between men and principles—awake!—attend to your situation, and redress yourselves. If the present moment be lost, every future effort is in vain; and your threats then will be as empty as your entreaties now.

"I would advise you, therefore, to come to some final opinion, upon what you can bear, and what you will suffer. If your determination be in any proportion to your wrongs, carry your appeal from the justice to the fears of government—change the milk and water style of your last memorial; assume a bolder tone—decent, but lively—spirited and determined; and suspect the man who would advise to more moderation and longer forbearance. Let two or three men, who can feel as well as write, be appointed to draw up your last remonstrance; for I would no longer give it the sueing, soft, unsuccessful epithet of memorial. Let it be represented (in language that will neither dishonour you by its rudeness, nor betray you by its fears) what has been promised by Congress, and what has been performed; how long and how patiently you have suffered; how little you have asked, and how much of that little has been denied. Tell them that though you were the first, and would wish to be the last, to encounter danger; though despair itself can never drive you into dishonour, it may drive you from the field; that the wound often irritated, and never healed, may at length become incurable; and that the slightest mark of indignity from Congress now, must operate like the grave, and part you for ever; that in any political event, the army has its alternative. If peace, that nothing shall separate you from your arms but death; if war, that courting the auspices and inviting the directions of your illustrious leader, you will retire to some unsettled country, smile in your turn, and 'mock when their fear cometh on.'

"But let it represent also, that should they comply with the request of your late memorial, it would make you more happy, and them more respectable: that while the war should continue, you would follow their standard into the field—and when it came to an end, you would withdraw into the shade of private life, and give the world another subject of wonder and applause—an army victorious over its enemies—victorious over itself."

[Anonymous]

This artful address found in almost every bosom such congenial sentiments, as prepared the way for its favourable reception. It operated like a torch on combustible materials. The passions of the army quickly caught the flame it was well calculated to excite. Every appearance threatened that the proposed convention of the officers would produce an explosion which might tarnish the reputation of the army, disturb the peace of the country, and, under certain circumstances, most probably terminate in the subversion of the recent liberties of the new formed states.

Accustomed as Washington had been to emergencies of great delicacy and difficulty, yet none had occurred, which called more pressingly than the present, for the utmost exertion of all his powers. He knew well that it was much easier to avoid intemperatemeasures than to recede from them after they had been adopted. He therefore considered it as a matter of the last importance, to prevent the meeting of the officers on the succeeding day, as proposed in the anonymous summons.

The sensibilities of the army were too high to admit of this being forbidden by authority, as a violation of discipline; but the end was

1782 and 1783: Prospects of peace

answered in another way, and without irritation. The commander in chief, in general orders, noticed the anonymous summons as a disorderly proceeding, not to be countenanced; and the more effectually to divert the officers from paying any attention to it, he requested them to meet for the same nominal purpose, but on a day four days subsequent to the one proposed by the anonymous addresser.

The intervening period was improved in preparing the officers for the adoption of moderate measures. Gen. Washington sent for one officer after another, and enlarged in private on the fatal consequences, and particularly on the loss of character, which would result from the adoption of intemperate resolutions. His whole personal influence was excited to calm the prevailing agitation.

When the officers assembled, their venerable chief preparing to address them, found his eye-sight to fail him, on which he observed, "My eyes have grown dim in my country's service, but I never doubted of its justice," and proceeded as follows:

"Gentlemen,

"By an anonymous summons, an attempt has been made to convene you together—how inconsistent with the rules of propriety!—how unmilitary!—and how subversive of all order and discipline, let the good sense of the army decide.

"In the moment of this summons, another anonymous production was sent into circulation; addressed more to the feelings of passions, than to the reason & judgment of the army.—The author of the piece, is entitled to much credit for the goodness of his pen:—and I could wish he had as much credit for the rectitude of his heart—for, as men we see thro' different optics, and are induced by the reflecting faculties of the mind, to use different means to attain the same end:—the author of the address, should have had more charity, than to mark for suspicion, the man who should recommend moderation and longer forbearance—or, in others words, who should not think as he thinks, and act as he advises.—But he had another plan in view, in which candor and liberality of sentiment, regard to justice, and love of ountry, have no part, and he was right, to insinuate the darkest suspicion, to effect the blackest designs.

"That the address is drawn with great art, and is designed to answer the most insidious purposes.—That it is calculated to impress the mind, with an idea of premeditated injustice in the sovereign power of the United States, and rouse all those resentments which must unavoidably flow from such a belief.—That the secret mover of this scheme (whoever he may be) intended to take advantage of the passions, while they were warmed by the recollection of mind which is so necessary to give dignity & stability to measures, is rendered too obvious, by the mode of conducting the business to need other proof than a reference to the proceeding.

"Thus much, gentlemen, I have thought it incumbent on me to observe to you, to shew upon what principles I opposed the irregular and hasty meeting which was proposed to have been held on Tuesday last:—and not because I wanted a disposition to give you every opportunity, consistent with your own honor, and the dignity of the army, to make known your grievances.—If my conduct heretofore, has not evinced to you, that I have been a faithful friend to the army, my declaration of it at this time would be equally unavailing & improper.—But as I was among the first who embarked in the cause of our common country—As I have never left your side one moment, but when called from you, on public duty—As I have been the constant companion & witness of your distresses, and not among the last to feel, & acknowledge your merits—As I have ever considered my own military reputation as inseperably connected with that of the army—As my Heart has ever expanded with joy, when I have heard its praises—and my indignation has arisen, when the mouth of detraction has been opened against it—it can scarcely be supposed, at this late stage of the war, that I am indifferent to its interests.

"But—how are they to be promoted? The way is plain, says the anonymous addresser—If war continues, remove into the unsettled country—there establish yourselves, and leave an ungrateful country to defend itself—But who are they to defend?—Our wives, our children, our farms, and other property which we leave behind us.—or—in this state of hostile seperation, are we to take the two first (the latter cannot be removed)—to perish in a wilderness, with hunger cold & nakedness?—If peace takes place, never sheath your sword says he untill you have obtained full and ample justice—This dreadful alternative, of either deserting our country in the extremest hour of her distress, or turning our arms against it, (which is the apparent object, unless Congress can be compelled into instant compliance) has something so shocking in it, that humanity revolts at the idea.

"My God! What can this writer have in view, by recommending such measures?—Can he be a friend to the army?—Can he be a friend to this country?—Rather is he not an insidious foe?—Some emissary, perhaps, from New York, plotting the ruin of both, by sowing the seeds of discord & seperation between the civil & military powers of the continent?—And what compliment does he pay to our understandings, when he recommends measures in either alternative, impracticable in their nature?

1782 and 1783: Prospects of peace

"But here, gentlemen, I will drop the curtain;—and because it would be as imprudent in me to assign my reasons for this opinion, as it would be insulting to your conception, to suppose you stood in need of them.— A moment's reflection will convince every dispassionate mind of the physical impossibility of carrying either proposal into execution.

"There might, gentlemen, be an impropriety in my taking notice, in this address to you, of an anonymous production—but the manner in which that performance has been introduced to the army—the effect it was intended to have, together with some other circumstances, will amply justify my observations on the tendency of that writing.—With respect to the advice given by the author—to suspect the man, who shall recommend moderate measures and longer forbearance—I spurn it—as every man, who regards that liberty, & reveres that justice for which we contend, undoubtedly must—for if men are to be precluded from offering their sentiments on a matter, which may involve the most serious and alarming consequences, that can invite the consideration of Mankind; reason is of no use to us—the freedom of speech may be taken away—and, dumb & silent we may be led, like sheep, to the slaughter.

"I cannot, in justice to my own belief, & what I have great reason to conceive is the intention of Congress, conclude this address, without giving it as my decided opinion; that that honourable body, entertain exalted sentiments of the services of the army;—and, from a full conviction of its merits & sufferings, will do it complete justice:—That their endeavors, to discover & establish funds for this purpose, have been unwearied, and will not cease, till they have succeeded, I have succeeded, I have not a doubt. But, like all other large bodies, where there is a variety of different interests to reconcile, their deliberations are slow.—Why then should we distrust them?—and, in consequence of that distrust, adopt measures, which may cast a shade over that glory which, has been so justly acquired; and tarnish the reputation of an army which is celebrated thro' all Europe, for its fortitude and patriotism?—and for what is this done?—to bring the object we seek for nearer?—No!—most certainly, in my opinion, it will cast it at a greater distance.—

"For myself (and I take no merit in giving the assurance, being induced to it from principles of gratitude, veracity & Justice)—a grateful sence of the confidence you have ever placed in me—a recollection of the chearful assistance, & prompt obedience I have experienced from you, under every vicisitude of fortune,—and the sincere I feel for an army I have so long had the honor to command, will oblige me to declare, in this public & solemn manner, that, in the attainment of compleat justice for all your toils & dangers, and in the gratification of every wish, so far as may be done consistently with the great duty I owe my country, and those powers we are bound to respect, you may freely command my services to the utmost of my abilities.

"While I give you these assurances, and pledge my self in the most unequivocal manner, to exert whatever ability I am possessed of, in your favor—let me entreat you, gentlemen, on your part, not to take any measures, which, viewed in the calm light of reason, will lessen the dignity, & sully the glory you have hitherto maintained—let me request you to rely on the plighted faith of your country, and place a full confidence in the purity of the intentions of Congress; that, previous to your dissolution as an Army they will cause all your accounts to be fairly liquidated, as directed in their resolutions, which were published to you two days ago—and that they will adopt the most effectual measures in their power, to render ample justice to you, for your faithful and meritorious Services.—And let me conjure you, in the name of our common country—as you value your own sacred honor—as you respect the rights of humanity; as you regard the military & national character of America, to express your utmost horror & detestation of the man who wishes, under any specious pretences, to overturn the liberties of our country, & who wickedly attempts to open the flood gates of civil discord, & deluge our rising empire in blood.

"By thus determining—& thus acting, you will pursue the plain & direct road to the attainment of your wishes.—You will defeat the insidious designs of our enemies, who are compelled to resort from open force to secret artifice.—You will give one more distinguished proof of unexampled patriotism & patient virtue, rising superior to the pressure of the most complicated sufferings;—And you will, by the dignity of your conduct, afford occasion for posterity to say, when speaking of the glorious example you have exhibited to mankind, "had this day been wanting, the world has never seen the last stage of perfection to which human nature is capable of attaining."

The address being ended, Washington withdrew. No person was hardy enough to oppose the advice he had given. The impression made by his address was irresistible. The happy moment was seized. While the minds of the officers, softened by the eloquence of their beloved commander, were in a yielding state, a resolution was offered and adopted, in which they assured him "that they reciprocated his affectionate expressions with the greatest sincerity of which the heart was capable."

Before they dispersed, they unanimously adopted several other resolutions, in which they declared—"That no circumstance of distress or danger should induce a conduct that might tend to sully the reputation and glory they had acquired at the price of their blood and eight years faithful service—

That they continued to have an unshaken confidence in the justice of Congress and their country—That they viewed with abhorrence, and rejected with disdain, the infamous proposition contained in a late anonymous address to the officers of the army."

The storm which had been long gathering was suddenly dissipated. The army acquired additional reputation, and the commander in chief gave a new proof to the goodness of his heart, and the soundness of his judgment. Perhaps in no instance did the United States receive from heaven a more signal deliverance through the hands of Washington, than in the happy termination of this serious transaction. If ambition had possessed a single corner of his heart, the opportunity was too favourable, the temptation too splendid, to have been resisted. But his soul was superior to such views, and his love of country so ardent, and at the same time so pure, that the charms of power, though recommended by the imposing appearance of procuring justice for his unrewarded army, made no impression on his unshaken mind. He viewed the character of a patriot as superior to that of a sovereign. To be elevated to supreme power, was less in his esteem than to be a good man.

Instead of turning the discontents of an unpaid army to his own aggrandizement, he improved the late events to stimulate Congress to do them justice. His letter to their President on this occasion was as follows:

"Sir, the result of the proceedings of the grand convention of the officers, which I have the honour of enclosing to your excellency for the inspection of Congress, will, I flatter myself, be considered as the last glorious proof of patriotism which could have been given, by men who could have aspired to the distinction of a patriot army; and will not only confirm their claim to the justice, but will increase their title to the gratitude of their country.

"Having seen the proceedings on the part of the army terminate with perfect unanimity, and in a manner entirely consonant to my wishes; being impressed with the liveliest sentiments of affection for those who have so long, so patiently, and so cheerfully suffered and fought under my immediate direction; having from motives of justice, duty, and gratitude, spontaneously offered myself as an advocate for their rights; and, having been requested to write to your excellency, earnestly entreating the most speedy decision of Congress upon the subjects of the late address from the army to that honourable body; it now only remains for me to perform the task I have assumed, and to intercede in their behalf, as I now do, that the sovereign power will be pleased to verify the predictions I have pronounced of, and the confidence the army have reposed in, the justice of their country.

"And here I humbly conceive it is altogether unnecessary (while I am pleading the cause of an army which have done and suffered more than any other army ever did in the defence of the rights and liberties of human nature), to expatiate on their claims to the most ample compensation for their meritorious services, because they are known perfectly to the whole world, and because (although the topics are inexhaustible, enough has already been said on the subject. To prove these assertions, to evince that my sentiments have ever been uniform, and to show what my ideas of the rewards in question have always been, I appeal to the archives of Congress, and call on those sacred deposites to witness for me. And in order that my observations and arguments in favour of a future adequate provision for the officers of the army may be brought to remembrance again, and considered in a single point of view, without giving Congress the trouble of having recourse to their files, I will beg leave to transmit herewith an extract from a representation made by me to a committee of Congress, so long ago as the 29th of January, 1778, and also the transcript of a letter to the President of Congress, dated near Pasaic Falls, October 11th, 1780.

"That in the critical and perilous moment when the last mentioned communication was made, there was the utmost danger a dissolution of the army would have taken place, unless measures similar to those recommended had been adopted, will not admit a doubt. That the adoption of the resolution granting half pay for life has been attended with all the happy consequences I had foretold, so far as respected the good of the service, let the astonishing contrast between the state of the army at this instant, and at the former period, determine. And that the establishment of funds, and security of the payment of all the just demands of the army, will be the most certain means of preserving the national faith, and future tranquillity of this extensive continent, is my decided opinion.

"By the preceding remarks it will readily be imagined, that instead of retracting and reprehending (from farther experience and reflection), the mode of compensation so strenuously urged in the enclosures, I am more and more confirmed in the sentiment; and if in the wrong, suffer me to please myself with the grateful delusion.

"For if, besides the simple payment of their wages, a farther compensation is not due to the sufferings and sacrifices of the officers, then have I been mistaken indeed. If the whole army have not merited whatever a grateful people can bestow, then have I been beguiled by prejudice, and built opinion on the basis of error. If this country should not in the

1782 and 1783: Prospects of peace

event perform every thing which has been requested in the late memorial to Congress, then will my belief become vain, and the hope that has been excited, void of foundation. And if (as has been suggested for the purpose of inflaming their passions), the officers of the army are to be the only sufferers by this revolution; "if retiring from the field they are to grow old in poverty, wretchedness, and contempt-if they are to wade through the vile mire of dependency, and owe the miserable remnant of that life to charity, which has hitherto been spent in honour;" then shall I have learned what ingratitude is; then shall I have realized a tale which will embitter every moment of my future life.

"But I am under no such apprehensions: a country rescued by their arms from impending ruin, will never leave unpaid the debt of gratitude. Should any intemperate or improper warmth have mingled itself amongst the foregoing observations, I must entreat your Excellency and Congress, it may attributed to the effusion of an honest zeal in the best of causes, and that my peculiar situation may be my apology; and I hope I need not on this momentous occasion make any new protestations of personal disinterestedness, having ever renounced for myself the idea of pecuniary reward. The consciousness of having attempted faithfully to discharge my duty, and the approbation of my country, will be a sufficient recompense for my services.

"I have the honour to be, &c. &c.

"Geo: WASHINGTON "His Excellency the President in Congress."

This energetic letter, connected with recent events, induced Congress to decide on the claims of the army. These were liquidated, and the amount acknowledged to be due from the United States.

Soon after these events, intelligence of a general peace was received. The reduction of the army was therefore resolved upon, but the mode of effecting it required deliberation. To avoid the inconveniences of dismissing a great number of soldiers in a body, furloughs were freely granted on the application of individuals, and after their dispersion, they were not enjoined to return. By this arrangement a critical moment was got over. A great part of an unpaid army was dispersed over the states without tumult or disorder.

While the veterans serving under the immediate eye of their beloved commander in chief, manifested the utmost good temper and conduct, a mutinous disposition broke out among some new levies stationed at Lancaster, in Pennsylvania. About 80 of this description marched in a body to Philadelphia, where they were joined by some other troops, so as to amount in the whole to 300. They marched with fixed bayonets to the state house, in which Congress and the state executive council

1782 and 1783: Prospects of peace

held their sessions. They placed guards at every door, and threatened the president and council of the state with letting loose an enraged soldiery upon them, unless they granted their demands in twenty minutes.

As soon as this outrage was known to Washington, he detached Gen. Howe with a competent force to suppress the mutiny. This was effected without bloodshed before his arrival. The mutineers were too inconsiderable to commit extensive mischief; but their disgraceful conduct excited the greatest indignation in the breast of the commander in chief, which was expressed in a letter to the president of Congress in the following words:

"While I suffer the most poignant distress in observing that a handful of men, contemptible in numbers, and equally so in point of service (if the veteran troops of the southward have not been seduced by their example), and who are not worthy to be called soldiers, should disgrace themselves and their country as the Pennsylvania mutineers have done, by insulting the sovereign authority of the United States, and that of their own, I feel an inexpressible satisfaction that even this behaviour cannot stain the name of the American soldiery. It cannot be imputable to, or reflect dishonour on, the army at large; but on the contrary, it will, by the striking contrast it exhibits, hold up to public view the other troops in the most advantageous point of light.

"Upon taking all the circumstances into consideration, I cannot sufficiently express my surprise and indignation at the arrogance, the folly, and the wickedness, of the mutineers; nor can I sufficiently admire the fidelity, the bravery, and patriotism, which must forever signalize the unsullied character of the corps of our army. For when we consider that these Pennsylvania levies who have now mutinied are recruits and soldiers of a day, who have not borne the heat and burden of the war, and who can have in reality very few hardships to complain of; and when we at the same time recollect that those soldiers who have lately been furloughed from this army, are the veterans who have patiently endured hunger, nakedness, and cold; who have suffered and bled without as murmur, and who, with perfect good order, have retired to their homes without a settlement of their accounts or a farthing of money in their pockets; we shall be as much astonished at the virtues of the latter, as we are struck with detestation of the proceedings of the former."

While arrangements were making for the final dismission of the army, Gen. Washington was looking forward with anxiety to the future destinies of the United States. Much of his attention was devoted to a serious consideration of such establishments as the independence of his country required. On these subjects, he freely communicated with Congress, and

1782 and 1783: Prospects of peace

recommended that great diligence should be used in forming a well regulated and disciplined militia during peace, as the best means for securing the future tranquillity and respectability of the nation. He also addressed the following circular letter to the Governors of each of the States:

"HEAD-QUARTERS, Newburgh, June 18, 1783.

"Sir, the object for which I had the honour to hold an appointment in the service of my country, being accomplished, I am now preparing to resign it into the hands of Congress, and return to that domestic retirement, which, it is well known, I left with the greatest reluctance; a retirement for which I have never ceased to sigh through a long and painful absence, in which (remote from the noise and trouble of the world), I meditate to pass the remainder of life, in a state of undisturbed repose: but, before I carry this resolution into effect, I think it a duty incumbent on me to make this my last official communication, to congratulate you on the glorious events which heaven has been pleased to produce in our favour; to offer my sentiments respecting some important subjects, which appear to me to be intimately connected with the tranquillity of the United States; to take my leave of your excellency as a public character; and to give my final blessing to that country, in whose service I have spent the prime of my life; for whose sake I have consumed so many anxious days and watchful nights, and whose happiness, being extremely dear to me, will always constitute no inconsiderable part of my own.

"Impressed with the liveliest sensibility on this pleasing occasion, I will claim the indulgence of dilating the more copiously on the subject of our mutual felicitation. When we consider the magnitude of the prize we contended for, the doubtful nature of the contest, and the favourable manner in which it has terminated; we shall find the greatest possible reason for gratitude and rejoicing. This is a theme that will afford infinite delight to every benevolent and liberal mind, whether the event in contemplation be considered as a source of present enjoyment, or the parent of future happiness; and we shall have equal occasion to felicitate ourselves on the lot that Providence has assigned us, whether we view it in a natural, a political, or a moral point of light.

"The citizens of America, placed in the most enviable condition, as the sole lords and proprietors of a vast tract of continent, comprehending all the various soils and climates of the world, and abounding with all the necessaries and conveniences of the world, are now, by the late satisfactory pacification, acknowledged to be possessed of absolute freedom and independency: they are from this period to be considered as the actors on a most conspicuous theatre, which seems to be peculiarly designed by Providence for the display of human greatness and felicity. Here they are not only surrounded with every thing that can contribute to the completion of private and domestic enjoyment; but heaven has crowned all its other blessings, by giving a surer opportunity for political happiness, than any other nation has ever been favoured with.

"Nothing can illustrate these observations more forcibly than a recollection of the happy conjuncture of times and circumstances, under which our republic assumed its rank among the nations.—The foundation of our empire was not laid in a gloomy age of ignorance and superstition, but at an epocha when the rights of mankind were better understood and more clearly defined, than at any former period. Researches of the human mind after social happiness have been carried to a great extent; the treasures of knowledge acquired by the labours of philosophers, sages, and legislators, through a long succession of years, are laid open for us, and their collective wisdom may be happily applied in the establishment of our forms of government. The free cultivation of letters, the unbounded extension of commerce, the progressive refinement of manners, the growing liberality of sentiment; and, above all, the pure and benign light of revelation, have had a meliorating influence on mankind, and increased the blessings of society. At this auspicious period, the United States came into existence as a nation; and if their citizens should not be completely free and happy, the fault will be entirely their own.

"Such is our situation, and such are our prospects. But notwithstanding the cup of blessing is thus reached out to us; notwithstanding happiness is ours, if we have a disposition to seize the occasion, and make it our own; yet it appears to me there is an option still left to the United States of America, whether they will be respectable and prosperous, or contemptible and miserable as a nation. This is a time of their political probation: this is the moment when the eyes of the whole world are turned upon them: this is the time to establish or ruin their national character for ever: this is the favourable moment to give such a ton to the federal government, as will enable it to answer the ends of its institution; or, this may be the illfated moment for relaxing the powers of the union, annihilating the cement of the confederation, and exposing us to become the sport of European politics, which may play one state against another, to prevent their growing importance, and to serve their own interested purposes.

"For, according to the system of policy the states shall adopt at this moment, they will stand or fall; and, by their confirmation or lapse, it is yet to be decided, whether the revolution must ultimately be considered as a blessing or a curse;—a blessing or a curse, not to the present age alone, for with our fate will the destiny of unborn millions be involved.

"With this conviction of the importance of the present crisis, silence in me would be a crime; I will therefore speak to your excellency the language of freedom and sincerity, without disguise. I am aware, however, those who differ from me in political sentiments may, perhaps, remark, I am stepping out of the proper line of my duty; and they may possibly ascribe to arrogance or ostentation, what I know is alone the result of the purest intention.

"But the rectitude of my own heart, which disdains such unworthy motives; the part I have hitherto acted in life; the determination I have formed of not taking any share in public business hereafter; the ardent desire I feel, and shall continue to manifest, of quietly enjoying in public life, after all the toils of war, the benefits of a wise and liberal government, will, I flatter myself, sooner or later, convince my countrymen, that I could have no sinister views in delivering with so little reserve the opinions contained in this address.

"There are four things which I humbly conceive are essential to the well being, I may even venture to say to the existence of the United States as an independent power.

"1st. An indissoluble union of the states under one federal head.

"2dly. A sacred regard to public justice.

"3dly. The adoption of a proper peace establishment. And,

"4thly. The prevalence of that pacific and friendly disposition among the people of the United States, which will induce them to forget their local prejudices and policies; to make those mutual concessions to the general prosperity; and, in some instances, to sacrifice their individual advantages to the interest of the community.

"These are the pillars on which the glorious fabric of our glorious independency and national character must be supported. Liberty is the basis-and whoever would dare to sap the foundation, or overturn the structure, under whatever specious pretext he may attempt it, will merit the bitterest execration, and the severest punishment, which can be inflicted by his injured country.

"On the first three articles I will make a few observations; leaving the last to the good sense and serious consideration of those immediately concerned.

"Under the first head, although it may not be necessary or proper for me in this place to enter into a particular disquisition of the principles of the union, and to take up the great question which has been frequently agitated, whether it be expedient and requisite for the states to delegate a larger proportion of power to Congress, or not; yet it will be a part of my duty, and that of every true patriot, to assert, without reserve, and to insist upon the following positions:—

"That unless the states will suffer Congress to exercise those prerogatives they are undoubtedly invested with by the constitution, every thing must very rapidly tend to anarchy and confusion:

"That it is indispensable to the happiness to the individual states, that there should be lodged, somewhere, a supreme power to regulate and govern the general concerns of the confederated republic, without which the union cannot be of long duration:

"That there must be a faithful and pointed compliance on the part of every state with the late proposals and demands of Congress, or the most fatal consequences will ensue:

"That whatever measures have a tendency to dissolve the union, or contribute to violate or lessen the sovereign authority, ought to be considered as hostile to the liberty and independency of America, and the authors of them treated accordingly.

"And, lastly, unless we can be enabled by the concurrence of the states to participate of the fruits of the revolution, and apply the essential benefits of civil society, under a form of government so free and uncorrupted, so happily guarded against the danger of oppression, as has been devised and adopted by the articles of confederation, it will be a subject of regret, that so much blood and treasure has been lavished for no purpose; that so many sufferings have been encountered without a compensation, and that so many sacrifices have been made in vain.

"Many other considerations might here be adduced to prove, that without an entire conformity to the spirit of the union, we cannot exist as an independent power. It will be sufficient for my purpose to mention but one or two, which seem to me of the greatest importance.

"It is only in our united character, as an empire, that our independence is acknowledged, that our power can be regarded, or our credit supported among foreign nations. The treaties of the European powers with the United States of America will have no validity on a dissolution of the union. We shall be left nearly in a state of nature; or we may find, by our own unhappy experience, that there is a natural and necessary progression from the extreme of anarchy to the extreme of tyranny; and that arbitrary power is most easily established on the ruins of liberty abused to licentiousness.

"As to the second article, which respects the performance of public justice, Congress have, in their late address to the United States, almost exhausted the subject; they have explained their ideas so fully, and have enforced the obligations the states are under to render complete justice to all the public creditors, with so much dignity and energy, that, in my opinion, that no real friend to the honour and independency of America can hesitate a single moment respecting the propriety of complying with the just and honourable measures proposed.

"If their arguments do not produce conviction, I know of nothing that will have greater influence, especially when we reflect that the system referred to, being the result of the collected wisdom of the continent, must be esteemed, if not perfect, certainly the least objectionable of any that could be devised; and that, if it should not be carried into immediate execution, a national bankruptcy, with all its deplorable consequences, will take place before any different plan can possibly be proposed or adopted; so pressing are the present circumstances, and such is the alternative now offered to the states.

"The ability of the country to discharge the debts which have been incurred in its defence, is not to be doubted; and inclination, I flatter myself, will not be wanting. The path of our duty is plain before us; honesty will be found, on every experiment, to be the best and only true policy. Let us then, as a nation, be just; let us fulfill the public contracts which Congress had undoubtedly a right to make for the purpose of carrying on the war, with the same good faith we suppose ourselves bound to perform our private engagements.

"In the mean time, let an attention to the cheerful performance of their proper business, as individuals, and as members of society, be earnestly inculcated on the citizens of America; then will they strengthen the bands of government, and be happy under its protection. Every one will reap the fruits of his labours: every one will enjoy his own acquisitions, without molestation and without danger.

"In this state of absolute freedom and perfect security, who will grudge to yield a very little of his property to support the common interests of society, and ensure the protection of our government? Who does not remember the frequent declarations at the commencement of the war, That we should be completely satisfied, if, at the expense of one half, we could defend the remainder of our possessions? Where is the man to be found, who wishes to remain in debt, for the defence of his own person and property, to the exertions, the bravery, and the blood of others, without making one generous effort to pay the debt of honour and of gratitude? In what part of the continent shall we find any man, or body of men, who would not blush to stand up and propose measures purposely calculated to rob the soldier of his stipend, and the public creditor of his due?

"And were it possible that such a flagrant instance of injustice could ever happen, would it not excite the general indignation, and tend to bring down the authors of such measures the aggravated vengeance of heaven? If, after all, a spirit of disunion, or a temper of obstinacy and perverseness should manifest itself in any of the states; if such an ungracious disposition should attempt to frustrate all the happy effects that might be expected to flow from the union; if there should be a refusal to comply for requisitions for funds to discharge the annual interest of the public debts; and if that refusal should revive all those jealousies, and produce all those evils, which are now happily removed, Congress, who have in all their transactions shown a great degree of magnanimity and justice, will stand justified in the sight of God and man! And that state alone, which puts itself in opposition to the aggregate wisdom of the continent, and follows such mistaken and pernicious councils, will be responsible for all the consequences.

"For my own part, conscious of having acted while a servant of the public, in the manner I conceived best suited to promote the real interests of my country; having in consequence of my fixed belief, in some measure pledged myself to the army, that their country would finally do them complete and ample justice; and not wishing to conceal any instance of my official conduct from the eyes of the world, I have thought proper to transmit to your excellency the enclosed collection of papers, relative to the half-pay and commutation granted by Congress, to the officers of the army. From these communications my decided sentiment will be clearly comprehended, together with the conclusive reasons which induced me, at an early period, to recommend the adoption of this measure in the most earnest and serious manner.

"As the proceedings of Congress, the army, and myself, are open to all, and contain, in my opinion, sufficient information to remove the prejudices and errors which may have been entertained by any, I think it unnecessary to say any thing more than just to observe, that the resolutions of Congress, now alluded to, are as undoubtedly and absolutely binding upon the United States, as the most solemn acts of confederation or legislation.

"As to the idea which, I am informed, has in some instances prevailed, that the half-pay and commutation are to be regarded merely in the odious light of a pension, it ought to be exploded for ever: that provision should be viewed,, as it really was, a reasonable compensation offered by Congress, at a time when they had nothing else to give to officers of the army, for services then to be performed. It was the only means to prevent a total dereliction of the service. It was a part of their hire; I may be

1782 and 1783: Prospects of peace

allowed to say, it was the price of their blood, and of your independency. It is therefore more than a common debt; it is a debt of honour; it can never be considered as a pension, or gratuity, nor cancelled until it is fairly discharged.

"With regard to the distinction between officers and soldiers, it is sufficient that the uniform experience of every nation of the world combined with our own, proves the utility and propriety of the discrimination. Rewards in proportion to the aid the public draws from them, are unquestionably due to all its servants. In some lines, the soldiers have perhaps, generally, had as ample compensation for their services, by the large bounties which have been paid them, as their officers will receive in the proposed commutation; in others, if, besides the donation of land, the payment of arrearages of cloathing and wages (in which articles all the component parts of the army must be put upon the same footing), we take into estimate the bounties many of the soldiers have received, and the gratuity of one year's full pay, which is promised to all, possibly their situation (every circumstance being duly considered), will not be deemed less eligible than that of the officers.

"Should a farther reward, however, be judges equitable, I will venture to assert, no man will enjoy greater satisfaction than myself, in an exemption from taxes for a limited time (which has been petitioned for I some instances), or any other adequate immunity or compensation granted to the brave defenders of their country's cause. But neither the adoption or the rejection of this proposition will, in any manner, affect, much less militate against, the act of Congress, by which they have offered five years full pay, in lieu of the half-pay for life, which had been before promised to the officers of the army.

"Before I conclude the subject on public justice, I cannot omit to mention the obligations this country is under to that meritorious class of veterans, the non-commissioned officers and privates, who have been discharged for inability, in consequence of the resolution of Congress, of the 23rd of April, 1782, on an annual pension for life. Their peculiar sufferings, their singular merits and claims to that provisions, need only to be known, to interest the feelings of humanity in their behalf. Nothing but a punctual payment of their annual allowance, can rescue them from the most complicated misery; and nothing could be a more melancholy and distressing sight, than to behold those who have shed their blood, or lost their limbs in the service of their country, without a shelter, without a friend, and without the means of obtaining any of the comforts or necessaries of life, compelled to beg their bread daily from door to door.

Suffer me to recommend those of this description, belonging to your state, to the warmest patronage of your excellency and your legislature.

"It is necessary to say but a few words on the third topic which was proposed, and which regards particularly the defence of the republic-as there can be little doubt but Congress will recommend a proper peace establishment for the United States, in which a due attention will be paid to the importance of placing the militia of the Union upon a regular and respectable footing. If this should be the case, I should beg leave to urge the great advantage of it in the strongest terms.

"The militia of this country must be considered as the palladium of our security, and the first effectual resort in case of hostility. It is essential, therefore, that the same system should pervade the whole; that the formation and discipline of the militia of the continent should be absolutely uniform; and that the same species of arms, accoutrements, and military apparatus, should be introduced in every part of the United States. No one, who has not learned it from experience, can conceive the difficulty, expense, and confusion, which result from a contrary system, or the vague arrangements which have hitherto prevailed.

"If, in treating of political points, a greater latitude than usual has been taken in the course of the address; the importance of the crisis, and the magnitude of the objects in discussion, must be my apology. It is, however, neither my wish nor expectation, that the preceding observations should claim any regard, except so far as they shall appear to be dictated by a good intention, consonant to the immutable rules of justice; calculated to produce a liberal system of policy, and founded on whatever experience may have been acquired, by a long and close attention to public business.

"Here I might speak with more confidence, from my actual observations; and if it would not swell this letter (already too prolix), beyond the bounds I had prescribed myself, I could demonstrate to every mind, open to conviction, that in less time, and with much less expense than has been incurred, the war might have been brought to the same happy conclusion, if the resources of the continent could have properly been called forth; that the distresses and disappointments which have very often occurred, have, in too many instances, resulted more from a want of energy in the continental government, than a deficiency of means in the particular states; that the efficacy of the measures, arising from the want of an adequate authority in the supreme power, from a partial compliance with the requisitions of Congress, in some of the states, and from a failure of punctuality in others, while they tended to damp the zeal of those who were more willing to exert themselves, served also to accumulate the expenses of the war, and to frustrate the best concerted plans; and

1782 and 1783: Prospects of peace

that the discouragement occasioned by the complicated difficulties and embarrassments, in which our affairs were by this means involved, would have long ago produced the dissolution of any army, less patient, less virtuous, and less persevering, than that which I have had the honour to command.

"But while I mention those things which are notorious facts, as the defects of our federal constitution, particularly in the prosecution of a war, I beg it may be understood, that as I have ever taken a pleasure in gratefully acknowledging the assistance and support I have derived from every class of citizens; so shall I always be happy to do justice to the unparalleled exertions of the individual states, on many interesting occasions.

"I have thus freely disclosed what I wished to make known, before I surrendered up my public trust to those who committed it to me. The task is now accomplished; I now bid adieu to your excellency, as the chief magistrate of your state; at the same time, I bid a last farewell to the cares of office, and all the employments of public life.

"It remains, then, to be my final and only request, that your excellency will communicate these sentiments to your legislature, at their next meeting; and that they may be considered as the legacy of one who has ardently wished, on all occasions, to be useful to his country, and who, even in the shade of retirement, will not fail to implore the divine benediction upon it.

"I now make it my earnest prayer, that God would have you, and the state over which you preside, in his holy protection; that he would incline the hearts of the citizens to cultivate a spirit of subordination and obedience to government; to entertain a brotherly affection and love for one another; for their fellow-citizens for the United States at large, and particularly for their brethren who have served in the field; and, finally, that he would most graciously be pleased to dispose us all to do justice, to love mercy, and to demean ourselves with that charity, humility, and pacific temper of the mind, which were the characteristics of the divine author of our blessed religion; without an humble imitation of whose example, in these things, we can never hope to be a happy nation.

"I have the honour to be, "with much esteem and respect,

"Sir, "your excellency's most obedient,

"and most humble servant,

"Geo: WASHINGTON."

The second of November was fixed for discharging that part of the army which was engaged to serve during the war. On that day, Gen. Washington issued his farewell orders to the armies of the United States

1782 and 1783: Prospects of peace

in the most endearing language. After giving them his advice respecting their future conduct, and imploring the choicest of heaven's blessings in their favour, he bade them an affectionate farewell.

On the 25th of the same month, the British evacuated New-York, and Gen. Washington made his public entry into it, where he was received with every mark of respect and attention.

The hour now approached in which it became necessary for the American chief to take leave of his officers who had been endeared to him by a long series of common sufferings and dangers. This was done in a solemn manner. The officers, having previously assembled for the purpose, Gen. Washington joined them, and calling for a glass of wine, thus addressed them: "With an heart full of love and gratitude, I now take leave of you. I most devoutly wish that your latter days may be as prosperous and happy as your former ones have been glorious and honourable."

Having drank he added—"I cannot come to each of you, to take my leave, but shall be obliged to you, if each of you will come and take me by the hand." Gen. Knox being next, turned to him. Incapable of utterance, Washington grasped his hand and embraced him. The officers came up successively, and he took an affectionate leave of each of them. Not a word was articulated on either side. A majestic silence prevailed. The tear of sensibility glistened in every eye. The tenderness of the scene exceeded all description.

When the last of the officers had taken his leave, Washington left the room and passed through the corps of light infantry, to the place of embarkation. The officers followed in a solemn mute procession, with dejected countenances. On his entering the barge to cross the North river, he turned towards the companions of his glory, and by waving his hat, bid them a silent adieu. Some of them answered this last signal of respect and affection with tears; and all of them hung upon the barge which conveyed him from their sight, till they could no longer distinguish in it the person of their beloved commander in chief.

The army being disbanded, Washington proceeded to Annapolis, then the seat of Congress, to resign his commission. On his way thither, he, of his own accord, delivered to the comptroller of accounts in Philadelphia, an account of the expenditure of all the public money he had ever received. This was in his own hand writing, and every entry was made in a very particular manner. Vouchers were produced for every item except for secret intelligence and service, which amounted to no more than 1,982 pounds 10 sterling. The whole which in the course of eight years of war, had passed through his hands, amounted to only 14,479 pounds 18s 9d. Nothing was charged or retained for personal services; and actual disbursements had been managed with such economy and fidelity, that they were all covered by the above moderate sum.

After accounting for all his expenditures of public money (secret service money for obvious reasons excepted), with all the exactness which established forms required from the inferior officers of his army, he hastened to resign into the hands of the fathers of his country, the powers with which they had invested him. This was done in a public audience. Congress received him as the founder and guardian of the republic.

While he appeared before them, they silently retraced the scenes of danger and distress through which they had passed together. They recalled to mind the blessings of freedom and peace purchased by his arm. They gazed with wonder on their fellow-citizen who appeared more great and worthy of esteem in resigning his power, than he had done in gloriously using it. Every heart was big with emotion. Tears of admiration and gratitude burst from every eye. The general sympathy was felt by the resigning hero, and wet his cheek with a manly tear. After a decent pause, he addressed Thomas Mifflin, the President of Congress, in the following words:

"Mr. President,

"The great events on which my resignation depended, having at length taken place, I have now the honour of offering my sincere congratulations to Congress, and of presenting myself before them to surrender into their hands the trust committed to me, and to claim the indulgence of retiring from the service of my country.

"Happy in the confirmation of our independence and sovereignty, and pleased with the opportunity afforded the United States of becoming a respectable nation, I resign with satisfaction the appointment I accepted with diffidence; a diffidence in my abilities to accomplish so arduous a task, which, however, superseded by a confidence in the rectitude of our cause, the support of the supreme power of the union, and the patronage of Heaven.

"The successful termination of the war has verified the most sanguine expectations; and my gratitude for the interposition of Providence, and the assistance I have received from my country-men, increases with every review of the momentous contest.

"While I repeat my obligations to the army in general, I should do injustice to my own feelings, not to acknowledge in this place, the peculiar services and distinguished merits of the persons who have been attached to my person during the war. It was impossible the confidential choice officers to compose my family should have been more fortunate.

1782 and 1783: Prospects of peace

Permit me, Sir, to recommend in particular, those who have continued in the service to the present moment, as worthy of the favourable notice and patronage of Congress.

"I consider it as an indispensable duty to close this last solemn act of my official life, by commending the interest of our dearest country to the protection of Almighty God, and those who have the superintendence of them to his holy keeping.

"Having now finished the work assigned me, I retire from the great theatre of action; and, bidding an affectionate farewell to this august body, under whose orders I have long acted, I here offer my commission, and take any leave of all the employments of public life."

This address being ended, Gen. Washington advanced and delivered his commission into the hands of the President of Congress, who replied as follows:

"The United States in Congress assembled, receive with emotions too affecting for utterance, the solemn resignation of the authorities under which you have led their troops with success, through a perilous and doubtful war.

"Called upon by your country to defend its invaded rights, you accepted the sacred charge before it had formed alliances, and whilst it was without friends or a government to support you.

"You have conducted the great military contest with wisdom and fortitude, invariable regarding the rights of the civil power through all disasters and changes. You have by the love and confidence of your fellow-citizens, enabled them to display their martial genius, and transmit their fame to posterity: you have persevered till these United States, aided by a magnanimous king and nation, have been enabled under a just Providence, to close the war in safety, freedom, and independence; on which happy event we sincerely join you in congratulations.

"Having defended the standard of liberty in this new world; having taught a lesson useful to those who inflict, and to those who feel oppression, you retire from the great theatre of action with the blessings of your fellow-citizens; but the glory of your virtues will not terminate with your military command, it will continue to animate remotest ages. We feel with you our obligations to the army in general, and will particularly charge ourselves with the interest of those confidential officers who have attended your person to this affecting moment.

"We join you in commending the interests of our dearest country to the protection of Almighty God, beseeching him to dispose the hearts and minds of its citizens to improve the opportunity afforded them of becoming a happy and respectable nation; and for you, we address to

1782 and 1783: Prospects of peace

Him our earnest prayers, that a life so beloved, may be fostered with all his care; that your days may be happy as they have been illustrious, and that he will finally give you that reward which this world cannot give."

The military services of Gen. Washington, which ended with this interesting day, were as great as ever were rendered by any man to any nation. They were at the same time disinterested. How dear would not a mercenary man have sold such toils, such dangers, and above all, such successes? What schemes of grandeur and of power would not an ambitious man have built upon the affections of the people and of the army? The gratitude of America was so lively, that any thing asked by her resigning chief, would have been readily granted.

He asked nothing for himself, his family, or relations; but indirectly solicited favours for the confidential officers who were attached to his person. These were young gentlemen without fortune, who had served him in the capacity of Aid de Camp. To have omitted the opportunity which then offered, of recommending them to their country's notice, would have argued a degree of insensibility in the breast of their friend. The only privilege distinguishing him from other private citizens, which the retiring Washington did or would receive from his grateful country, was a right of sending and receiving letters free of postage.

The American chief, having by his own voluntary act, become one of the people, hastened with ineffable delight to his seat at Mount Vernon, on the banks of the Potowmac. There, in a short time, the most successful General in the world, became the most diligent farmer in Virginia.

To pass suddenly from the toils of the first commission in the United States to the care of a farm—to exchange the instruments of war, for the instruments of husbandry, and to become at once the patron and example of ingenious agriculture, would to most men have been a difficult task. But to the elevated mind of Washington, it was natural and delightful. From his example, let the commanders of armies learn, that the fame which is acquired by the sword, without guilt or ambition, may be preserved without power or splendour in private life.

10

General Washington, on retiring from public life devotes himself to agricultural pursuits. Favours inland navigation. Declines offered emoluments from it. Urges an alteration of the fundamental rules of the society of the Cincinnati. Regrets the defects of the Federal system, and recommends a revisal of it. Is appointed a member of the continental convention for that purpose, which, after hesitation, he accepts. Is chosen President thereof. Is solicited to accept the Presidency of the United States. Writes sundry letters expressive of the conflict in his mind, between duty and inclination. Answers applicants for offices. His reluctance to enter on public life.

THE sensations of Washington on retiring from public business are thus expressed:

"I feel as a wearied traveller must do, who, after treading many a painful step with a heavy burden on his shoulders, is eased of the latter, having reached the haven to which all the former were directed, and from his house top is looking back and tracing with an eager eye, the meanders by which he escaped the quicksands and mires which lay in his way, and into which none but the All Powerful Guide and Dispenser of human events, could have prevented his falling.

"I have become a private citizen on the banks of the Potowmac, and, under the shadow of my own vine and in own fig-tree, free from the bustle of a camp, and the busy scenes of public life, I am solacing myself with those tranquil enjoyments of which the soldier, who is ever in pursuit of fame—the statesman, whose watchful days and sleepless nights are spent in devising schemes to promote the welfare of his own, perhaps the ruin of other countries, as if this globe was insufficient for us all—and the courtier, who is always watching the countenance of his prince, in the hope of catching a gracious smile, can have very little conception. I have not only retired from all public employments, but am retiring within myself, and shall be able to view the solitary walk, and tread the paths of private life with heartfelt satisfaction. Envious of none, I am determined to be pleased with all; and this, my dear friend, being the order of my march, I will move gently down the stream of life, until I sleep with my fathers."

Agriculture, which had always been the favourite employment of Washington, was now resumed with increasing delight. The energies of his active mind were devoted to this first and most useful art. No improvements in the construction of farming utensils, no valuable experiments in husbandry, escaped his attention. He saw with regret, the miserable system of cultivation which prevailed too generally in his Native country, and wished to introduce a better. With this view, he engaged in a correspondence with some of the distinguished agriculturists in Great-Britain, particularly the celebrated Arthur Young.

He traced the different states of agriculture in the two countries, in a great degree to the following obvious principles. In Great-Britain, land was dear, and labour cheap. In America the reverse took place to such a degree, that manuring land was comparatively neglected, on the mistaken, shortsighted idea, that it was cheaper to clear and cultivate new fields, than to improve and repair such as were old. To this radical error, which led to idleness and a vagabond dispersed population, he opposed the whole weight of his influence. His example and recommendations tended to revolutionize the agriculture of his country, as his valour had revolutionized its government.

The extension of inland navigation occupied much of Washington's attention, at this period of exemption from public cares. Soon after peace was proclaimed, he made a tour as far west as Pittsburgh, and also traversed the western parts of New-England and New-York, and examined for himself the difficulties of bringing the trade of the west to different points on the Atlantic. Possessed of an accurate knowledge of the subject, he corresponded with the governors of different, states, and other influential characters.

To them he suggested the propriety of making "by public authority," an appointment of commissioners of integrity and ability, whose duty it should be, after accurate examination, to ascertain the nearest and best portages between such of the eastern and western rivers as headed near to each other, though they ran in opposite directions; and also to trace the rivers west of the Ohio, to their sources and mouths, as they respectively emptied either into the Ohio, or the lakes of Canada, and to make an accurate map of the whole, with observations on the impediments to be overcome, and the advantages to be acquired on the completion of the work.

The views of Washington in advocating the extension of inland navigation were grand, and magnificent. He considered it as an effectual mean of cementing the union of the states. In his letter to the Governor of Virginia he observed:

"I need not remark to you, sir, that the flanks and rear of the United States are possessed by other powers, and formidable ones too; nor need I press the necessity of applying the cement of interest to bind all parts of the union together by indissoluble bonds—especially of binding that part of it which lies immediately west of us, to the middle states. For what ties, let me ask, should we have upon those people; how entirely unconnected with them shall we be, and what troubles may we not apprehend, if the Spaniards on their right, and great Britain on their left, instead of throwing impediments in their way as they do now, should hold out lures for their trade and alliance?

When they get strength, which will be sooner than most people conceive, what will be the consequence of their having formed those commercial connexions with both or either of those powers? It needs not, in my opinion, the gift of prophecy to foretell." After stating the same thing to a member of Congress, he proceeds, "It may be asked, how we are to prevent this? Happily for us the way is plain. Other immediate interests, as well as remote political advantages, point to it; whilst a combination of circumstances render the present time more favourable than any other to accomplish it. Extend the inland navigation of the eastern waters; communicate them as near as possible with those which run westward; open these to the Ohio; open also such as extend from the Ohio towards lake Erie; and we shall not only draw the produce of the western settlers, but the peltry and fur trade of the lakes also, to our ports; thus adding an immense increase to our ex-ports, and binding those people to us by a chain which never can be broken."

The Virginia legislature acted on the recommendation of Gen. Washington, to the extent of his wishes; and in consequence thereof, works of the greatest utility have been nearly accomplished.

They went one step farther and vested in him at the expense of the state, one hundred and fifty shares in the navigation of the rivers Potowmac and James. The act for this purpose was introduced with the following preamble: "Whereas it is the desire of the representatives of this commonwealth, to embrace ever suitable occasion of testifying their sense of the unexampled merits of George Washington, Esq. towards his country; and it is their wish in particular that those great works for its improvement, which, both springing from the liberty which he has been so instrumental in establishing, and as encouraged by his patronage, will be durable monuments of' his glory, may be made monuments also of the gratitude of his country. Be it enacted," &c. To the friend who conveyed to Washington the first intelligence of this bill, he replied—

"It is not easy for me to decide, by which my mind was most affected upon the receipt of' your letter of the sixth instant, surprise or gratitude. Both were greater than I had words to express. The attention aid good wishes which the assembly have evidenced by their act for vesting in me one hundred and fifty shares in the navigation of the rivers Potowmac and James, is more than mere compliment. There is an unequivocal and substantial meaning annexed. But believe me, sir, no circumstance has happened since left the walks of public life, which has so much embarrassed me. On the one hand, I consider this act as noble and unequivocal proof of the good opinion, the affection, and disposition of my country to serve me; and I should be hurt, if by declining the acceptance of it, my refusal should be construed into disrespect or the smallest slight upon the generous intention of the legislature, or that an ostentatious display of disinterestedness or public virtue was the source of refusal.

"On the other hand, it is really my wish to have my mind and my actions, which are the result of reflection, as free and independent as the air, that I may be more at liberty to express my sentiments, and if necessary to suggest what may occur to me under the fullest conviction, that although my judgment may be arraigned, there will be no suspicion that sinister motives had the smallest influence in the suggestion. Not content then with the bare consciousness of my having, in all this navigation business, acted upon the clearest conviction of the political importance of the measure, I would wish that every individual who may hear that it was a favourite plan of mine, may know also that I had no other motive for promoting it than the advantage of which I conceived it would be productive to the union at large, and to this state in particular, by cementing the eastern and western territory together, at the same time, that it will give vigor to and, increase our commerce, and be a convenience to our citizens.

"How would this matter be viewed then by the eye of the world, and what opinion would be formed, when it comes to be related that G_____ W_____ exerted himself to effect, this work, and that G_____ W_____ has received twenty thousand Dollars, and five thousand pounds sterling of the public money as an interest therein? Would not this, (if I am entitled to any merit for the part I have performed, and without it there is no foundation for the act,) deprive me of the principal thing which is laudable in my conduct?

"Would it not in some respects be considered in the same light as a pension? And would not the apprehensions of this induce me to offer my sentiments in future with the more reluctance? In a word, under whatever pretence, and however customary these gratuities may be in other countries, should I not thenceforward be considered as a dependent? One moment's thought of which would give me more pain, than I should receive pleasure from the product of all the tolls, was every farthing of them vested in me."

To the Governor of the state, on receiving from him an official copy of the aforesaid act, Washington replied as follows:

"Your excellency having been pleased to transmit me a copy of the act appropriating to my benefit certain shares in the companies for opening the navigation of James and Potowmac rivers; I take the liberty of returning to the general assembly, through your hands, the profound and grateful acknowledgments inspired by so signal a mark of their beneficent intentions towards me. I beg you, sir, to assure them that I am filled on this occasion with every sentiment which can flow from a heart warm with love to my country, sensible to every token of its approbation and affection, and solicitous to testify in every instance a respectful submission to its wishes.

"With these sentiments in my bosom, I need not dwell on the anxiety I feel, in being obliged, in this instance, to decline a favour which is rendered no less flattering by the manner in which it is conveyed, than it is affectionate in itself. In explaining this, I pass over a comparison of my endeavours in the public service, with the many honourable testimonies of approbation which I have already so far over-rated and overpaid them; reciting one consideration only, which supersedes the necessity of recurring to every other.

"When I was first called to the station with which I was honoured during the late conflict for our liberties, to the diffidence which I had so many reasons to feel in accepting it, I thought it my duty to join a firm resolution to shut my hand against every pecuniary recompense. To this resolution I have invariably adhered, and from it, (of I had the inclination,) I do not consider myself at liberty now to depart.

"Whilst I repeat, therefore, my fervent acknowledgments to the legislature for their very kind sentiments and intentions in my favour, and at the same time beg them to be persuaded, that a remembrance of this singular proof of their goodness towards me will never cease to cherish returns of the warmest affection and, gratitude; I must pray that their act, so far as it has for its Object my personal emolument, may not have its effect; but if it should please the general assembly to permit me to turn the destination of the fund vested in me, from my private emolument to objects of a public nature, it will be my study in selecting these, to prove the sincerity of my gratitude for the honour conferred upon me, by preferring such as may appear most subservient to the enlightened and patriotic views of the legislature."

The wishes suggested in this letter were sanctioned by the legislature; and, at a subsequent time, the trust was executed by conveying the shares to the use of a seminary of learning in the vicinity of each river.

Near the close of the revolutionary war, the officers of the American army, with a view of perpetuating their friendships, formed themselves into a society, to be named after the famous Roman patriot, Cincinnatus. At the head of the society, Gen. Washington was placed. By the rules of their institution, the honours of the society were to be hereditary in their respective families, and distinguished individuals' might be admitted as honorary members for life. These circumstances, together with the union of the officers of the army, gave an alarm to the community; several individuals of which supposed that the hereditary part of the institution would be a germ of nobility. It was the usual policy of Washington to respect the opinions of the people, in matters indifferent, or of small magnitude, though he might think them mistaken. Having ascertained to his own satisfaction, that a degree of jealousy pervaded the mass of the people, respecting the probable tendency of this perpetual hereditary society, he successfully exerted his influence to new model its rules, by relinquishing the hereditary principle and the power of adopting honorary members. The result proved the wisdom of the measure; for all jealousies of the society henceforward were done away, and the members thereof were received as brethren, by the most suspicious of their fellow-citizens.

When Washington, at the close of the revolutionary war, became a private citizen, his country confidently anticipated every possible blessing from peace, independence, and self-government. But experience soon proved the inefficacy of existing systems for promoting national happiness, or preserving national dignity. Congress had neither the power nor the means of doing justice to public creditors, nor of enforcing the respect of foreign nations.—Gold and silver vanished—commerce languished—property was depreciated—and credit expired. The lovers of liberty and independence began to be less sanguine in their hopes from the American revolution, and to fear that they had built a visionary fabric of government on the fallacious ideas of public virtue.

For the first five or six years immediately following peace, the splendour which surrounded the infant states from their successful struggle in the cause of independence and self-government, was daily darkening. This state of things could not be indifferent to Washington. He was among the first to discover the cause, and to point out the remedy. The inefficient support he received while commander in chief, proved the inefficacy of the articles of confederation, for raising and supporting a requisite military force. The experience of the first years of peace, proved their total inadequacy for the purpose of national government From want of vigour in the federal head, the United States were fast dwindling into separate sovereignties, unconnected by any bond of union, equal to public exigency. The private letters of Washington at this time, show his anxiety for his country's welfare, and his wisdom in pointing out a remedy for its degradation.

In one of them he observes:

"The confederation appears to me to be little more than a shadow without the substance, and Congress a nugatory body, their ordinances being little attended to. To me it is a solecism in politics; indeed it is one of the most extraordinary things in nature, that we should confederate as a nation, and yet be afraid to give the rulers of that nation, who are the creatures of our own making, appointed for a limited and short duration, and who are amenable for every action, recallable at any moment, and subject to all the evils which they may be instrumental in producing sufficient powers to order and direct the affairs of the same. By such policy the wheels of government are clogged, and our brightest prospects, and that high expectation, which was entertained of us by the wondering world, are turned into astonishment; and from the high ground on which we stood, we are descending into the vale of confusion and darkness.

"That we have it in our power to become one of the most respectable nations upon earth, admits, in my humble opinion, of no doubt, if we would but pursue a wise, just, and liberal policy towards one another, and would keep good faith with the rest of the world. That our resources are ample, and increasing, none can deny; but while they are grudgingly applied, or not applied at all, we give a vital stab to public faith, and will sink in the eyes of Europe into contempt."

In another:

"It is one of the evils of democratic governments, that the people, not always seeing, and frequently misled, must often feel before they are set right, But evils of this nature seldom fall to work their own cure. It is to be lamented, nevertheless, that the remedies are so slow, and that those who wish to apply them seasonably, are not attended to before they suffer in person, in interest, and in reputation. I am not without hopes that matters will soon take a favourable turn in the federal constitution. The discerning part of the community have long since seen the necessity of giving adequate powers to Congress for national purposes, and those of a different description must yield to it ere long."

In a letter to Mr. Jay, Gen. Washington observed:

"Your sentiments that our affairs are drawing rapidly to a crisis, accord with my own. What the event will be, is also beyond the reach of my foresight. We have errors to correct; we have probably had too good an opinion of human nature in forming our confederation. Experience has taught us that men will not adopt and carry into execution, measures the best calculated for their own good, without the intervention of coercive power. I do not conceive we can subsist long as a nation, without lodging somewhere a power which will pervade the whole union in as energetic a manner, as the authority of the state governments extends over the several states. To be fearful of investing Congress, constituted as that body is, with ample authorities for national purposes, appears to me the very climax of popular absurdity and madness. Could Congress exert them for the detriment of the people, without injuring themselves in an equal or greater proportion? Are not their interests inseparably connected with those of their constituents? By the rotation of appointment, must they not mingle frequently with the mass of citizens? Is it not rather to be apprehended, if they were possessed of the powers before described, that the individual members would be induced to use them on many occasions, very timidly and inefficaciously, for fear of losing their popularity and future election?

"We must take human nature as we find it—perfection falls not to the share of mortals. Many are of opinion, that Congress have too frequently made use of the suppliant humble tone of requisition, in applications to the states, when they had a right to assert their imperial dignity, and command obedience. Be that as it may, requisitions are a perfect nullity, where thirteen sovereign, independent, disunited states, are in the habit of discussing, and refusing or complying with them at their option. Requisitions are actually little better than a jest and a bye-word throughout the land. If you tell the legislatures they have violated the treaty of peace, and invaded the prerogatives of the confederacy, they will laugh in your face. What then is to be done? Things cannot go on in the same train for ever. It is much to be feared, as you observe, that the better kind of people, being disgusted with these circumstances, will have their minds prepared for any revolution whatever. We are apt to run from one extreme into another. To anticipate and prevent disastrous contingencies, would be the part of wisdom and patriotism.

"What astounding changes are a few years capable of producing! I am told that even respectable characters speak of a monarchical form of government, without horror. From thinking, proceeds speaking; thence to acting is often but a single step. But how irrevocable and tremendous! What a triumph for our enemies to verify their predictions! What a triumph for the advocates of despotism to find that we are incapable of governing ourselves, and that systems founded on the basis of equal liberty, are merely ideal and fallacious! Would to God that wise measures may be taken in time, to avert the consequences we have but too much reason to apprehend.

"Retired as I am from the world, I frankly acknowledge, I cannot feel myself an unconcerned spectator. Yet having happily assisted in bringing the ship into port, and having been fairly discharged, it is not my business to embark again on a sea of troubles.

"Nor could it be expected that my sentiments and opinions would have much weight on the minds of my countrymen. They have been neglected, though given as a last legacy, in the most solemn manner. I had then, perhaps, some claims to public attentions. I consider myself as having none at present."

Illumination, on the subject of enlarging the powers of Congress, was gradual. Washington, in his extensive correspondence and intercourse with the leading characters of the different states, urged the necessity of a radical reform in the existing system of government. The business was at length seriously taken up, and a proposition was made by Virginia, for electing deputies to a federal convention, for the sole purpose of revising the Federal system of government.

While this proposition was under consideration, an event took place, which pointed out the propriety of its adoption. The pressure of evils in a great degree resulting from the imbecility of government, aided by erroneous opinions, which confound liberty with licentiousness, produced commotions in Massachusetts, which amounted to treason and rebellion. On this occasion, Washington expressed himself in a letter as follows:—

"The commotions and temper of numerous bodies in the eastern country, present a state of things equally to be lamented and deprecated. They exhibit a melancholy verification of what our Transatlantic foes have predicted, and of another thing perhaps, which is still more to be regretted, and is yet more unaccountable, that mankind when left to themselves, are unfit for their own government. I am mortified beyond expression, when I view the clouds which have spread over the brightest morn that ever dawned upon my country. In a word, I am lost in amazement, when I behold what intrigue the interested. Views of desperate characters, ignorance and jealousy of the minor part, are capable of affecting, as a scourge on the major part of our fellow-citizens of the union; for it is hardly to be supposed, that the great body of the people, though they will not act, can be so short-sighted, or enveloped in darkness, as not to see rays of a distant sun through all this mist of intoxication and folly.

"You talk, my good sir, of employing influence to appease the present tumults in Massachusetts. I know not where that influence is to be found, nor, if attainable, that it would be a proper remedy for these disorders. Influence is not government. Let us have a government by which our lives, liberties, and properties, will be secured, or let us know the worst at once. Under these impressions, my humble opinion is, that there is a call for decision. Know precisely what the insurgents aim at. If they have real grievances, redress them if possible, or acknowledge the justice of them, and your inability to do it in the present moment. If they have not, employ the force of government against them at once. If this is inadequate, all will be convinced that the superstructure is bad, or wants support.

"To be more exposed in the eyes of tile world, and more contemptible, is hardly possible. To delay one or the other of these expedients, is to exasperate on the one hand, or to give confidence on the other, and will add to their numbers; for like snow-balls such bodies increase by every movement, unless there is something in the way to obstruct and crumble them before their weight is too great and irresistible.

"These are my sentiments. Precedents are dangerous things. Let the reins of government, then, be braced and held with a steady hand, and every violation of the constitution be reprehended. If defective, let it be amended, but not suffered to be trampled upon while it has an existence."

Virginia placed the name of Washington at the head of her delegates for the proposed convention. Letters poured in upon him from all sides, urging his acceptance of the appointment. In answer to one from Mr. Madison, who had been the principal advocate of the measure in the Virginia legislature, Gen. Washington replied—

"Although I have bid a public adieu to the public walks of life, and had resolved never more to tread that theatre, yet, if upon any occasion so interesting to the well-being of our confederacy, it had been the wish of the Assembly that I should be an associate in the business of revising the Federal systems I should, from a sense of the obligation I am under for repeated proofs of confidence in me, more than from any opinion I could entertain of my usefulness, have obeyed its call; but it is now out of my power to do this with any degree of consistency The cause I will mention.

"I presume, sir, that you heard first that I was appointed, and have since been re-chosen, President of the Society of the Cincinnati; and you may have understood also, that the triennial general meeting of this body is to be held in Philadelphia the first Monday in May next. Some particular reasons, combining with the peculiar situation of my private concerns, the necessity of paying attention to them, a wish for retirement, and relaxation from public cares, and rheumatic pains, which begin to feel very sensibly, induced me, on the 31st ultimo, to address a circular letter to each state society, informing them of my intention not to be at the next meeting, and of my desire not to be re-chosen President. The Vice-president is also informed of this, that the business of the society may not be impeded by my absence. Under these circumstances it will readily be perceived, that I could not appear at the same time and place, on any other occasion, without giving offence to a very respectable and deserving part of the community—the late officers of the American army."

The meeting of the convention was postponed to a day subsequent to that of the meeting of the Cincinnati. This removed one of the difficulties in the way of Washington's acceptance of a seat in the convention, and, joined with the importance of the call, and his own eager desire to advance the public interest, finally induced his compliance with the wishes of his friends.

The convention met in Philadelphia, in May, and unanimously chose George Washington their President. On the 17th of September, 1787, they closed their labours, and submitted the result to Congress, with their opinion "that it should be submitted to a convention of delegates chosen in each state by the people thereof, under the recommendation of its legislature for their assent, and ratification." By this new form of Government, ample powers were given to Congress without the intervention of the states, for every purpose that national dignity, interest, or happiness, required. The ablest pens and most eloquent tongues were employed for, and against, its acceptance. In this animated contest, Washington took no part. Having with his sword vindicated the right of his country to self-government, and having with his advice aided in digesting an efficient form of government, which he most thoroughly approved, it would seem as though he wished the people to decide for themselves, whether to accept or reject it.

The constitution being accepted by eleven states, and preparatory measures being taken for bringing it into operation, all eyes were turned

Retirement from public life

to Washington, as being the fittest man for the office of President of the United States. His correspondents began to press his acceptance of the high office, as essential to the well-being of his country.

To those who think that Washington was like other men, it will scarcely appear possible, that supreme magistracy possessed no charms sufficient to tempt him from his beloved retirement, when he was healthy and strong, and only fifty seven years old; but if an opinion can be formed of his real sentiments, from the tenour of his life and confidential communications to his most intimate friends, a conviction will be produced, that his acceptance of the Presidency of the United States was the result of a victory obtained by a sense of duty over his inclinations, and was a real sacrifice of the latter, to the former.

In a letter to Col. Henry Lee, Washington observes:

"Notwithstanding my advanced season of life, my increasing fondness for agricultural amusements, and my growing love of retirement, augment and confirm my decided predilection for the character of a private citizen; yet it will be no one of these motives, nor the hazard to which my former reputation might be exposed, nor the terror of encountering new fatigues and troubles, that would deter me from an acceptance, but a belief that some other person who had less pretence and less inclination to be excused, could execute all the duties full as satisfactorily as myself. To say more would be indiscreet, as a disclosure of a refusal before-hand might incur the application of the fable, in which the fox is represented as undervaluing the grapes he could not reach. You will perceive, my dear sir, by what is here observed, (an which you will be pleased to consider in the light of a confidential communication,) that my inclinations will dispose and decide me to remain as I am, unless a clear and insurmountable conviction should be impressed on my mind, that some very disagreeable consequences must in all human probability result from the indulgence of my wishes."

In a letter to Col. Hamilton, Washington observes:

"If I am not grossly deceived in myself, I should unfeignedly rejoice, in case the electors, by giving their votes to some other person, would save me from the dreadful dilemma of being forced to accept or refuse. If that may not be, I am in the next place, earnestly desirous of searching out the truth, and of knowing whether there does not exist a probability that the government would just as happily and effectually be carried into execution, without my aid, as with it. I am truely solicitous to obtain all the previous information which the circumstances will afford, and to determine, (when the determination can no longer be postponed,) according to the principles of right reason, and the dictates of a clear conscience, without too great a reference to the unforeseen consequences which may affect my person or reputation. Until that period, I may fairly hold myself open to conviction, though I allow your sentiments to have weight in them; and I shall not pass by your arguments, without giving them as dispassionate a consideration as I can possibly bestow upon them.

"In taking a survey of the subject, in whatever point of light I have been able to place it, I will not suppress the acknowledgment, my dear sir, that 1 have always felt a kind of gloom upon my mind, as often as I have been taught to expect I might, and, perhaps, must be called upon ere long to make the decision. You will, I am well assured, believe the assertion, (though I have little expectation it would gain credit from those who are less acquainted with me,) that if I should receive the appointment, and should be prevailed upon to accept it, the acceptance would be attended with more difficulty and reluctance, than I ever experienced before. It would be, however, with a fixed and sole determination of lending whatever assistance might be in my power to promote the public weal, in hopes that at a convenient and early period, my services might be dispensed with; and that I might be permitted once more to retire, to pass an unclouded evening, after the stormy day of life, in the bosom of domestic tranquility."

In a letter to Gen. Lincoln, Washington observes:

"I may, however, with great sincerity, and I believe without offending against modesty and propriety, say to you, that I most heartily wish the choice to which you allude, might not fall upon me; and that if it should, I must reserve to myself the right of making up my final decision, at the last moment when it can be brought into one view, and when the expediency or inexpediency of a refusal can be more judiciously determined than at present. But be assured, my dear sir, if, from any inducement, I shall be persuaded ultimately to accept, it will not be, (so far as I know my own heart,) from any of a private or personal nature. Every personal consideration conspires to rivet me, (if I may use the expression,) to retirement. At my time of life, and under my circumstances, nothing in this world can ever draw me from it, unless it be a conviction that the partiality of my country men had made my services absolutely necessary, joined to a fear that my refusal might induce a belief that I preferred the conservation of my own reputation and private ease, to the good of my country. After all, if I should conceive myself in a manner constrained to accept, I call heaven to witness, that this very act would be the greatest sacrifice of my personal feelings and wishes, that ever I have been called upon to make. It would be to forego repose and domestic enjoyment, for trouble, perhaps for public obloquy; for I should consider myself as entering upon an unexplored field, enveloped on every side with clouds and darkness.

"From this embarrassing situation, I had naturally supposed, that my declarations at the close of the war would have saved me, and that my sincere intentions then publicly made known, would have effectually precluded me for ever afterwards. from being looked upon as a candidate for any office. This hope, as a last anchor of worldly happiness in old age, I had carefully preserved, until the public papers and private letters from my correspondents in almost every quarter, taught me to apprehend that I might soon be obliged to answer the question, whether I would go again into public life or not."

In a letter to the Marquis de la Fayette, Washington Observes:

"Your sentiments indeed coincide much more nearly with those of my other friends, that with my own feelings. In truth, my difficulties increase and magnify as I draw towards the period, when, according to the common belief, it will be necessary for me to give a definitive answer in one way or other. Should circumstances render it in a manner inevitably necessary to be in the affirmative, be assured, my dear sir, I shall assume the task with the most unfeigned reluctance, and with a real diffidence, for which I shall probably receive no credit from the world. If I know my own heart, nothing short of a conviction of duty, will induce me again to take an active part in public affairs. And in that case, if I can form a plan for my own conduct, my endeavours shall be unremittingly exerted, (even at the hazard of former fame or present popularity,) to extricate my country from the embarrassments in which it is entangled through want of credit, and to establish a general system of policy, which, if pursued, will ensure permanent felicity to the commonwealth. I think I see a path as clear and as direct as a ray of light, which leads to the attainment of that object. Nothing but harmony, honesty, industry, and frugality, are necessary to make us a great and a happy people. Happily the present posture of affairs and the prevailing disposition of my countrymen, promise to co-operate in establishing those four great and essential pillars of public felicity."

Before the election of a President came on, so universal was the expectation that Washington would be elected, that numerous applications were made to him, in anticipation for offices in the government, which would be in his gift. To one of such applicants he wrote as follows:—

"Should it become absolutely necessary for me to occupy the station in which your letter presupposes me, I have determined to go into it perfectly free from all engagements of every nature whatsoever. A conduct in conformity to this resolution, would enable me in balancing the various pretensions of different candidates for appointments, to act with a sole reference to justice, and the public good. This is in substance, the answer that I have given to all applications, (and they are not few,) which have already been made."

11

President Washington: Washington elected President. On his way to the seat of government at New-York, receives the most flattering marks of respect. Addresses Congress. The situation of the United States in their foreign and domestic relations, at the inauguration of Washington. Fills up offices solely with a view to the public good. Proposes a treaty to the Creek Indians, which is at first rejected. Col. Willet induces the heads of the nation 'to come New-York, to treat there. The North-Western Indians refuse a treaty, but after defeating Generals Harmar and Sinclair, they are defeated by Gen. Wayne. They then submit, and agree to treat. A new system is introduced for meliorating their condition.

It was intended that the new government should commence its operations on the 4th of March, 1789; but from accidental causes, the elections of Gen. Washington to the Presidency was officially announced to him at Mount Vernon, till the 14th of next April. This was done by Charles Thomson, Secretary of the late Congress who presented to him the certificate signed the President of the Senate of the United States, stating that George Washington was unanimously elected President. This unexpected delay was regretted by the public, but not by the newly elected President. In a letter to Gen. Knox, he observed—

"As to myself, the delay may be compared to a reprieve; for in confidence I tell you, (with the world it would obtain credit,) that my movements to the chair of government will be accompanied by feelings not unlike those of a culprit who is going to the place of his execution. So unwilling am I in the evening of life, nearly consumed in public cares, to quit a peaceful abode for an ocean of difficulties, without that competency of political skill, abilities and inclination, which are necessary to manage the helm. I am sensible that I am embarking the voice of the people, and a good name of my own, on this voyage, but what returns will be made for them, Heaven alone can foretell. Integrity and firmness are all I can promise. These, be the voyage long or short, shall never forsake me, I may be deserted by all men; for of the consolations which are to be derived from these, under any circumstances, the world cannot deprive me."

On the second day after, receiving notice of his appointment, Washington set out for New-York. On his way thither, the road was crowded with numbers anxious to see the man of the people. Escorts of militia and of gentlemen of the first character and station, attended him from state to state, and he was every where received with the highest honours which a grateful and admiring people could confer. Addresses of congratulation were presented to him by the inhabitants of almost every place of consequence through which he passed, to all of which he returned such modest, unassuming answers, as were in every respect suitable to his situation. So great were the honours with which he was loaded, that they could scarcely have failed to produce haughtiness in the mind of any ordinary man; but nothing of the kind was ever discovered in this extraordinary age. On all occasions he behaved to all men with the affability of one citizen to another. He was truly great in deserving the plaudits of his country, but much greater in not being elated by them. Of the numerous addresses which were present-ed on this occasion, one subscribed by <u>Dennis Ramsay, the mayor of Alexandria</u>, in the name of the people of that city, who were the neighbours of Mr. Washington, was particularly and universally ally admired. It was in the following words:

"To George Washington Esq. President of the United States,

"Again your country commands your care. Obedient to its wishes, unmindful of your ease, we see you again relinquishing the bliss of retirement, and this too, at a period of life when nature itself seems to authorize a preference of repose. Not to extol your glory as a soldier; not to pour forth our gratitude for past services; and not to acknowledge the justice of the unexampled honour which has been conferred upon you by the spontaneous and unanimous suffrage of three millions of freemen, in your election to the supreme magistracy, nor to admire the patriotism which directs your conduct, do your neighbours and friends now address you. Themes less splendid, but more endearing, impress our minds. The first and best of citizens must leave us; our aged 1789 must lose their ornament; our youth their model; our agriculture its improver; our commerce its friend; our infant academy its protector; our poor their benefactor; and the interior navigation of the Potowmac, (an event, replete with the most extensive utility, already by your unremitted ex-ertions brought into partial use,) its institutor and promoter.

"Farewell. Go, and make a grateful people happy, a people who will be doubly grateful when they contemplate this recent sacrifice for their interest.

"To that Being who maketh and unmaketh at his will, we commend you; and after the accomplishment of the arduous business to which you are called, may he restore to us the best of men, and the most beloved fellow-citizen."

To this Mr. Washington returned the following answer:

Gentlemen,

"Although I ought not to conceal, yet I cannot describe the painful emotions which I felt, in being called upon to determine whether I would accept or refuse the Presidency of the United States. The unanimity in the choice; the opinion of my friends communicated from different parts of Europe as well as from America; the apparent wish of those who were not entirely satisfied with the constitution in its present form, and an ardent desire on my own part to be instrumental in connecting the good will of my countrymen towards each other, have induced an acceptance. Those who know me best, (and you, my fellow-citizens, are, from your situation, in that number,) 1789 know better than any others, my love of retirement is so great that no earthly consideration, short of a conviction of duty, could have prevailed upon me to depart from my resolution "never more to take any share in transactions of a public nature;" for at my age, and in my circumstances, what prospects or advantages could I propose to myself from embarking again on the tempestuous and uncertain ocean of public life?

"I do not feel myself under the necessity of making public declarations in order to convince you, gentlemen, of my attachment to yourselves, and regard for your interests. The whole tenour of my life has been open to your inspection, and my past actions, rather than my present declara-tions, must be the pledge of my future conduct.

"In the mean time, I thank you most sincerely for the expressions of kindness contained in your valedictory address. 1$ is true, just after having bade adieu to my domestic connexions, this ten-der proof of your friendship is but too well calcu-lated still further to awaken my sensibility, and increase my regret at parting from the enjoy-ment of private life.

"All that now remains for me, is to commit myself and you to the protection of that beneficent Being, who on a former occasion hath happily brought us together, after a long and distressing separation. Perhaps the same gracious Providence will again indulge me. Unutterable sensations must then be left to more expressive silence, while from an aching heart I bid all my affectionate friends and kind neighbours farewell."

Gray's bridge over the Schuylkill, which Mr. Washington had to pass, was highly decorated with laurels and evergreens. At each end of it were erected magnificent arches, composed of lau-rels, emblematical of the ancient Roman triumphal arches, and on each side of the bridge was a laurel shrubbery. As Mr. Washington passed the bridge, a youth ornamented with sprigs of laurel, assisted by machinery, let drop above his head, though unperceived by him, a civic crown of laurel. Upwards of 20,000 citizens lined the fences, fields, and avenues, between the Schuylkill and Philadel-phia. Through these he was conducted to the city by a numerous and respectable body of the citizens, where he partook of an elegant en-tertainment provided for him. The pleasures of the day were succeeded by a handsome display of fireworks in the evening.

When Mr. Washington crossed the Delaware, and landed on the Jersey shore, he was saluted with three cheers by the inhabitants of the vicinity. When he came to the brow of the hill on his way to Trenton, a triumphal arch was erected on the bridge by the direction of the ladies of the place. The crown of the arch was highly orna-mented with laurels and flowers, and on it was displayed in large figures, "December 26th, 1776." On the sweep of the arch beneath, was this inscription—" The Defender of the Mothers will also protect their Daughters."

On the north side were ranged a number of female children dressed in white, with garlands of flowers on their heads, and baskets of flowers on their arms; in the second row stood the young women, and behind them the married ladies of the vicinity. The instant he passed the arch, the children began to sing following ode:

"Welcome mighty chief! once more
"Welcome to this grateful shore.
"Now no mercenary foe Aims again the fatal blow,
"Aims at thee the fatal blow,
"Virgins fair, and matrons grave,
"These thy conquering arm did save!
"Build for thee triumphal bowers:
"Strew, ye fair, his way with flowers;
"Strew your hero's way with flowers."

As they sung the last lines, they strewed their flowers on the road before their beloved deliverer. His situation on this occasion, contrasted with what he had in December, 1776, felt on the same spot, when the affairs of America were at the lowest ebb of depression, filled him with sensations that cannot be described. He was rowed across the hay from Elizabethtown to New-York, in an elegant barge, by thirteen pilots. All the vessels in the harbour hoisted their flags. Stairs were erected and decorated for his reception, On his landing, universal joy diffused itself through every order of the people, and he was received and congratulated by the Governor of the state, and offi-cers of the corporation. He was conducted from the landing place to the house which had been fitted up for his reception, and was followed by an elegant procession of militia in their uniforms and by a great number of citizens. In the evening the houses of the inhabitants were brilliantly illuminated.

A day was fixed soon after his arrival, for his taking the oath of office, which was in the follow-ing words. "I do solemnly swear, that I will faithfully execute the office of President of the United States; and will to the best of my ability preserve, protect, and defend the constitution of the United States."

On this occasion he was wholly clothed in American manufactures. In the morning of the day appointed for this purpose, the clergy of different denominations assembled their congregations in their respective places of worship, and offered up public prayers for the President and people of the United States. About noon a procession, followed by a multitude of citizens, moved from the President's house to Federal Hall. When they came within a short distance from the Hall, the troops formed a line on both sides of the way, through which Mr. Washington, accompanied by the Vice-President, Mr. John Adams, passed into the Senate chamber. Immediately after, accompanied by both houses, he went into the gallery fronting Broad-street, and before them and an immense concourse of citizens, took the oath prescribed by the constitution, which was administered by R. R. Livingston, the Chancellor of the state of New-York. An awful silence prevailed among the spectators during this part of the ceremony. It was a minute of the most sublime political joy. The Chancellor then proclaimed him President of the United States. This was answered by the discharge of 13 guns: and by the effusions of shouts from near 10,000 grateful and affectionate hearts. The President bowed most respectfully to the people, and the air resounded again with their acclamations. He then retired to the Senate Chamber, where he made the following speech to both houses.

"Fellow citizens of the Senate and of the House of Representatives,

"Among the vicissitudes incident to life, no event could have filled me with greater anxieties than that of which the notification was transmitted by your order, and received on the 14th day of the present month.

On the one hand, I was summoned by my country, whose voice I can never hear but with veneration and love, from a retreat which I had chosen with the fondest predilection, and, in my flattering hopes, with an immutable decision, as the asylum of my declining years: a retreat which was rendered every day more necessary as well as more dear to me, by the addition of habit to inclination, and of frequent interruptions in my health to the gradual waste committed on it by time. On the other hand, the magnitude and difficulty of the trust to which the voice of my country called me, being sufficient to awaken in the wisest and most experienced of her citizens a distrustful scrutiny into his qualifications, could not but overwhelm with despondence one who, inheriting inferior endowments from nature, and unpractised in the duties of civil administration, ought to be pecu-liarly conscious of his own deficiencies.

"In this conflict of emotions, all I dare aver is, that it has been my faithful study to collect my duty from a just appreciation of every circumstance by which it might be effected. All I dare hope is, that, if in accepting this task, I have been too much swayed by a grateful remembrance of former circumstances, or by an affectionate sensibility to this transcendent proof of the confidence of my fellow citizens; and have thence too little consulted my incapacity, as well as disinclination for the weighty and untried cares before me; my ERROR will be palliated by the motives which misled me, and its consequences be judged by my country with some share of the partiality in which they originated.

"Such being the impressions under which I have, in obedience to the public summons, repaired to the present station; it will be peculiarly improper to emit, in this first official act, my fervent supplications to that Almighty Being who rules over the universe; who presides in the councils of nations; and whose providential aids can supply every human defect, that his benediction may consecrate to the liberties and happiness of the people of the United States, a government instituted by themselves for these essential purposes; and may enable every instrument employed in its administration, to execute with success, the functions allotted to his charge.

"In tendering this homage to the great Author of every public and private good, I assure myself that it expresses your sentiments not less than my own; nor those of my fellow-citizens at large, less than either. No people can be bound to acknowledge and adore the invisible hand which conducts the affairs of men, more than the people of the United States. Every step by which they have advanced to the character of an independent nation seems to have been distinguished by some token of providential agency; and in the important revolution just accomplished in the system of their united government, the tranquil deliberations and voluntary consent of so many distinct communities, from which the event has resided, cannot be compared with the means by which most governments have been established, without some return of pious gratitude along with an humble anticipation of the future blessings which the past seem to presage.

"These reflections, arising out of the present crisis, have forced themselves too strongly on my mind to be suppressed. You will join with me, I trust, in thinking that There are none, under the influence of which the proceedings of a new and free government can more auspiciously com-mence.

"By the article establishing the executive department, it is made the duty of the president 'to recommend to your consideration, such measures as he shall judge necessary and expedient.' The circumstances under which I now meet you will acquit me from entering into that subject, further than to refer to the great constitutional charter under which you are assembled, and which, in defining your powers, designates the objects to which your attention is to be given. It will be more consistent with those circumstances, and far more congenial with the feelings which actuate me, to substitute in place of a recommendation of particular measures, the tribute that is due to the talents, the rectitude, and the patriotism, which adorn the characters selected to devise and adopt them.

"In these honourable qualifications, I behold the surest pledges that, as on one side, no local prejudices or attachments, no separate views nor party animosities, will misdirect the comprehensive and equal eye which ought to watch over this great assemblage of communities and interests: so, on another, that the foundations of our national policy will be laid in the pure and immutahle principles, of private morality; and the preeminence of free government be exemplified by all the attributes which can win the affections of its citizens, and command the respect of time world.

"I dwell on this prospect with every satisfaction which an ardent love for my country can inspire; since there is no truth more thoroughly established than that there exists, in the economy and course of nature, an indissoluble union between virtue and happiness; between duty and advantage; between the genuine maxims of an honest and magnanimous policy, and the solid rewards of public prosperity and felicity: since we ought to be no less persuaded that the propitious smiles of heaven can never be expected on a nation that disregards the eternal rules of order and right, which heaven itself has ordained: and since the preservation of the sacred fire of liberty, and the destiny of the republican model of government, are justly considered as DEEPLY, perhaps as FINALLY, staked on the experiment intrusted to the hands of the American people.

"Besides the ordinary objects submitted to your care, it will remain with your judgment to decide, how far an exercise of the occasional power delegated by the fifth article of the constitution is rendered expedient, at the present juncture, by the nature of objections which have, been urged against the system, or by the degree of inquietude which has given birth to them. Instead of undertaking particular recommendations on this subject, in which I could be guided by no lights derived from official opportunities, I shall again give way to my entire confidence in your. discernment and pursuit of the public good: for I assure myself that whilst you carefully avoid every alteration which might endanger the benefits of a united and effective government, or which ought to await the future lessons of experience; a reverence for the characteristic rights of freemen, and a regard for the public harmony, will sufficiently influence your deliberations on the question how far the former can be more impregnably fortified, or the latter be safely and advantageously promoted.

"To the preceding observations I have one to add, which will be most properly addressed to the house of representatives. It concerns myself and will therefore be as brief as possible. When I was first honoured with a call into the service of my country, then on the eve of an arduous struggle for its liberties, the light, in which I contemplated my duty required that I should renounce every pecuniary compensation. From this resolution I have in no instance departed. And being still under the impressions which produced it, I must decline, as inapplicable to myself, any share in the personal emoluments which may be indispensable included in a permanent provision for the executive department; and must accordingly pray that the pecuniary estimates for the station in which I am placed, may, during my continuance in it, be limited to each actual expenditures as the public good may be thought to require.

"Having thus imparted to you my sentiments, as they have been awakened by the occasion which brings us together, I shall take my present leave; but not without resorting once more to the benign Parent of the human race, in humble supplication, that since he has been pleased to favour the American people with opportunities for deliberating in perfect tranquillity, and dispositions for deciding with unparralleled unanimity on a form of government for the security of their union, and the advancement of their happiness; so his diving blessing may be equally

President Washington

conspicuous in the enlarged views, the temperate consultations, and the wise measures on which the success of this government must depend."

"In their answer to this speech, the senate say:

"The unanimous suffrage of the elective body in your favour, is peculiarly expressive of the gratitude, confidence, and affection of the citizens of America, and is the highest testimonial at once of your merit, and their esteem. We are sensible, sir, that nothing but the voice of your fellow-citizens could have called you from a retreat, chosen with the fondest predilection, endeared by habit, and consecrated to the repose of declining years. We rejoice, and with us all America, that, in obedience to the call of our common country, you have returned once more to public life. In you all parties confide; in you all interests unite; and we have no doubt that your past services, great as they have been, will be equalled by your future exertions; and that your prudence and sagacity as a statesman, will tend to avert the dangers to which we were exposed, to give stability to the present government, and dignity and splendour to that country, which your skill and valour as a soldier, so eminently contributed to raise to independence and to empire."

The affection for the person and character of the President with which the answer of the house of representatives glowed, promised that between this branch of the legislature also and the executive, the most harmonious co-operation in the public service might be expected.

"The representatives of the people of the United States," says this address, "present their congratulations on the event by which your fellow-citizens have attested the pre-eminence of your merit. You have long held the first place in their esteem. You have often received tokens of their affection. You now possess the only proof that remained of their gratitude for your services, of their reverence for your wisdom, and of their confidence in your virtues. You enjoy the highest, because the truest honour, of being the first magistrate, by the unanimous choice of the freest people on the face of the earth.

"We well know the anxieties with which you must have obeyed the summons from the repose reserved for your declining years, into public scenes of which you had taken your leave for ever. But obedience was due to the occasion. It is already applauded by the universal joy which welcomes you to your station. And we cannot doubt that it will be rewarded with all the satisfaction with which an ardent love for your fellow-citizens must review successful efforts to promote their happiness.

"This anticipation is not justified merely by the past experience of your signal services. It is particularly suggested by the pious impressions under which you commence your administration; and the enlightened maxims by which you mean to conduct it. We feel with you the strongest obligations to adore the invisible hand which has led the American people through so many difficulties; to cherish a conscious responsibility for the destiny of republican liberty; and to seek the only sure means of preserving and recommending the precious deposit in a system of legislation founded on the principles of an honest policy, and directed by the spirit of a diffusive patriotism.

"In forming the pecuniary provisions for the executive department, we shall not lose sight of a wish resulting from motives which give it a peculiar claim to our regard. Your resolution, in a moment critical to the liberties of your country, to renounce all personal emolument, was among the many presages of your patriotic services, which have been amply fulfilled; and your scrupulous adherence now to the law then imposed whilst it increase the lustre of a character which has so many titles to admiration.

"Such are the sentiments with which we have thought fit to address you. They flow from our own hearts, and we verily believe that among the millions we represent, there is not a virtuous citizen whose heart will disown them.

"All that remains is, that we join in your fervent supplications for the blessing of Heaven on our country; and that we add our own for the choicest of these blessings on the most beloved of her citizens."

The President and Congress then attended on divine service.

In the evening a very ingenious and splendid show of fireworks was exhibited. Betwixt the fort and the Bowling-Green stood conspicuous, a superb and brilliant transparent painting, in the centre of which was the portrait of the President, represented under the emblem of fortitude; on the right hand was Justice, representing the Senate of the United States, and on his left Wisdom, representing the House of Representatives.

When Washington commenced his administration, the condition of the United States was so embarrassed as to excite many fears for the success of the new government. The treasury was empty. Large debts were due both by the old Congress and individuals to foreigners, and also from the United States to its own citizens, and from citizens to citizens. Every effort made by the former government to pay, or even to fund its debts, had failed, from the imbecility of the federal system. Great discontents prevailed in the United States, for the party opposed to the new constitution was strong and numerous. Several of these were elected to seats in the new Congress. Some were clamorous for a new convention, and the most moderate for amendments of what had been modified. Two states, North-Carolina and Rhode-Island, by refusing an acceptance of the constitution, were without the pale of its operations.

Animosities prevailed to a great degree between the United States and Great-Britain. Each charged the other with a breach of their late treaty. In support of these charges, one party urged the severities practised towards the loyalists, and that some of the states had interposed legal impediments to the recovery of debts due to British subjects.

The other recriminated by alleging, that the British, on their departure from the United States, had carried off with them several thousands of negroes belonging to the Americans; and continued to possess sundry posts within the acknowledged limits of the United States; and that from these posts they encouraged and instigated the neighbouring Indians to make war on their northwestern frontier settlements.

Spain, from their circumstance of their owning the land on each side of the mouth of the Mississippi, claimed the exclusive navigation of that river; while the western inhabitants of the United States looked to their country for a vindication of their common right to the use of this highway of nature. The boundaries of the United States towards the territories of Spain in the south, and towards those of Britain in the north-east, were both unsettled and in dispute.

The whole regular effective force of the United States, was less than six hundred men. Their trade was restricted much more than when they formed a part of the British empire. They had neither money to purchase, nor a naval force to compel the friendship of the Barbary powers; and were therefore exposed to capture whenever they ventured to trade in the Mediterranean, the coasts of which offered the best markets for some of their valuable commodities.

The military strength of the northern Indians who inhabited the country between the Lakes, the Mississippi, and the Ohio, was computed at 5000 then, and of these 1,500 were at open war with the United States. The Creeks, in the south-west, who could bring 6,000 fighting men into the field, were at war with Georgia.

These were but a part of the embarrassments under which the United States laboured when Gen. Washington was called to the helm. The redress of most of them required legislative interference, as well as executive aid. To point out the particular agency of the President in removing these embarrassments, and generally meliorating the condition of the United States, is peculiarly the province of the biographer of Washington.

Congress having organized the great departments of government, it became the duty of the President to designate proper persons to fill them.

In discharging this delicate and difficult trust, Washington kept himself free from every engagement, and uniformly declined giving decisive answers to applicants, having previously resolved to nominate persons to offices with a sole view to the public good, and to bring forward those who, upon every consideration, and from the best information he could obtain, were in his judgment most likely to answer the great end.

Under these impressions he placed Col. Hamilton at the head of the Treasury Department.

At the head of the Department of Foreign Affairs, he placed Mr. Thomas Jefferson.

General Knox was continued in the Department of War, which he had filled under the old Congress.

The office of Attorney General was assigned to Mr. Edmund Randolph. These composed the cabinet council of the first President.

The judicial department was filled as follows:

John Jay, of New-York, Chief Justice. John Rutledge, of South Carolina, James Wilson, of Pennsylvania, William Cushing, of Massachusetts, Robert Harrison, of Maryland, and John Blair, of Virginia, Associate Judges.

The officers who had been appointed by the individual states to manage the revenue, which, under the old system, was paid into the state treasury, were re-appointed to corresponding offices under the new constitution, by which the revenue had been transferred from the local to the general treasury of the union.

It was among the first cares of Washington to make peace with the Indians. Gen. Lincoln, Mr. Griffin, and Col. Humphreys, very soon after the inauguration of the President, were deputed by him to treat with the Creek Indians. These met with McGillvray, and other chiefs of the nation, with about 2,000 men, at the Rock Landing, on the frontiers of Georgia. The negociations were soon broken off by McGillvray, whose personal interests and connexion with Spain were supposed to have been the real cause of their abrupt and unsuccessful termination.

The next year brought round an accomplishment of the President's wishes, which had failed in the first attempt. Policy and interest concurred in recommending every prudent measure for detaching the Creek Indians from all connexion with the Spaniards, and cementing their friendship with the United States. Negociations carried on with them in the vicinity of the Spanish settlements, promised less than negociations conducted at the seat of government.

To induce a disposition favourable to this change of place, the President sent Col. Willet, a gallant and intelligent officer of the late army, into the Creek country, apparently on private business, but with a letter of introduction to McGillvray, and with instructions to take occasional opportunities to point out the distresses which a war with the United States would bring on the Creek nation, and the indiscretion of their breaking off the negociation at the Rock Landing; and to exhort him to repair with the chiefs of his nation to New-York, in order to effect a solid and lasting peace. Willet performed these duties with so much dexterity, that McGillvray, with the chiefs of his nation, were induced to come to New-York, where fresh negociations commenced, which, on the 7th of August, 1790, terminated in the establishment of peace.

The pacific overtures made by Washington to the Indians of the Wabash and the Miamis, failed of success. Long experience had taught the President, that on the failure of negociations with Indians, policy, economy, and even humanity, required the employment of a sufficient force to carry offensive war into their country, and lay waste their settlements.

The accomplishment of this was no easy matter. The Indian nations were numerous, accustomed to war, and not without discipline. They were said to be furnished with arms and ammunition from the British posts held within the United States, in violation of the treaty of peace. Generals Harmar and Sinclair were successively defeated by the Indians; and four or five years elapsed before they were subdued. This was accomplished by Gen. Wayne, in 1794.

Soon after that event, a peace was concluded, under his auspices, between these Indians and the United States. In the progress of this last Indian war, repeated overtures of peace were made to the Northwestern Indians, but rejected. About the same period a new system was commenced for turning them off from hunting to the employments of civilized life, by furnishing them with implements and instructions for agriculture and manufactures.

In this manner, during the Presidency of George Washington, peace was restored to the frontier settlements both in the north and south-west, which has continued ever since, and it is likely to do so, while, at the same time, the prospect of meliorating the condition of the savages is daily brightening; for the system first began by Washington with the view of civilizing these fierce sons of nature, have been ever since steadily pursued by all his successors. Indian wars are now only known from the records or recollection of past event; and it probable that the day is not far distant when the United States will receive a considerable accession of citizens from the civilized red men of the forest.

12

President Washington: Gen. Washington attends to the foreign relations of the United States. Negotiates with Spain. Difficulties in the way. The free navigation of the Mississippi is granted by a treaty made with Major Pinckney. Negotiations with Britain. Difficulties in the way. War probable. Mr. Jay's mission. His treaty with Great-Britain. Opposition thereto. Is ratified. Washington refuses papers to House of Representatives. British posts in United States evacuated. Negotiations with France. Genet's arrival. Assumes illegal powers, in violation of the neutrality of the United States. Is flattered by the people, but opposed by the executive. Is recalled. Gen. Pinckney sent as public minister to adjust disputes with France. Is not received. Washington declines a re-election, and addresses the people. His last address to the national legislature. Recommends a navy, a military academy, and other public institutions.

Events which had taken place before the inauguration of Washington, embarrassed his negotiations for the adjustments of the political relations between the United States and Spain.

In the year 1779, Mr. Jay had been appointed by the old Congress to make a treaty with the Catholic Majesty; but his best endeavours for more than two years were ineffectual. In a fit of despondence, while the revolutionary war was pressing, he had been authorized to agree "to relinquish, and in future forbear to use the navigation of the river Mississippi, from the point where it leaves the United States, down to the ocean."

After the war was ended, a majority of Congress had agreed to barter away for twenty-five years, their claim to this navigation. A long and intricate negotiation between Mr. Gardoqui, the Minister of his Catholic Majesty, and the Secretary of Foreign Affairs, had taken place at New-York, in the interval between the establishment of peace and of the new constitution of the United States; but was rendered abortive from the inflexible adherence of Mr. Gardoqui to the exclusion of the citizens of the United States from navigating the Mississippi below their southern boundary.

This unyielding disposition of Spain, the inability of the United States to assert their claims to the navigation of this river, and especially the facility which the old Congress had shown to recede from it for a term of years, had soured the minds of the western settlers. Their impatience transported them so far beyond the bounds of policy, that they sometimes dropped hints of separating from the Atlantic States, and attaching themselves to the Spaniards.

In this critical state of things, the President found abundant exercise for all his prudence. The western inhabitants were, in fact, thwarting his views in their favor, and encouraging Spain to persist in refusing that free navigation, which was so ardently desired both by the President and the people. The adherence of Spain to the exclusive use of the lower Mississippi, and the impolitic discontents of the western inhabitants, were not the only embarrassments of Washington, in negotiating with the court of Madrid.

In 1793, four Frenchmen left Philadelphia, empowered by Mr. Genet, the Minister of the French Republic, to prepare an expedition in Kentucky against New-Orleans. Spain, then at war with France, was at peace with the United States. Washington was officially bound to interpose his authority to prevent the raising of an armed force from among his fellow-citizens to commit hostilities on a peaceable neighboring power. Orders were accordingly given to the civil authority in Kentucky, to use all legal means to prevent this expedition; but the execution of these orders was so languid, that it became necessary to call in the aid of the regular army. Gen. Wayne was ordered to establish a military post at Fort Massac on the Ohio, for the purpose of forcibly stopping any body of armed men, who, in opposition to remonstrances, should persist in going down that river.

Many of high-spirited Kentuckians were so exasperated against the Spaniards, as to be very willing to second the views of the French Minister, and under his auspices to attack New-Orleans. The navigation of the Mississippi was so necessary for conveying to proper markets the surplusage of their luxuriant soil, that to gain this privilege, others were willing to receive it from the hands of the Spaniards at the price of renouncing all political connexion with the United States.

While these opposite modes of seeking a remedy for the same evil were pursuing by persons of different temperaments, a remonstrance from the inhabitants of Kentucky were presented to Washington and Congress. This demanded the use of the Mississippi as a natural right, and at the same time charged the government with being under the influence of a local policy, which had prevented all serious efforts for the acquisition of a right which was essential to the prosperity of the western people. It spoke the language of an injured people, irritated by the maladministration of their public servants; and hinted the probability of a dismemberment of the union, if their natural rights were not vindicated by government. To appease these discontents; to restrain the French from making war on the Spaniards with a force raised and embodied in the United States; and at the same time, by fair negotiation, to obtain the free use of the Mississippi from the court of Madrid, was the task assigned to Washington.

Difficult and delicate as it was, the whole was accomplished. Anterior to the receipt of the Kentucky remonstrance, the President, well knowing the discontents of the interior people, and that the publication of them would obstruct his views, had directed the Secretary of State to give assurances to the Governor of Kentucky, that every exertion was making to obtain for the western people the free navigation they so much desired. The strong arm of government was successfully exerted to frustrate the expedition projected by the French Minister against New Orleans; and, while these matters were pending, Major Thomas Pinckney was appointed Envoy Extraordinary to the court of Madrid; and in the year 1795, he concluded a treaty with his Catholic Majesty, in which the claims of the United States on the subject of boundary, and the navigation of the Mississippi, were fully conceded.

By these events, the discontents of the western people were done away. Tranquillity was restored between the Atlantic and western states; and all points in controversy between the United States and Spain were satisfactorily adjusted. The most important of these, the free navigation of the Mississippi, had been the subject of discussion in the hands of different negotiators, for almost the whole of the immediately preceding fifteen years.

Great were the difficulties Washington had to encounter in amicably settling all matters with Spain; but much greater stood in the way of a peaceable adjustment of various grounds of controversy between the United States and Great-Britain.

Each of these two nations charged the other with a breach of the treaty of peace, in 1783, and each supported the charge against the other, with more solid arguments than either alleged in their own defence.

President Washington: Foreign relations

The peace terminated the calamities of the war, but was far from terminating the resentments which were excited by it. Many in the United States believed that Great-Britain was their natural enemy, and that her views of subjecting the United States to her empire, were only for the present suspended. Soon after the peace, Mr. John Adams had been deputed by the old Congress to negotiate a treaty between the United States and Great-Britain; but the latter declined to meet this advance of the former. While he urged on the court of Great-Britain, the necessity they were under by the late treaty to evacuate their posts on the south side of the lakes of Canada, they retorted that some of the states had, in violation of the same treaty, passed laws interposing legal impediments to the recovery of debts due to British subjects.

Washington's love of country was not weakened by partiality to his country. In a letter to a member of Congress, he observed—

"It was impolitic and unfortunate, if not unjust, in those states to pass laws, which, by fair construction, might be considered as infractions of the treaty of peace. It is good policy at all times, to place one's adversary in the wrong. Had we observed good faith, and the western posts had been withheld from us by Great-Britain, we might have appealed to God and man for justice.

"What a misfortune," said he, in another letter, "that the British should have so well grounded a pretext for their palpable infractions; and what a disgraceful part, out of the choice of difficulties before us, are we to act!"

In the first years of Washington's presidency, he took informal measures to sound the British cabinet, and to ascertain its views respecting the United States. To Mr. Gouverneur Morris, who had been carried by private business to Europe, this negotiation was entrusted. He conducted it with ability; but found no disposition in the court of Great-Britain to accede to the wishes of the United States. In about two years more, when the stability and energy of the as administered by Washington became a matter of public notoriety, the British, of their own motion, sent Mr. Hammond their first minister to the United States. This advance induced the President to nominate Mr. Thomas Pinckney as Minister Plenipotentiary to the court of Great-Britain.

About this time war commenced between France and Great-Britain. The correct, sound judgment of Washington instantly decided that a perfect neutrality was the right, the duty, and the interest of the United States, and of this he gave public notice by a proclamation, in April, 1793. Subsequent events have proved the wisdom of this measure, though it was then reprobated by many.

The war between the late enemies and friends of the United States, revived revolutionary feelings in the breasts of the citizens, and enlisted the strongest passions of human nature against the one, and in favour of the other. A wish for the success of France was almost universal; and many were willing to hazard the peace of their country, by taking an active part in the war in her favour. The proclamation was at variance with the feelings and the passions of a large portion of the citizens. To compel the observance of neutrality under these circumstances, was no easy matter. Hitherto Washington had the people with him; but in this case a large proportion was on the other side. His resolution was nevertheless unshaken; and at the risk of popularity he persisted in promoting the real good of his fellow-citizens, in opposition to their own mistaken wishes and views.

The tide of popular opinion ran as strongly against Britain as in favour of France. The former was accused of instigating the Indians to acts of hostility against the United States; of impressing their sailors; of illegally capturing their ships; and of stirring up the Algerines against them. The whole of this hostility was referred to a jealousy of the growing importance of the United States. Motions were made in Congress for sequestering debts due to British subjects; for entering into commercial hostility with Great-Britain, and even for interdicting all intercourse with her, till she pursued other measures with respect to the United States.

Every appearance portended immediate war between the two countries. The passionate admirers of France wished for it; while others, more attached to British systems, dreaded a war with Great-Britain, as being likely to throw the United States into the arms of France.

In this state of things, when war seemed inevitable, the President composed the troubled scene by nominating John Jay, in April 1794, Envoy Extraordinary to the court of London. By this measure a truce was obtained, and that finally ended in an adjustment of the points in controversy between the two countries. The exercise of the constitutional right of the President to negotiate, virtually suspended all hostile legislative measures; for these could not with delicacy or propriety be urged, while the executive was in the act of treating for an amicable adjustment of differences.

A treaty between the United States and Great-Britain was the result of this mission. This was pronounced by Mr. Jay, "to be the best that was attainable, and which he believed it for the interest of the United States to accept." While the treaty was before the Senate for consideration, a member, contrary to the rules of that body, furnished an editor of a newspaper with a copy of it. This being published, operated like a spark of fire applied to combustible materials. The angry passions which for some short time had been smothered, broke out afresh. Some went so far as to pronounce the treaty a surrender of their power to their late enemy, Great-Britain, and a dereliction of their tried friend and ally, France. The more moderate said, that too much was given, and too little received.

Meetings of the people were held at Boston, New-York, Philadelphia, Charleston, and several other places, in which the treaty was pronounced to be unworthy of acceptance, and petitions were agreed upon and forwarded to the President, urging him to refuse his signature to the obnoxious instrument.

These agitations furnished matter for serious reflection to the President, but they did not affect his conduct, though they induced a reiterated examination of the subject. In a private letter to a friend, after reciting the importance of the crisis, he added—

"There is but one straight course, and that is to seek truth and to pursue it steadily."

It is probable that he had early made up his mind to ratify the treaty as better than none, and infinitely better than war; but regretted that it was so generally disliked, and considered by many as made with a design to oppress the French Republic. Under the weight of his high responsibility, he consoled himself, "that in time when passion shall have yielded to reason, the current may possibly turn." Peace with all the world was his policy, where it could be preserved with honour. War he considered as an evil of such magnitude, as never to be entered upon without the most imperious necessity.

The mission of Mr. Jay was his last effort for the preservation of peace with Great-Britain. The rejection of the treaty which resulted from this mission, he considered as the harbinger of war; for negotiation having failed to redress grievances, no alternative but war was left. By this prudent conduct, the rising states were preserved in peace, but the bickerings of the citizens among themselves, and their animosities against Great-Britain, still continued.

The popularity of the President for the present was diminished; but on this he had counted. In a letter to Gen. Knox, he observes—

"Next to a conscientious discharge of my public duties, to carry along with me the approbation of my constituents, would be the highest gratification of which my mind is susceptible. But the latter being secondary, I cannot make the former yield to it, unless come criterion more infallible than partial, (if they are not party,) meetings, can be discovered as the touchstone of public sentiment. If any person on earth could, or the Great Power above would erect the standard of infallibility in political opinions, no being that inhabits this terrestrial globe, would resort to it with more eagerness than myself, so long as I remain a servant of the public. But as I have hitherto found no better guide than upright intentions, and close investigation, I shall adhere to them while I keep the watch."

After the treaty was duly ratified, an attempt was made to render it a dead letter, by refusing the appropriations of money necessary to carry it into effect. Preparatory to this, a motion was made for the adoption of a resolution to request the President to lay before the House of Representatives a copy of his instructions to Mr. Jay, together with the correspondence and other documents relative to the treaty with Great-Britain.

This involved a new question, where the treaty making power was constitutionally lodged? The debate was animated and vehement. Appeals were made both to reason and passion. After a discussion of more than twenty days, the motion was carried in the affirmative by a majority of 25 votes. When the resolution was presented to the President, he replied "That he would take to consider it."

His situation was peculiarly delicate; the passions of the people were strongly excited against the treaty; the popularity of the demand being solely for information; the large majority by which the vote was carried; the suspicions that would probably attach in case of refusal, that circumstances had occurred in the course of the negotiation which the President was afraid to publish, added to other weighty considerations, would have induced minds of an ordinary texture, to yield to the request.

With Washington, popularity was only a secondary object. To follow the path of duty and the public good was a primary one. He had sworn to "preserve, protect and defend the constitution." In his opinion the treaty making power was exclusively given by the people in convention to the executive, and that the public good required that it should be so exercised. Under the influence of these solemn obligations, he returned the following answer to the resolution which had been presented to him.

Gentlemen of the House of Representatives,

"With the utmost attention I have considered your resolution of the 24th inst. requesting me to lay before your house a copy of the instructions to the minister of the United States, who negotiated the treaty with the king of Great-Britain, together with the correspondence and other documents relative to that treaty, excepting such of the said papers as any the existing negotiation may render improper to be disclosed.

"In deliberating upon this subject, it was impossible for me to lose sight of the principle which some have avowed in its discussion, or to avoid extending my views to the consequences which must flow from the admission of that principle.

"I trust that no part of my conduct has ever indicated a disposition to withhold any information which the constitution has enjoined it upon the President as a duty to give, or which could be required of him by either house of Congress as a right; and with truth I affirm, that it has been, as it will continue to be, while I have the honour to preside in the government, my constant endeavour to harmonize with the other branches thereof, so far as the trust delegated to me by the people of the United States, and my sense of the obligation it imposes, "to preserve, protect, and defend the constitution," will permit.

"The nature of foreign negotiations requires caution, and their success must often depend on secrecy; and even when brought to a conclusion, a full disclosure of all the measures, demands, or eventual concessions, which may have been proposed or contemplated, would be extremely impolitic; for this might have a pernicious influence on future negotiations, or produce immediate inconveniences, perhaps danger and mischief, to other persons. The necessity of such caution and secrecy was one cogent reason for vesting the power of making treaties in the President, with the advice and consent of the Senate, the principle on which that body was formed confining it to a small number of members.

"To admit then a right in the House of Representatives to demand, and to have as a matter of course, with all the papers respecting a negotiation with a foreign power, would be to establish a dangerous precedent.

"It does not occur that the inspection of the papers asked for, can be relative to any purpose under the cognizance of the House of Representatives, except that of an impeachment, which the resolution has not expressed. I repeat that I have no disposition to withhold any information which the duty of my station will permit, or the public good shall require, to be disclosed; and in fact all the papers affecting the negotiation with Great-Britain were laid before the Senate when the treaty itself was communicated for their consideration and advice.

"The course which the debate has taken on the resolution of the house, leads to some observations on the mode of making treaties under the constitution of the United States.

"Having been a member of the general convention, and knowing the principles on which the constitution was formed, I have ever entertained but one opinion upon this subject; and from the first establishment of the government to this moment, my conduct has exemplified that opinion—That the power of making treaties is exclusively vested in the President, by and with the advice and consent of the Senate, provided two-thirds of the Senators present concur; and that every treaty so made and promulgated, thenceforward becomes the law of the land.

"It is thus that the treaty-making power has been understood by foreign nations; and in all the treaties made with them we have declared, and they have believed, that when ratified by the President with the advice and consent of the Senate, they become obligatory. In this construction of the constitution, every House of Representatives has heretofore acquiesced, and, until the present time, not a doubt or suspicion has appeared to my knowledge that this construction was not the true one. Nay, they have more than acquiesced; for until now, without controverting the obligation of such treaties, they have made all the requisite provisions for carrying them into effect.

"There is also reason to believe that this construction agrees with the opinions entertained by the state conventions, when they were deliberating on the constitution, especially by those who objected to it; because there was not required in commercial treaties the consent of two-thirds of the whole number of the members of the Senate, instead of two-thirds of the Senators present; and because in treaties respecting territorial and certain other rights and claims, the concurrence of three-fourths of the whole number of the members of both houses respectively was not made necessary.

"It is a fact declared by the general convention, and universally understood, that the constitution of the United States was the result of a spirit of amity and mutual concession; and it well known that under this influence, the smaller states were admitted to an equal representation in the Senate with the larger states, and that this branch of the government was invested with great powers; for on the equal participation of those powers, the sovereignty and political safety of the smaller states were deemed essentially to depend.

"If other proofs than these, and the plain letter of the constitution itself, be necessary to ascertain the point under consideration, they may be found in the journals of the general convention, which I have deposited in the office of the department of state. In these journals it will appear that a proposition was made 'that no treaty should be binding on the United States which was not ratified by a law;' and that the proposition was explicitly rejected.

"As therefore it is perfectly clear to my understanding, that the assent of the House of Representatives is not necessary to the validity of a treaty; as the treaty with Great-Britain exhibits in itself all the objects requiring legislative provision, and on these the papers called for can throw no light; and as it is essential to the due administration of the government, that the boundaries fixed by the constitution between the different departments should be preserved with "just regard to the constitution and to the duty of my office, under all the circumstances of this case, forbid a compliance with your request."

Though the call for papers was unsuccessful, the favourers of the resolution for that purpose opposed the appropriations necessary to carry the treaty into effect; but, from the firmness of the President, the ground was altered. The treaty was ratified, and proclaimed to the public as constitutionally obligatory on the citizens. To refuse appropriations for carrying it into effect, would not only incur the high responsibility of breaking the public faith, but make a schism in the government between the executive and legislative departments.

After long and vehement debates, in which argument and passion were both resorted to, with the view to exposing the merits and demerits of the treaty, the resolution for bringing in the laws necessary to carry it into effect, was carried by a majority of three. Though in this discussion Washington had no direct agency, yet the final result in favour of the treaty was the consequence of the measures he had previously adopted. For having ratified the treaty and published it to the world as the law of the land, and having in his answer to the request of the House of Representatives, proved that he had a constitutional right so to do, could not be withheld without hazarding the most serious consequences.

The treaty which was thus carried into operation, produced more good and less evil than was apprehended. It compromised ancient differences, produced amicable dispositions, and a friendly intercourse. It brought round a peaceable surrender of the British posts, and compensation for American vessels illegally captured. Though it gave up some favourite principles, and some of its articles relative to commerce were deemed unequal, yet from Britain, as a great naval power holding valuable colonies and foreign possessions, nothing better, either with or without treaty, could have been obtained.

After the lapse of ten years has cooled the minds both of the friends and enemies of the treaty, most men will acknowledge that the measures adopted by Washington with respect to it were founded in wisdom; proceeded from the purest patriotism; were carried through with uncommon firmness; and finally eventuated in advancing the interests of the country.

Thorny and difficult as was the line of policy proper to be pursued by Washington with respect to Britain, it was much more so in regard to France. The revolution in France, and the establishment of the constitution of the United States, were nearly contemporary events. Till about the year 1793, perfect harmony subsisted between the two countries; but

President Washington: Foreign relations

from the commencement of the war between France and England, the greatest address was requisite to prevent the United States from being involved in war with one or the other, and sometimes with both. Good will to France, and hatred to Britain, which had prevailed more or loess from the peace of 1783, revived with a great increase of force on the breaking out of war between the two countries.

These dispositions were greatly increased by the arrival of Mr. Genet, the first Minister Plenipotentiary from the republic of France to the United States. He landed April 8th, 1793, at Charleston, S.C. the contiguity of which to the West-Indies, fitted it to be a convenient resort for privateers. By the Governor of the state, Wm. Moultrie, and the citizens, he was received with ardour approaching to enthusiasm. During his stay, which was for several days, he received unequivocal proofs of the warmest attachment to his person, his country, and its cause.

Encouraged by these evidences of the good wishes of the people for the success of the French revolution, he undertook to authorize the fitting and arming of vessels in that port, enlisting men, and giving commissions to vessels to cruise and commit hostilities on nations with whom the United States were at peace. The captures made by these cruisers were to be tried, condemned and sold under the authority of Genet, who had not yet been recognized as a public Minister by the government.

Similar marks of enthusiastic attachment were lavished on Genet as he passed through the country between Charleston and Philadelphia. At Gray's ferry, over the Schuylkill, he was met by crowds who flocked to do honour to the first ambassador of a republican allied nation. On the day after his arrival in Philadelphia, he received addresses from societies and the inhabitants, who expressed their gratitude for the aids furnished by the French nation to the United States in their late struggle for liberty and independence, and unbounded exultation at the success of the French arms. Genet's answers to these addresses were well calculated to preserve the idea of a complete fraternity between the two nations, and that their interests were the same.

After Genet had been thus accredited by the citizens of Philadelphia, he was presented to the President, and received with expressions of a sincere and cordial regard for his nation. In the conversations which took place on the occasion, Mr. Genet gave the most explicit assurances that France did not wish to engage the United States in the war between his country and Great-Britain.

While Mr. Genet was receiving these flattering marks of attention from the people, the British minister preferred a long catalogue of complaints against his proceedings at Charleston. This was founded on the acts

President Washington: Foreign relations

already mentioned, which were calculated to make the United States instruments of hostility in the hands of France, against those with whom she was at war. These were further aggravated by actual hostilities in the territories of the United States. The ship Grange, a British vessel, was captured by the French frigate l'Ambuscade, within the Capes of the Delaware, while on her way from Philadelphia to the ocean. Of this ship, and of other illegal prizes which were in the power of the American government, the British minister demanded restitution.

The cabinet council of Washington was unanimous that every independent nation was exclusively sovereign in its own territories, and that the proceedings complained of were unwarranted usurpations of sovereignty, and violations of neutrality; and therefore must in future be prevented. It was also agreed that the efficacy of the laws should be tried against those citizens of the United States who had joined in the offences complained of. The restitution of the Grange was also agreed to; but on the propriety of enforcing the restitution of prizes made on the high seas, there was a diversity of sentiment, the Secretaries of the Treasury and War being for it, and the Secretary of State and the Attorney General against it.

The principles on which a concurrence of sentiment had taken place being considered as settles, the Secretary of State was desired to communicate them to the Ministers of France and of Britain; and circular letters were written to the Governors of the several states, requiring them to co-operate with force, if necessary, to execute the rules which had been agreed upon.

Mr. Genet was highly dissatisfied with these determinations, and considered them as subversive of the treaty between the United States and France. His representations induced a re-consideration of the subject; but on the most dispassionate review of it, no reason appeared for an alteration of any part of the system. The minister of France was further informed that, in the opinion of the President, the vessels which had been illegally equipped, should depart from the ports of the United States.

Mr. Genet, adhering to his own construction of the treaty between France and the United States, would not acquiesce in those decisions of the government. Intoxicated with the flattering attentions he had received, and ignorant of the firmness of the executive, he seems to have expected that the popularity of his nation and its cause, would enable him to undermine the executive, or render it subservient to his views.

About this time, two citizens of the United States who had been engaged in Charleston by Mr. Genet, to cruise in the service of France, were arrested by the civil authority, in pursuance of the determination formed by government to prosecute persons who had offended against the laws. Mr. Genet demanded their release as French citizens, in the most extraordinary terms. This was refused; but on trial they were acquitted by the verdict of a jury.

The Minister of the French Republic was encouraged to this line of opposition, by a belief that the sentiments of the people were in his favour. So extravagant was their enthusiastic devotedness to France; so acrimonious were their expressions against all the powers at war with the new republic, that a person less sanguine than Mr. Genet might have cherished the hope of being able to succeed so far with the people, as, with their support, ultimately to triumph over the opposition he experienced. At civic festivals, the ensigns of France were displayed in union with those of America; at these the cap of liberty passed from head to head, and toasts were given expressive of the fraternity of the two nations

The proclamation of neutrality was treated as a royal edict, which demonstrated the disposition of the government to break its connexions with France, and dissolve the friendship which united the people of the two republics. The scenes of the revolutionary war were brought into view; the effects of British hostility against the United States, and of French aids both in men and money in their favour, were painted in glowing colours. The enmity of Britain to the United States was represented as continuing undiminished; and in proof of it their detention of the western posts, and their exciting from these stations the neighbouring Indians to make war on the frontier settlers, were urged with great vehemence, and contrasted with the amicable dispositions professed by the French republic.

It was indignantly asked, should a friend and an enemy be treated with equal favour? By declamations of this kind daily issuing from the press, the public mind was so inflamed against the executive, that Genet, calculating on the partialities of the people, openly insulted the government; and, adhering to his own construction of the treaty, that he had a right to do as he had done, threatened to appeal to the sovereign people against their President.

To preserve neutrality in such a crisis, was no easy matter. Washington, adhering to the principles avowed in his late proclamation, and embodied in the declaration of independence, "that the United States would hold all mankind enemies in war and friends in peace," exerted all his authority and influence to keep the balance even between the belligerents.

It was at length resolved by Washington to instruct Mr. Morris, the Minister of the United States at Paris, to request the recall of Mr. Genet; and that Mr. Morris should be furnished with all the necessary documents

President Washington: Foreign relations

to evince the propriety of the request. What was asked was granted; and Mr. Genet's conduct was disapproved by his government. Mr. Fauchet was appointed his successor, who was succeeded by Mr. Adet. The latter brought with him the colours of France, which he was directed to present to the United States. To answer the animated speech of Mr. Adet on his presenting the colours, required address—The occasion required something affectionate and complimentary to the French nation; and yet the guarded policy of Washington forbade the utterance of any sentiments which might be improper in the chief magistrate of a neutral country, when addressing the representative of one of the belligerent powers.

Impressed with this double view, the President made the following reply:

"Born, sir, in a land of liberty; having early learned its value; having engaged in a perilous conflict to defend it; having, in a word, devoted the best years of my life to secure its permanent establishment in my own country; my anxious recollections; my sympathetic feelings; and my best wishes, are irresistibly attracted, whensoever, in any country, I see an oppressed nation unfurl the banners of freedom.

"But above all, the events of the French revolution have produced the deepest solicitude, as well as the highest admiration. To call your nation brave, were to pronounce but common praise. Wonderful people! Ages to come will read with astonishment the history of your brilliant exploits. I rejoice that the period of your toils and of your immense sacrifices is approaching. I rejoice that the interesting revolutionary movements of so many years have issued have issued in the formation of a constitution designed to give permanency to the great object for which you have contended. I rejoice that liberty, which you have so long embraced with enthusiasm; liberty, of which you have been the invincible defenders, now finds an asylum in the bosom of a regularly organized government; a government, which, being formed to secure the happiness of the French people, corresponds with the ardent wishes of my heart, while it gratifies the pride of every citizen of the United States by its resemblance to their own. On these glorious events, accept, sir, my sincere congratulations.

"In delivering to you these sentiments, I express not my own feelings only, but those of my fellow-citizens, in relation to the commencement, the progress, and the issue, of the French revolution; and they will certainly join with me in purest wishes to the Supreme Being, that the citizens of our sister Republic, our magnanimous allies, may soon enjoy in peace that liberty which they have purchased at so great a price, and all the happiness that liberty can bestow.

"I receive, sir, with lively sensibility, the symbol of the triumphs and of the infranchisements of your nation, the Colours of France, which you have now presented to the United States. The transaction will be announced to Congress, and the colours will be deposited with the archives of the United States, which are at once the evidence and the memorials of their freedom and independence. May these be perpetual! And may the friendship of the two republics be commensurate with their existence!"

The successors of Genet continued to tread in his steps, but with less violence. They made frequent complaints of particular cases of hardship which grew out of the war, and out of the rules which had been established by the executive with regard to ships of war, cruisers, and their prizes. They complained particularly that in the treaty with Great-Britain, the principle of "free ships making free goods," was given up; and urged the injustice, while French cruisers were restrained by treaty from taking English goods out of American bottoms, that English cruisers should be liberated from the same restraint.

In vain did the executive show a willingness to release France from the pressure of a situation in which she had voluntarily placed herself. Private explanations were made, that neither the late treaty made with Britain, nor the arrangements growing out of it, furnished any real cause of complaint to France. With the same conciliatory view, Washington appointed Gen. Pinckney Minister Plenipotentiary to the French republic, "to maintain that good understanding, which, from the commencement of the alliance, had subsisted between the two nations, and to efface unfavourable impressions, banish suspicion, and restore that cordiality which was at once the evidence and pledge of a friendly union."

The Directory having inspected his letter of credence, announced their haughty determination, "not to receive another Minister from the United States, until after a redress of grievances demanded of the American government, which the French republic had a right to expect from it." This was followed by a written mandate to Gen. Pinckney, to quit the territories of the republic. To complete the system of hostility, American vessels, wherever found, were captured by French cruisers.

From this mission Washington expected an adjustment of all points in dispute between France and the United States. In his opinion, the failure of it was owing to a belief that the American people were in unison with France, and in opposition to their own government; and that high-toned measures on the part of France, would induce a change of rulers in the United States.

President Washington: Foreign relations

Before the result of the mission was known, Washington had at his own request ceased to be President. Having made peace with the Indians, and adjusted all matters in dispute with both Spain and Britain, and hoping that an accommodation would soon take place with France, after eight years service in the high office of President, at the commencement of which period he found the United States in a miserable state of depression, and at its conclusion, left them advancing with gigantic steps in agriculture, commerce, wealth, credit, and reputation, and being in the sixty-sixth year of his age; he announced his intention of declining a re-election, in full time for the people to make up their mind in the choice of his successor. This was done in an address to the people of the United States in the following words:

"Friends and Fellow-Citizens,

"The period for a new election of a citizen to administer the executive government of the United States being not far distant, and the time actually arrived when your thoughts must be employed in designating the person who is to be clothed with that important trust, it appears to me proper, especially as it may conduce to a more distinct expression of the public voice, that I should now apprize you of the resolution I have formed, to decline being considered among the number of those out of whom the choice is to be made.

"I beg you at the same time to do me the justice to be assured, that this resolution has not been taken, without a strict regard to all the considerations appertaining to the relation which binds a dutiful citizen to his country; and that in withdrawing the tender of service, which silence in my situation might imply, I am influenced by no diminution of zeal for your future interest; no deficiency of grateful respect for your past kindness; but am supported by a full conviction, that the step is compatible with both.

"The acceptance of, and continuance hitherto in, the office to which your suffrages have twice called me, have been an uniform sacrifice of inclination to the opinion of duty, and to a deference for what appeared to be your desire. I constantly hoped that it would have been much earlier in my power, consistently with motives which I was not at liberty to disregard, to return to that retirement from which I had been reluctantly drawn. The strength of my inclination to do this, previous to the last election, had even led to the preparation of an address to declare it to you; but mature reflection on the then perplexed and critical posture of our affairs with foreign nations, and the unanimous advice of persons entitled to my confidence, impelled me to abandon the idea.

"I rejoice, that the state of your concerns, external as well as internal, no longer renders the pursuit of inclination incompatible with the sentiment of duty, or propriety; and am persuaded, whatever partiality may be retained for my services, that, in the present circumstances of our country, you will not disapprove my determination to retire.

"The impressions, with which I first undertook the arduous trust, were explained on the proper occasion. In the discharge of this trust, I will only say, that I have, with good intentions, contributed towards the organization and administration of the government the best exertions of which a very fallible judgment was capable. Not unconscious, in the outset, of the inferiority of my qualifications, experience in my own eyes, perhaps still more in the eyes of others, has strengthened the motives to diffidence of myself; and every day the increasing weight of years admonishes me more and more, that the shade of retirement is as necessary to me as it will be welcome. Satisfied, that, if any circumstances have given peculiar value to my services, they were temporary, I have the consolation to believe, that, while choice and prudence invite me to quit the political scene, patriotism does not forbid it.

"In looking forward to the moment, which is intended to terminate the career of my public life, my feelings do not permit me to suspend the deep acknowledgment of that debt of gratitude, which I owe to my beloved country for the many honors it has conferred upon me; still more for the steadfast confidence with which it has supported me; and for the opportunities I have thence enjoyed of manifesting my inviolable attachment, by services faithful and persevering, though in usefulness unequal to my zeal. If benefits have resulted to our country from these services, let it always be remembered to your praise, and as an instructive example in our annals, that under circumstances in which the passions, agitated in every direction, were liable to mislead, amidst appearances sometimes dubious, vicissitudes of fortune often discouraging, in situations in which not unfrequently want of success has countenanced the spirit of criticism, the constancy of your support was the essential prop of the efforts, and a guarantee of the plans by which they were effected. Profoundly penetrated with this idea, I shall carry it with me to my grave, as a strong incitement to unceasing vows that Heaven may continue to you the choicest tokens of its beneficence; that your union and brotherly affection may be perpetual; that the free constitution, which is the work of your hands, may be sacredly maintained; that its administration in every department may be stamped with wisdom and virtue; than, in fine, the happiness of the people of these States, under the auspices of liberty, may be made complete, by so careful a preservation and so prudent a use of this blessing, as will acquire to them the glory of recommending it to the applause, the affection, and adoption of every nation, which is yet a stranger to it.

"Here, perhaps I ought to stop. But a solicitude for your welfare which cannot end but with my life, and the apprehension of danger, natural to that solicitude, urge me, on an occasion like the present, to offer to your solemn contemplation, and to recommend to your frequent review, some sentiments which are the result of much reflection, of no inconsiderable observation, and which appear to me all-important to the permanency of your felicity as a people. These will be offered to you with the more freedom, as you can only see in them the disinterested warnings of a parting friend, who can possibly have no personal motive to bias his counsel. Nor can I forget, as an encouragement to it, your indulgent reception of my sentiments on a former and not dissimilar occasion.

"Interwoven as is the love of liberty with every ligament of your hearts, no recommendation of mine is necessary to fortify or confirm the attachment.

"The unity of Government, which constitutes you one people, is also now dear to you. It is justly so; for it is a main pillar in the edifice of your real independence, the support of your tranquillity at home, your peace abroad; of your safety; of your prosperity; of that very Liberty, which you so highly prize. But as it is easy to foresee, that, from different causes and from different quarters, much pains will be taken, many artifices employed, to weaken in your minds the conviction of this truth; as this is the point in your political fortress against which the batteries of internal and external enemies will be most constantly and actively (though often covertly and insidiously) directed, it is of infinite moment, that you should properly estimate the immense value of your national Union to your collective and individual happiness; that you should cherish a cordial, habitual, and immovable attachment to it; accustoming yourselves to think and speak of it as of the Palladium of your political safety and prosperity; watching for its preservation with jealous anxiety; discountenancing whatever may suggest even a suspicion, that it can in any event be abandoned; and indignantly frowning upon the first dawning of every attempt to alienate any portion of our country from the rest, or to enfeeble the sacred ties which now link together the various parts.

"For this you have every inducement of sympathy and interest. Citizens, by birth or choice, of a common country, that country has a right to concentrate your affections. The name of american, which belongs to you, in your national capacity, must always exalt the just pride of Patriotism, more than any appellation derived from local discriminations. With slight shades of difference, you have the same religion, manners, habits, and political principles. You have in a common cause fought and triumphed together; the Independence and Liberty you possess are the work of joint counsels, and joint efforts, of common dangers, sufferings, and successes.

"But these considerations, however powerfully they address themselves to your sensibility, are greatly outweighed by those, which apply more immediately to your interest. Here every portion of our country finds the most commanding motives for carefully guarding and preserving the Union of the whole.

"The North, in an unrestrained intercourse with the South, protected by the equal laws of a common government, finds, in the productions of the latter, great additional resources of maritime and commercial enterprise and precious materials of manufacturing industry. The South, in the same intercourse, benefiting by the agency of the North, sees its agriculture grow and its commerce expand. Turning partly into its own channels the seamen of the North, it finds its particular navigation invigorated; and, while it contributes, in different ways, to nourish and increase the general mass of the national navigation, it looks forward to the protection of a maritime strength, to which itself is unequally adapted. The East, in a like intercourse with the West, already finds, and in the progressive improvement of interior communications by land and water, will more and more find, a valuable vent for the commodities which it brings from abroad, or manufactures at home. The West derives from the East supplies requisite to its growth and comfort, and, what is perhaps of still greater consequence, it must of necessity owe the secure enjoyment of indispensable outlets for its own productions to the weight, influence, and the future maritime strength of the Atlantic side of the Union, directed by an indissoluble community of interest as one nation. Any other tenure by which the West can hold this essential advantage, whether derived from its own separate strength, or from an apostate and unnatural connexion with any foreign power, must be intrinsically precarious.

"While, then, every part of our country thus feels an immediate and particular interest in Union, all the parts combined cannot fail to find in the united mass of means and efforts greater strength, greater resource, proportionably greater security from external danger, a less frequent interruption of their peace by foreign nations; and, what is of inestimable value, they must derive from Union an exemption from those broils and wars between themselves, which so frequently afflict neighbouring countries not tied together by the same governments, which their own rivalships alone would be sufficient to produce, but which opposite foreign alliances, attachments, and intrigues would stimulate and embitter. Hence, likewise, they will avoid the necessity of those overgrown military establishments, which, under any form of government, are inauspicious to liberty, and which are to be regarded as particularly hostile to Republican Liberty. In this sense it is, that your Union ought to be considered as a main prop of your liberty, and that the love of the one ought to endear to you the preservation of the other.

"These considerations speak a persuasive language to every reflecting and virtuous mind, and exhibit the continuance of the union as a primary object of Patriotic desire. Is there a doubt, whether a common government can embrace so large a sphere? Let experience solve it. To listen to mere speculation in such a case were criminal. We are authorized to hope, that a proper organization of the whole, with the auxiliary agency of governments for the respective subdivisions, will afford a happy issue to the experiment. It is well worth a fair and full experiment. With such powerful and obvious motives to Union, affecting all parts of our country, while experience shall not have demonstrated its impracticability, there will always be reason to distrust the patriotism of those, who in any quarter may endeavour to weaken its bands.

"In contemplating the causes, which may disturb our Union, it occurs as matter of serious concern, that any ground should have been furnished for characterizing parties by Geographical discriminations, Northern and Southern, Atlantic and Western; whence designing men may endeavour to excite a belief, that there is a real difference of local interests and views. One of the expedients of party to acquire influence, within particular districts, is to misrepresent the opinions and aims of other districts. You cannot shield yourselves too much against the jealousies and heart-burnings, which spring from these misrepresentations; they tend to render alien to each other those, who ought to be bound together by fraternal affection. The inhabitants of our western country have lately had a useful lesson on this head; they have seen, in the negotiation by the Executive, and in the unanimous ratification by the Senate, of the treaty with Spain, and in the universal satisfaction at that event, throughout the United States, a decisive proof how unfounded were the suspicions propagated among them of a policy in the General Government and in the Atlantic States unfriendly to their interests in regard to the mississippi; they have been witnesses to the formation of two treaties, that with Great Britain, and that with Spain, which secure to them every thing they could desire, in respect to our foreign relations, towards confirming their prosperity. Will it not be their wisdom to rely for the preservation of these advantages on the union by which they were procured? Will they not henceforth be deaf to those advisers, if such there are, who would sever them from their brethren, and connect them with aliens?

"To the efficacy and permanency of your Union, a Government for the whole is indispensable. No alliances, however strict, between the parts can be an adequate substitute; they must inevitably experience the infractions and interruptions, which all alliances in all times have experienced. Sensible of this momentous truth, you have improved upon your first essay, by the adoption of a Constitution of Government better calculated than your former for an intimate Union, and for the efficacious management of your common concerns. This Government, the offspring of our own choice, uninfluenced and unawed, adopted upon full investigation and mature deliberation, completely free in its principles, in the distribution of its powers, uniting security with energy, and containing within itself a provision for its own amendment, has a just claim to your confidence and your support. Respect for its authority, compliance with its laws, acquiescence in its measures, are duties enjoined by the fundamental maxims of true Liberty. The basis of our political systems is the right of the people to make and to alter their Constitutions of Government. But the Constitution which at any time exists, till changed by an explicit and authentic act of the whole people, is sacredly obligatory upon all. The very idea of the power and the right of the people to establish Government presupposes the duty of every individual to obey the established Government.

"All obstructions to the execution of the Laws, all combinations and associations, under whatever plausible character, with the real design to direct, control, counteract, or awe the regular deliberation and action of the constituted authorities, are destructive of this fundamental principle, and of fatal tendency. They serve to organize faction, to give it an artificial and extraordinary force; to put, in the place of the delegated will of the nation, the will of a party, often a small but artful and enterprising minority of the community; and, according to the alternate triumphs of different parties, to make the public administration the mirror of the ill-concerted and incongruous projects of faction, rather than the organ of consistent and wholesome plans digested by common counsels, and modified by mutual interests.

"However combinations or associations of the above description may now and then answer popular ends, they are likely, in the course of time and things, to become potent engines, by which cunning, ambitious, and unprincipled men will be enabled to subvert the power of the people, and to usurp for themselves the reins of government; destroying afterwards the very engines, which have lifted them to unjust dominion.

"Towards the preservation of your government, and the permanency of your present happy state, it is requisite, not only that you steadily discountenance irregular oppositions to its acknowledged authority, but also that you resist with care the spirit of innovation upon its principles, however specious the pretexts. One method of assault may be to effect, in the forms of the constitution, alterations, which will impair the energy of the system, and thus to undermine what cannot be directly overthrown. In all the changes to which you may be invited, remember that time and habit are at least as necessary to fix the true character of governments, as of other human institutions; that experience is the surest standard, by which to test the real tendency of the existing constitution of a country; that facility in changes, upon the credit of mere hypothesis and opinion, exposes to perpetual change, from the endless variety of hypothesis and opinion; and remember, especially, that, for the efficient management of our common interests, in a country so extensive as ours, a government of as much vigor as is consistent with the perfect security of liberty is indispensable. Liberty itself will find in such a government, with powers properly distributed and adjusted, its surest guardian. It is, indeed, little else than a name, where the government is too feeble to withstand the enterprises of faction, to confine each member of the society within the limits prescribed by the laws, and to maintain all in the secure and tranquil enjoyment of the rights of person and property.

"I have already intimated to you the danger of parties in the state, with particular reference to the founding of them on geographical discriminations. Let me now take a more comprehensive view, and warn you in the most solemn manner against the baneful effects of the spirit of party, generally.

"This spirit, unfortunately, is inseparable from our nature, having its root in the strongest passions of the human mind. It exists under different shapes in all governments, more or less stifled, controlled, or repressed; but, in those of the popular form, it is seen in its greatest rankness, and is truly their worst enemy.

'The alternate domination of one faction over another, sharpened by the spirit of revenge, natural to party dissension, which in different ages and countries has perpetrated the most horrid enormities, is itself a frightful despotism. But this leads at length to a more formal and permanent despotism. The disorders and miseries, which result, gradually incline the minds of men to seek security and repose in the absolute power of an individual; and sooner or later the chief of some prevailing faction, more able or more fortunate than his competitors, turns this disposition to the purposes of his own elevation, on the ruins of Public Liberty.

"Without looking forward to an extremity of this kind, (which nevertheless ought not to be entirely out of sight,) the common and continual mischiefs of the spirit of party are sufficient to make it the interest and duty of a wise people to discourage and restrain it.

"It serves always to distract the Public Councils, and enfeeble the Public Administration. It agitates the Community with ill-founded jealousies and false alarms; kindles the animosity of one part against another, foments occasionally riot and insurrection. It opens the door to foreign influence and corruption, which find a facilitated access to the government itself through the channels of party passions. Thus the policy and the will of one country are subjected to the policy and will of another.

"There is an opinion, that parties in free countries are useful checks upon the administration of the Government, and serve to keep alive the spirit of Liberty. This within certain limits is probably true; and in Governments of a Monarchical cast, Patriotism may look with indulgence, if not with favor, upon the spirit of party. But in those of the popular character, in Governments purely elective, it is a spirit not to be encouraged. From their natural tendency, it is certain there will always be enough of that spirit for every salutary purpose. And, there being constant danger of excess, the effort ought to be, by force of public opinion, to mitigate and assuage it. A fire not to be quenched, it demands a uniform vigilance to prevent its bursting into a flame, lest, instead of warming, it should consume.

"It is important, likewise, that the habits of thinking in a free country should inspire caution, in those intrusted with its administration, to confine themselves within their respective constitutional spheres, avoiding in the exercise of the powers of one department to encroach upon another. The spirit of encroachment tends to consolidate the powers of all the departments in one, and thus to create, whatever the form of government, a real despotism. A just estimate of that love of power, and proneness to abuse it, which predominates in the human heart, is sufficient to satisfy us of the truth of this position. The necessity of reciprocal checks in the exercise of political power, by dividing and distributing it into different depositories, and constituting each the Guardian of the Public Weal against invasions by the others, has been evinced by experiments ancient and modern; some of them in our country and under our own eyes. To preserve them must be as necessary as to institute them. If, in the opinion of the people, the distribution or modification of the constitutional powers be in any particular wrong, let it be corrected by an amendment in the way, which the constitution designates. But let there be no change by usurpation; for, though this, in one instance, may be the instrument of good, it is the customary weapon by which free governments are destroyed. The precedent must always greatly overbalance in permanent evil any partial or transient benefit, which the use can at any time yield.

"Of all the dispositions and habits, which lead to political prosperity, Religion and Morality are indispensable supports. In vain would that man claim the tribute of Patriotism, who should labor to subvert these great pillars of human happiness, these firmest props of the duties of Men and Citizens. The mere Politician, equally with the pious man, ought to respect and to cherish them. A volume could not trace all their connexions with private and public felicity. Let it simply be asked, Where is the security for property, for reputation, for life, if the sense of religious obligation desert the oaths, which are the instruments of investigation in Courts of Justice? And let us with caution indulge the supposition, that morality can be maintained without religion. Whatever may be conceded to the influence of refined education on minds of peculiar structure, reason and experience both forbid us to expect, that national morality can prevail in exclusion of religious principle.

"It is substantially true, that virtue or morality is a necessary spring of popular government. The rule, indeed, extends with more or less force to every species of free government. Who, that is a sincere friend to it, can look with indifference upon attempts to shake the foundation of the fabric?

"Promote, then, as an object of primary importance, institutions for the general diffusion of knowledge. In proportion as the structure of a government gives force to public opinion, it is essential that public opinion should be enlightened.

"As a very important source of strength and security, cherish public credit. One method of preserving it is, to use it as sparingly as possible; avoiding occasions of expense by cultivating peace, but remembering also that timely disbursements to prepare for danger frequently prevent much greater disbursements to repel it; avoiding likewise the accumulation of debt, not only by shunning occasions of expense, but by vigorous exertions in time of peace to discharge the debts, which unavoidable wars may have occasioned, not ungenerously throwing upon posterity the burthen, which we ourselves ought to bear. The execution of these maxims belongs to your representatives, but it is necessary that public opinion should cooperate. To facilitate to them the performance of their duty, it is essential that you should practically bear in mind, that towards the payment of debts there must be Revenue; that to have Revenue there must be taxes; that no taxes can be devised, which are not more or less inconvenient and unpleasant; that the intrinsic embarrassment, inseparable from the selection of the proper objects (which is always a choice of difficulties), ought to be a decisive motive for a candid construction of the conduct of the government in making it, and for a spirit of acquiescence in the measures for obtaining revenue, which the public exigencies may at any time dictate.

"Observe good faith and justice towards all Nations; cultivate peace and harmony with all. Religion and Morality enjoin this conduct; and can it be, that good policy does not equally enjoin it? It will be worthy of a free, enlightened, and, at no distant period, a great Nation, to give to mankind the magnanimous and too novel example of a people always guided by an exalted justice and benevolence. Who can doubt, that, in the course of time and things, the fruits of such a plan would richly repay any temporary advantages, which might be lost by a steady adherence to it? Can it be, that Providence has not connected the permanent felicity of a Nation with its Virtue? The experiment, at least, is recommended by every sentiment which ennobles human nature. Alas! is it rendered impossible by its vices?

"In the execution of such a plan, nothing is more essential, than that permanent, inveterate antipathies against particular Nations, and passionate attachments for others, should be excluded; and that, in place of them, just and amicable feelings towards all should be cultivated. The Nation, which indulges towards another an habitual hatred, or an habitual fondness, is in some degree a slave. It is a slave to its animosity or to its affection, either of which is sufficient to lead it astray from its duty and its interest. Antipathy in one nation against another disposes each more readily to offer insult and injury, to lay hold of slight causes of umbrage, and to be haughty and intractable, when accidental or trifling occasions of dispute occur. Hence frequent collisions, obstinate, envenomed, and bloody contests. The Nation, prompted by ill-will and resentment, sometimes impels to war the Government, contrary to the best calculations of policy. The Government sometimes participates in the national propensity, and adopts through passion what reason would reject; at other times, it makes the animosity of the nation subservient to projects of hostility instigated by pride, ambition, and other sinister and pernicious motives. The peace often, sometimes perhaps the liberty, of Nations has been the victim.

"So likewise, a passionate attachment of one Nation for another produces a variety of evils. Sympathy for the favorite Nation, facilitating the illusion of an imaginary common interest, in cases where no real common interest exists, and infusing into one the enmities of the other, betrays the former into a participation in the quarrels and wars of the latter, without adequate inducement or justification. It leads also to concessions to the favorite Nation of privileges denied to others, which is apt doubly to injure the Nation making the concessions; by unnecessarily parting with what ought to have been retained; and by exciting jealousy, ill-will, and a disposition to retaliate, in the parties from whom equal privileges are withheld. And it gives to ambitious, corrupted, or deluded citizens, (who devote themselves to the favorite nation,) facility to betray or sacrifice the interests of their own country, without odium, sometimes even with popularity; gilding, with the appearances of a virtuous sense of obligation, a commendable deference for public opinion, or a laudable zeal for public good, the base or foolish compliances of ambition, corruption, or infatuation.

"As avenues to foreign influence in innumerable ways, such attachments are particularly alarming to the truly enlightened and independent Patriot. How many opportunities do they afford to tamper with domestic factions, to practise the arts of seduction, to mislead public opinion, to influence or awe the Public Councils! Such an attachment of a small or weak, towards a great and powerful nation, dooms the former to be the satellite of the latter.

"Against the insidious wiles of foreign influence (I conjure you to believe me, fellow-citizens,) the jealousy of a free people ought to be constantly awake; since history and experience prove, that foreign influence is one of the most baneful foes of Republican Government. But that jealousy, to be useful, must be impartial; else it becomes the instrument of the very influence to be avoided, instead of a defence against it. Excessive partiality for one foreign nation, and excessive dislike of another, cause those whom they actuate to see danger only on one side, and serve to veil and even second the arts of influence on the other. Real patriots, who may resist the intrigues of the favorite, are liable to become suspected and odious; while its tools and dupes usurp the applause and confidence of the people, to surrender their interests.

"The great rule of conduct for us, in regard to foreign nations, is, in extending our commercial relations, to have with them as little political connexion as possible. So far as we have already formed engagements, let them be fulfilled with perfect good faith. Here let us stop.

"Europe has a set of primary interests, which to us have none, or a very remote relation. Hence she must be engaged in frequent controversies, the causes of which are essentially foreign to our concerns. Hence, therefore, it must be unwise in us to implicate ourselves, by artificial ties, in the ordinary vicissitudes of her politics, or the ordinary combinations and collisions of her friendships or enmities.

"Our detached and distant situation invites and enables us to pursue a different course. If we remain one people, under an efficient government, the period is not far off, when we may defy material injury from external annoyance; when we may take such an attitude as will cause the neutrality, we may at any time resolve upon, to be scrupulously respected; when belligerent nations, under the impossibility of making acquisitions upon us, will not lightly hazard the giving us provocation; when we may choose peace or war, as our interest, guided by justice, shall counsel.

"Why forego the advantages of so peculiar a situation? Why quit our own to stand upon foreign ground? Why, by interweaving our destiny with that of any part of Europe, entangle our peace and prosperity in the toils of European ambition, rivalship, interest, humor, or caprice?

"It is our true policy to steer clear of permanent alliances with any portion of the foreign world; so far, I mean, as we are now at liberty to do it; for let me not be understood as capable of patronizing infidelity to existing engagements. I hold the maxim no less applicable to public than to private affairs, that honesty is always the best policy. I repeat it, therefore, let those engagements be observed in their genuine sense. But, in my opinion, it is unnecessary and would be unwise to extend them.

"Taking care always to keep ourselves, by suitable establishments, on a respectable defensive posture, we may safely trust to temporary alliances for extraordinary emergencies.

"Harmony, liberal intercourse with all nations, are recommended by policy, humanity, and interest. But even our commercial policy should hold an equal and impartial hand; neither seeking nor granting exclusive favors or preferences; consulting the natural course of things; diffusing and diversifying by gentle means the streams of commerce, but forcing nothing; establishing, with powers so disposed, in order to give trade a stable course, to define the rights of our merchants, and to enable the government to support them, conventional rules of intercourse, the best that present circumstances and mutual opinion will permit, but temporary, and liable to be from time to time abandoned or varied, as experience and circumstances shall dictate; constantly keeping in view, that it is folly in one nation to look for disinterested favors from another; that it must pay with a portion of its independence for whatever it may accept under that character; that, by such acceptance, it may place itself in the condition of having given equivalents for nominal favors, and yet of being reproached with ingratitude for not giving more. There can be no greater error than to expect or calculate upon real favors from nation to nation. It is an illusion, which experience must cure, which a just pride ought to discard.

"In offering to you, my countrymen, these counsels of an old and affectionate friend, I dare not hope they will make the strong and lasting impression I could wish; that they will control the usual current of the passions, or prevent our nation from running the course, which has hitherto marked the destiny of nations. But, if I may even flatter myself, that they may be productive of some partial benefit, some occasional good; that they may now and then recur to moderate the fury of party spirit, to warn against the mischiefs of foreign intrigue, to guard against the impostures of pretended patriotism; this hope will be a full recompense for the solicitude for your welfare, by which they have been dictated.

"How far in the discharge of my official duties, I have been guided by the principles which have been delineated, the public records and other evidences of my conduct must witness to you and to the world. To myself, the assurance of my own conscience is, that I have at least believed myself to be guided by them.

"In relation to the still subsisting war in Europe, my Proclamation of the 22d of April 1793, is the index to my Plan. Sanctioned by your approving voice, and by that of your Representatives in both Houses of Congress, the spirit of that measure has continually governed me, uninfluenced by any attempts to deter or divert me from it.

"After deliberate examination, with the aid of the best lights I could obtain, I was well satisfied that our country, under all the circumstances of the case, had a right to take, and was bound in duty and interest to take, a neutral position. Having taken it, I determined, as far as should depend upon me, to maintain it, with moderation, perseverance, and firmness.

"The considerations, which respect the right to hold this conduct, it is not necessary on this occasion to detail. I will only observe, that, according to my understanding of the matter, that right, so far from being denied by any of the Belligerent Powers, has been virtually admitted by all.

"The duty of holding a neutral conduct may be inferred, without any thing more, from the obligation which justice and humanity impose on every nation, in cases in which it is free to act, to maintain inviolate the relations of peace and amity towards other nations.

"The inducements of interest for observing that conduct will best be referred to your own reflections and experience. With me, a predominant motive has been to endeavour to gain time to our country to settle and mature its yet recent institutions, and to progress without interruption to that degree of strength and consistency, which is necessary to give it, humanly speaking, the command of its own fortunes.

"Though, in reviewing the incidents of my administration, I am unconscious of intentional error, I am nevertheless too sensible of my defects not to think it probable that I may have committed many errors. Whatever they may be, I fervently beseech the Almighty to avert or mitigate the evils to which they may tend. I shall also carry with me the hope, that my Country will never cease to view them with indulgence; and that, after forty-five years of my life dedicated to its service with an upright zeal, the faults of incompetent abilities will be consigned to oblivion, as myself must soon be to the mansions of rest.

"Relying on its kindness in this as in other things, and actuated by that fervent love towards it, which is so natural to a man, who views it in the native soil of himself and his progenitors for several generations; I anticipate with pleasing expectation that retreat, in which I promise myself to realize, without alloy, the sweet enjoyment of partaking, in the midst of my fellow-citizens, the benign influence of good laws under a free government, the ever favorite object of my heart, and the happy reward, as I trust, of our mutual cares, labors, and dangers.

"United States, Sept. 17, 1796"

This valedictory address of the father of his country, was received in every part of the union with the most unbounded veneration, and recorded with the most pointed respect. Shortly after, the President, for the last time, met the national legislature in the senate chamber. His address on the occasion was highly dignified. He congratulated Congress on the internal situation of the United States; on the progress which had been made for preserving peace with the Indians, and meliorating their condition; and, after stating the measures which had been adopted in execution of the treaties with Britain, Spain and Algiers, and the negociations which were pending with Tunis and Tripoli, he observed:—

"To an active internal commerce, the protection of a naval force is indispensable. This is manifest with regard to wars in which a state is itself a party. But besides this, it is in our own experience, that the most sincere neutrality is not a sufficient guard against the depredations of nations at war. To secure respect to a neutral flag requires a naval force, organized and ready to vindicate it from insult or aggression. This may even prevent the necessity of going to war, by discouraging belligerent powers from committing such violations of the rights of the neutral party, as may first or last leave no other option. From the best information I have been able to obtain, it would seem as if our trade to the Mediterranean, without a protecting force, will always be insecure, and our citizens exposed to the calamities from which numbers of them have but just been relieved.

"These considerations invite the United States to look to the means, and to set about the gradual creation of a navy. The increasing progress of their navigation, promises them at no distant period, the requisite supply of seamen, and their means in other respects, favour the undertaking. It is an encouragement, likewise, that their particular situation will give a weight and influence to a moderate naval force in their hands. Will it not them be adviseable to begin without delay, to provide and lay up the materials for the building and equipping of ships of war, and to proceed in the work by degrees, in proportion as our resources shall render it practicable, without inconvenience; so that a future war of Europe may not find our commerce in the same unprotected state in which it was found by the present?"

He then recommended the establishment of national works for manufacturing implements of defence; of an institution for the improvement of agriculture; and pointed out the advantages of a military academy; of a national university; and the necessity of augmenting the salaries of the officers of the United States.

In respect to the disputes with France, he observed—"While in our external relations some serious inconveniences and embarrassments have been overcome, and others lessened, it is with much pain and deep regret I mention, that circumstances of a very unwelcome nature have lately occurred. Our trade has suffered, and is suffering, extensive injuries in the West-Indies, from the cruisers and agents of the French republic; and communications have been received from its Minister here, which indicate the danger of a further disturbance of our commerce by its authority; and which are in other respects far from agreeable.

"It has been my constant, sincere, and earnest wish, in conformity with that of our nation, to maintain cordial harmony, and a perfectly friendly understanding with that republic. This wish remains unabated, and I shall persevere in the endeavour to fulfill it, to the utmost extent of what shall be consistent with a just and indispensable regard to the rights and honour of our country; nor will I easily cease to cherish the expectation, that a spirit of justice, candour and friendship, on the part of the republic, will eventually ensure success.

"In pursuing this course, however, I cannot forget what is due to the character of our government and nation, or to a full and entire confidence in the good sense, patriotism, self-respect, and fortitude of my country-men."

This address was concluded in the following pathetic terms:

"The situation in which I now stand for the last time, in the midst of the representatives of the people of the United States, naturally recalls the period when the administration of the present form of government commenced; and I cannot omit the occasion to congratulate you and my country on the success of the experiment, nor to repeat my fervent supplications to the Supreme Ruler of the Universe, and sovereign arbiter of nations, that his providential care may still be extended to the United States; that the virtue and happiness of the people may be preserved; and that the government which they have instituted for the protection of their liberties may be perpetual."

13

Washington Retires: Washington rejoices at the prospect of retiring. Writes to the Secretary of State, denying the authenticity of letters said to be From him to J.P. Custis and Lund Washington, in 1776. Pays Respect to his successor, Mr. John Adams. Review of Washington's Administration. He retires to Mount Vernon. Resumes agricultural Pursuits. Hears with regret the aggression of the French republic. Corresponds on the subject of his taking the command of an army To oppose the French. Is appointed Lieutenant-General. His commission Is sent to him by the Secretary of War. His letter to President Adams on The receipt thereof. Directs the organization of the proposed army. Three Envoys Extraordinary sent to France, who adjust all disputes with Bonaparte, after the overthrow of the Directory. Gen. Washington dies. Is honoured by Congress, and by the citizens. His character

The pleasing emotions which are excited in ordinary men on their acquisition of power, were inferior to those which Washington felt on the resignation of it. To his tried friend, Gen. Knox, on the day preceding the termination of his office in a letter—"To the weary traveller who sees a resting place, and is bending his body thereon, I now compare myself. Although the prospect of retirement is most grateful to my soul, and I have not a wish to mix again in the great world, or to partake in its politics, yet I am not without regret at parting with (perhaps never more to meet) the few intimates whom I love. Among these be assured you are one."

The numerous calumnies of which Washington was the subject, drew from him no public animadversions, except in one case. A volume of letters, said to be from Gen. Washington to John Parke Custis and Lund Washington, were published by the British, in the year 1776, and were given to the public as being found in a small portmanteau, left in the care of his servant, who it was said by the editors, had been taken prisoner in Fort Lee. These letters were intended to produce in the public mind, impressions unfavourable to the integrity of Washington's motives, and to represent his inclinations as at variance with his profession and duty.

When the first edition of these spurious letters was forgotten, they were republished during Washington's civil administration, by some of his fellow-citizens who differed from him in politics. On the morning of the last day of his Presidency, he addressed a letter to the Secretary of State, in which, after enumerating all the facts and dates connected with the forgery, and declaring that he had hitherto deemed it unnecessary to take any formal notice of the imposition, he concluded as follows—

"But as I cannot know a more serious event may succeed to that which will this day take place, I have thought it a duty that I owed to myself, to my country, and to truth, now to detail the circumstances above recited, and to add my solemn declaration, that the letters herein described, are a base forgery; and that I never saw of heard of them until they appeared in print. The present letter I commit to your care, and desire it may be deposited in the office of the department of state, as a testimony of the truth to the present generation and to posterity."

The moment now approached which was to terminate the official character of Washington, and in which that of his successor, John Adams, was to commence. The old and new President walked in together to the House of Representatives, where the oath of office was administered to the latter. On this occasion Mr. Adams concluded an impressive speech with a handsome compliment to his predecessor, by observing, that though he was about to retire, "his name may still be a rampart, and the knowledge that he lives a bulwark against all open or secret enemies of his country."

The immense concourse of citizens who were present, gazed with love and affection on the retiring Washington, while cheerfulness overspread his countenance and joy filled his heart, on seeing another invested with the high authorities he so long exercised, and the way opened for his returning to the long wished-for happiness of domestic private life. After paying his most respectful compliments to the new President, he set out for Mount Vernon, the scene of enjoyment which he preferred to all others. His wished to travel privately were in vain; for wherever he passed, the gentlemen of the country took every occasion of testifying their respect for him. In his retirement he continued to receive the most flattering addresses from legislative bodies, and various classes of his fellow-citizens.

Washington retires

During the eight years administration of Washington, the United States enjoyed prosperity and happiness at home; and, by the energy of the government, regained among foreigners that importance and reputation, which, by its weakness, they had lost. The debts contracted in the revolutionary war, which, from the imbecility of the old government, had depreciated to an insignificant sum, were funded; and such ample revenues provided for the payment of the interest and the gradual extinction of the principal, that their real and nominal value were in a little time nearly the same. The government was so firmly established as to be cheerfully and universally obeyed.

The only exception was an insurrection in the western counties of Pennsylvania, which was quelled without bloodshed. Agriculture and commerce were extended far beyond what had ever before taken place. The Indians on the frontiers had been first compelled by force to respect the United States, and to continue in peace; and afterwards a humane system was commenced for teaching them to exchange the tomahawk and hatchet for the plough, the hoe, the shuttle, and the spinning-wheel. The free navigation of the Mississippi had been acquired with the consent of Spain, and all differences compromised with that power. The military posts which had been long held by Britain within the United States, were peaceably given up. The Mediterranean was opened to American vessels in consequence of treaties made with the Barbary powers.

Indeed, differences with all powers, either contiguous to or connected with the United States, had been amicably adjusted, with the exception of France. To accomplish this very desirable object, Washington made repeated advances; but it could not be obtained without surrendering the independence of the nation, and its right of self-government.

Washington, on returning to Mount-Vernon, resumed agricultural pursuits. These, with the society of men and books, gave to every hour innocent and interesting employment, and promised a serene evening of his life. Though he wished to withdraw not only from public office, but from all anxiety respecting public affairs, yet he felt too much for his country to be indifferent to its interests. He heard with regret the repeated insults offered by the French Directory to the United States, in the person of their ministers, and the injury done to their commerce by illegal capture of their vessels. These indignities and injuries, after a long endurance and a rejection of all advances for an accommodation, at length roused the government, in the hands of Mr. Adams, to adopt vigorous measures. To be in readiness to repel a threatened invasion, Congress authorized the formation of a regular army.

As soon as the adoption of this measure was probable, the eyes of all were once more turned on Washington as the most suitable person to be at its head. Letters from his friends poured in upon him, urging that he should accept the command. To one from President Adams, in which it was observed—"We must have your name if you will in any case permit us to use it; there will be more efficacy in it, than in many an army"

Washington replied as follows—"At the epoch of my retirement, an invasion of these states by any European power, or even the probability of such an event in my days, was so far from being contemplated by me, that I had no conceptions either that, or any other occurrence, would arrive in so short a period, which could turn my eyes from the shades of Mount-Vernon.

"But this seems to be the age of wonders; and it is reserved for intoxicated and lawless France, (for purposes far beyond the reach of human ken) to slaughter her own citizens, and to disturb the repose of all the world besides. From a view of the past; from the prospect of the present; and of that which seems to be expected, it is not easy for me to decide satisfactorily on the part it might best become me to act. In case of actual invasion by a formidable force, I certainly should not intrench myself under the cover of age and retirement, if my services should be required by my country to assist in repelling it. And if there be good cause to expect such an event, which certainly must be better known to the government than to private citizens, delay in preparing for it may be dangerous, improper, and not to be justified by prudence. The uncertainty, however, of the latter, in my mind, creates my embarrassment; for I cannot bring it to believe, regardless as the French are of treaties and of the laws of nations, and capable as I conceive them to be of any species of despotism and injustice, that they will attempt to invade this country, after such a uniform and unequivocal expression of the determination of the people in all parts to oppose them with their lives and fortunes. That they have been led to believe by their agents and partisans among us, that we are a divided people; that the latter are opposed to their own government; and that the show of a small force would occasion a revolt, I have no doubt; and how far these men, (grown desperate), will further attempt to deceive, and may succeed in keeping up the deception, is problematical. Without that, the folly of the Directory in such an attempt would, I conceive, be more conspicuous, if possible, than their wickedness.

"Having with candour made this disclosure of the state of my mind, it remains only for me to add, that to those who know me best it is best known, that should imperious circumstances induce me to exchange once more the smooth paths of retirement for the thorny ways of public life, at a period too when repose is more congenial to nature, that it would be productive of sensations which can be more easily conceived than expressed."

To the Secretary of War, writing on the same subject, Washington replied—"It cannot be necessary for me to premise to you, or to others who know my sentiments, that to quit the tranquility of retirement, and enter the boundless field of responsibility, would be productive of sensations which a better pen than I possess would find it difficult to describe. Nevertheless, the principle by which my conduct has been actuated through life, would not suffer me, in any great emergency, to withhold my services I could render when required by my country; especially in a case where its dearest rights are assailed by lawless ambition and intoxicated power, in contempt of every principle of justice, and in violation of solemn compact, and of laws which govern all civilized nations; and this too with the obvious intent to sow thick the seeds of disunion, for the purpose of subjugating our government, and destroying our independence and happiness.

"Under circumstance like these, accompanied by an actual invasion of our territory, it would be difficult for me at any time to remain an idle spectator, under the plea of age or retirement. With sorrow, it is true, I should quit the shades of my peaceful abode, and the ease and happiness I now enjoy, to encounter anew the turmoils of war, to which possibly my strength and powers might be found incompetent. These, however, should not be stumbling blocks in my own way."

"President Adams nominated Washington with the rank of Lieutenant-General, to the chief command of all the armies raised and to be raised in the United States. His commission was sent to him by Mr. McHenry, the Secretary of War, who was directed to repair to Mount Vernon, and to confer on the arrangements of the new army with its commander in chief. To the letter which President Adams sent with the commission by the Secretary of War, Washington, in two days, replied as follows:

"I had the honour, on the evening of the 11th instant, to receive from the hand of the Secretary of War, your favour of the 7th, announcing that you had, with the advice and consent of the Senate, appointed me 'Lieutenant-General and Commander in Chief of the armies raised, or to be raised, for the service of the United States.'

"I cannot express how greatly affected I am at this new proof of public confidence, and the highly flattering manner in which you have been pleased to make the communication. At the same time I must not conceal from you my earnest wish, that the choice had fallen upon a man less declined in years, and better qualified to encounter the usual vicissitudes of war.

"You know, sir, what calculation I had made relative to the probable course of events, on my retiring from office, and the determination I had consoled myself with, of closing the remnant of my days in my present peaceful abode. You will therefore be at no loss to conceive and appreciate the sensations I must have experienced, to bring my mind to any conclusion that would pledge me, at so late a period of late, to leave scenes I sincerely love, to enter upon the boundless field of public action, incessant trouble, and high responsibility.

"It was not possible for me to remain ignorant of, or indifferent to, recent transactions. The conduct of the Directory of France, towards our country; their insidious hostility to its government; their various practices to withdraw the affections of the people from it; the evident tendency of their acts, and those of their agents, to countenance and invigorate opposition; their disregard of solemn treaties and the laws of nations; their war upon our defenceless commerce; their treatment of our ministers of peace; and their demands, amounting to tribute, could not fail to excite in me corresponding sentiments with those my countrymen have so generally expressed in their affectionate addresses to you. Believe me, sir, no one can more cordially approve of the wise and prudent measures of your administration. They ought to inspire universal confidence, and will, no doubt, combined with the state of things, cal, from Congress such laws and means as will enable you to meet the full force and extent of the crisis.

"Satisfied, therefore, that you have sincerely wished and endeavoured to avert war, and exhausted, to the last drop, the cup of reconciliation, we can with pure hearts appeal to Heaven for the justice of our Cause; and may confidently trust the final result to that kind Providence who has heretofore, and so often, signally favoured the people of these United States.

"Thinking in this manner, and feeling how incumbent it is upon every person of every description, to contribute at all times to his country's welfare, and especially in a moment like the present, when every thing we hold dear and sacred is so seriously threatened; I have finally determined to accept the commission of Commander in Chief of the armies of the United States; with the reserve only, that I shall not be called into the field until the army is in a situation to require my presence, or it becomes indispensable by the urgency of circumstances.

"In making this reservation, I beg it to be understood, that I do not mean to withhold any assistance to arrange and organize the army, which you may think I can afford. I take the liberty also to mention, that I must decline having my acceptance considered as drawing after it any immediate charge upon the public; or that I can receive any emoluments annexed to the appointment, before entering a situation to incur expense."

The time of Washington after the receipt of this appointment, was divided between agricultural pursuits and the cares and attentions which were imposed by his new office. The organization of the army was, in a great measure, left to him. Much of his time was employed in making a proper selection of officers, and arranging the whole army in the best possible manner to meet the invaders at the water's edge; for he contemplated a system of continued attack, and frequently observed, "that the enemy must never be permitted to gain foothold on the shores of the United States."

Yet he always thought that an actual invasion of the country was very improbable. He believed that the hostile measures of France took their rise from an expectation that these measures would produce a revolution of power in the United States, favourable to the views of the French republic; and that when the spirit of the Americans was roused, the French would give up the contest. Events soon proved that these opinions were well founded; for no sooner had the United States armed, than they were treated with respect, and an indirect communication was made that France would accommodate all matters in dispute on reasonable terms.

Mr. Adams embraced these overtures, and made a second appointment of three envoys, extraordinary to the French republic. These, on repairing to France, found the Directory overthrown, and the government in the hands of Bonaparte, who had taken no part in the disputes which had brought the two countries to the verge of war. With him negociations were commenced, and soon terminated in a pacific settlement of all differences. The joy to which this event gave birth was great; but in it General Washington did not partake, for before accounts arrived of this amicable adjustment, he ceased to be numbered among the living.

On the 13th of December, 1799, his hair and neck were sprinkled with a light rain, while he was out of doors attending to some improvements on his estate. In the following night he was seized with an inflammatory affection of the windpipe, attended with pain, and a difficult deglutition, which was soon succeeded by fever, and a laborious respiration. He was bled in the night, but would not permit his family physician to be sent before day. About 11 o'clock A.M. Dr. Craik arrived, and rightly judging that the case was serious, recommended that two consulting physicians should be sent for. The united powers of all three were in vain; in about twenty-four hours from the time he was in his usual health, he expired without a struggle, and in the perfect use of his reason.

In every stage of his disorder he believed that he should die, and he was so much under this impression, that he submitted to the prescriptions of his physicians more from a sense of duty than expectation of relief. After he had given them a trial, he expressed a wish that he might be permitted to die without further interruption. Towards the close of his illness, he undressed himself and went to bed, to die there. To his friend and physician, Dr. Craik, he said, "I am dying, and have been dying for a long time, but I am not afraid to die." The equanimity which attended him through life, did not forsake him in death. He was the same in that moment as in all the past, magnanimous and firm; confiding in the mercy and resigned to the will of Heaven. He submitted to the inevitable stroke with the dignity of a man, the calmness of a philosopher, the resignation and confidence of a christian.

On the 18th, his body, attended by military honours and the offices of religion, was deposited in the family vault on his estate.

When intelligence reached Congress of the death of Washington, they instantly adjourned until the next day, when John Marshall, then a member of the House of Representatives, and since Chief Justice of the United States, and biographer of Washington, addressed the speaker in the following words:

"The melancholy event which was yesterday announced with doubt, has been rendered but too certain. Our Washington is no more. The hero, the patriot, and the sage of America; the man on whom in times of danger every eye was turned, and all hopes were placed, lives now only in his own great actions, and in the hearts of an affectionate and afflicted people.

"If, sir, it had even not been usual openly to testify respect for the memory of those whom Heaven has selected as its instruments for dispensing good to man, yet such has been the uncommon worth, and such the extraordinary incidents which have marked the life of him whose loss we all deplore, that the whole American nation, impelled by the same feelings, would call with one voice for a public manifestation of that sorrow, which is so deep and so universal.

"More than any other individual, and as to much as to one individual was possible, has he contributed to found this our wide spreading empire, and to give to the western world, independence and freedom.

"Having effected the great object for which he was placed as the head of our armies, we have seen him convert the sword into the ploughshare, and sink the soldier into the citizen.

Washington retires

"When the debility of our federal system had become manifest, and the bonds which connected this vast continent were dissolving, we have seen him the chief of those patriots who formed for us a constitution, which, by preserving the union, will, I trust, substantiate and perpetuate those blessings which our revolution had promised to bestow.

"In obedience to the general voice of his country, calling him to preside over a great people, we have seen him once more quit the retirement he loved, and in a season more stormy and tempestuous than war itself, with calm and wise determination pursue the true interests of the nation, and contribute more than any other could contribute, to the establishment of that system of policy which will, I trust, yet preserve our peace, our honour, and our independence.

"Having been twice been chosen the chief magistrate of a free people, we have seen him, at a time when his re-election with universal suffrage could not be doubted, afford to the world a rare instance of moderation, by withdrawing from his station to the peaceful walks of private life.

"However the public confidence may change, and the public affections fluctuate with respect to others, with respect to him they have, in war and in peace, in public and in private life, been as steady as his own firm mind, and as constant as his own exalted virtues.

"Let us then, Mr. Speaker, pay the last tribute of respect and affection to our departed friend. Let the grand council of the nation display those sentiments which the nation feels. For this purpose I hold in my hand some resolutions which I take the liberty of offering to the house.

"Resolved, That this House will wait on the President, in condolence of this mournful event.

"Resolved, That the Speaker's chair be shrouded with black, and that the members and officers of the house wear black during the session.

"Resolved, That a committee, in conjunction with one from the Senate, be appointed to consider on the most suitable manner of paying honour to the memory of the man, first in war, first in peace, and first in the hearts of his fellow-citizens."

The Senate of the United States, on this melancholy occasion, addressed to the President in these words:

"The Senate of the United States respectfully take leave, sir, to express to you their deep regret for the loss their country sustains in the death of Gen. George Washington.

"This event, so distressing to all our fellow-citizens, must be peculiarly heavy to you, who have long been associated with him in deeds of patriotism. Permit us, sir, to mingle our tears with yours. On this occasion it is manly to weep. To lose such a man, at such a crisis, is no common calamity to the world. Our country mourns a father. The Almighty Disposer of human events, has taken from us our greatest benefactor and ornament. It becomes us to submit with reverence to him 'who maketh darkness his pavillion.'

"With patriotic pride we review the life of our Washington, and compare him with those of other countries who have been pre-eminent in fame. Ancient and modern times are diminished before him. Greatness and guilt have too often been allied; but his fame is whiter than it is brilliant. The destroyers of nations stood abashed at the majesty of his virtues. It reproved the intemperance of their ambition, and darkened the splendour of victory. The scene is closed, and we are no longer anxious lest misfortune should sully his glory; he has travelled on to the end of his journey, and carried with him an increasing weight of honour; he has deposited it safely where misfortune cannot tarnish it—where malice cannot blast it. Favoured of Heaven, he departed without exhibiting the weakness of humanity. Magnanimous in death, the darkness of the grave could not obscure his brightness.

"Such was the man whom we deplore. Thanks to God, his glory is consummated. Washington yet lives on earth in his spotless example—his spirit is in Heaven.

"Let his countrymen consecrate the memory of the heroic general, the patriotic statesman, and the virtuous sage. Let them teach their children never to forget, that the fruits of his labours and his example are their inheritance."

14

Reflections on Washington's life and death

To this address, the President returned the following answer:

"I receive with the most respectful and affectionate sentiments, in this impressive address, the obliging expressions of your regret for the loss our country has sustained in the death of her most esteemed, beloved, and admired citizen.

"In the multitude of my thoughts and recollections on this melancholy event, you will permit me to say, that I have seen him in the days of adversity, in some of the scenes of his deepest distress, and most trying perplexities. I have also attended him in his highest elevation, and most prosperous felicity, with uniform admiration of his wisdom. moderation, and constancy.

"Among all our original associates in that memorable league of this continent, in 1774, which first expressed the sovereign will of a free nation in America, he was the only one remaining in the general government. Although with a constitution more enfeebled than his, at an age when he thought it necessary to prepare for retirement, I feel myself alone bereaved of my last brother, yet I derive a strong consolation from the unanimous disposition which appears in all ages and classes, to mingle their sorrows with mine, on the common calamity to the world.

"The life of our Washington cannot suffer by a comparison with those of other countries, who have been celebrated and exalted by fame. The attributes and decorations of royalty, could only have served to eclipse the majesty of those virtues which made him, from being a modest citizen, a more resplendent luminary. Misfortune, had he lived, could hereafter have sullied his glory only with those superficial minds who, believing that character and actions are marked by success alone, rarely deserve to enjoy it. Malice could never blast his honour, and envy made him a singular exception to her universal rule. For himself, he had lived long enough to life and to glory; for his fellow-citizens, if their prayers could have been answered, he would have been immortal; for me, his departure is at a most unfortunate moment. Trusting, however, in the wise and righteous dominion of Providence over the passions of man and the results of their actions, as well as over their lives, nothing remains for me but humble resignation.

"His example is now complete; and it will teach wisdom and virtue to magistrates, citizens, and men, not only in the present age, but in future generations, as long as our history shall be read. If a Trajan found a Pliny, a Marcus Aurelius can never want biographers, eulogists, or historians."

The committee of both houses appointed to devise the mode by which the nation should express its grief, reported the following resolutions, which were unanimously adopted.

"Resolved, by the Senate and House of Representatives of the United States of America, in Congress assembled, That a marble monument be erected by the United States at the capitol of the city of Washington, and that the family of General Washington be requested to permit his body to be deposited under it, and that the monument be so designed as to commemorate the great events of his military and political life.

"And be it further resolved, that there be a funeral procession from Congress-Hall, to the German Lutheran church, in memory of Gen. George Washington, on Thursday the 26th instant, and that an oration be prepared at the request of Congress, to be delivered before both houses that day; and that the President of the Senate, and Speaker of the House of Representatives, be desired to request one of the members of Congress to prepare and deliver the same.

"And be it further resolved, that it be recommended to the people of the United States, to wear crape on their left arm, as mourning, for thirty days.

"And be it further resolved, that the President of the United States be requested to direct a copy of these resolutions to be transmitted to Mrs. Washington, assuring her of the profound respect Congress will ever bear for her person and character, of their condolence on the late affecting dispensation of Providence; and entreating her assent to the interment of the remains of Gen. Washington in the manner expressed in the first resolution."

To the letter of President Adams, which transmitted to Mrs. Washington the resolution of Congress that she should be requested to permit the remains of Gen. Washington to be deposited under a marble monument, to be erected in the city of Washington, she replied very much in the style and manner of her departed husband, and in the following words—

"Taught by the great example which I have so long had before me, never to oppose my private wishes to the public will, I must consent to the request made by Congress, which you have had the goodness to transmit to me; and in doing this, I need not, I cannot say, what a sacrifice of individual feeling I make to a sense of public duty."

The honours paid to Washington at the seat of government, were but a small part of the whole. Throughout the United States, the citizens generally expressed, in a variety of ways, bot their grief and their gratitude. Their heart-felt distress resembled the agony of a large and affectionate family, when a bereaved wife and orphan children mingle their tears for the loss of a husband and father.

The people, from the impulse of their own minds, before they knew of similar intentions of their fellow-citizens, or of the resolution of Congress for a general mourning, assembled and passed resolutions, expressive of their high sense of the great worth of the deceased, and their grateful recollection of his important services. Orations were delivered, sermons preached, and elegies written, on the melancholy occasion. The best talents of the nation were employed, both in prose and verse. In writing and speaking, to express the national grief, and to celebrate the deeds of the departed father of the country.

In addition to the public honours which, in the preceding pages, have been mentioned as conferred on Washington in his life time, there were others of a private nature which flowed from the hearts of the people, and which neither wealth nor power could command. An infinity of children were called by his name. This was often done by people in the humble walks of life, who had never seen nor expected to see him; and who could have no expectations of favour from him. Villages, towns, cities, districts, counties, seminaries of learning, and other public institutions, were called Washington, in such numbers, and in such a variety of places, that the name no longer answered the end of distinction, unless some local or appropriating circumstances were added to the common appellation. Adventurous mariners, who discovered islands or countries in unexplored regions, availing themselves of the privilege of discoverers, planed the name of the American Chief in the remotest corners of the globe.

The person of George Washington was uncommonly tall. Mountain air, abundant exercise in the open country, the wholesome toils of the chase, and the delightful scenes of rural life, expanded his limbs to an unusual, but graceful and well-proportioned size. His exterior suggested to every beholder the idea of strength, united with manly gracefulness. His form was noble, and his port majestic. No man could approach him but with respect. His frame was robust, his constitution vigorous, and he was capable of enduring great fatigue. His passions were naturally strong; with them was his first contest, and over them his first victory. Before he undertook to command others, he had thoroughly learned to command himself.

The powers of his mind were more solid than brilliant. Judgment was his forte. To vivacity, wit, and the sallies of a lively imagination, he made no pretensions. His faculties resembled those of Aristotle, Bacon, Locke, and Newton; but were very unlike those of Voltaire. Possessed of a large proportion of common sense, directed by a sound practical judgment, he was better fitted for the exalted stations to which he was called, than many others, who, to a greater brilliancy of parts, frequently add the eccentricities of genius.

Truth and utility were his objects. He steadily pursued, and generally attained them. With this view he thought much, and closely examined every subject on which he was to decide, in all its relations. Neither passion, party, spirit, pride, prejudice, ambition, nor interest, influenced his deliberations. In making up his mind on great occasions, many of which occurred in which the fate of the army or nation seemed involved, he sought for information from all quarters, revolved the subject by night and by day and examined it in every point of view. [In a letter to Gen. Knox, written after the termination of the revolutionary war, Washington observed—"Strange as it may seem, it is nevertheless true, that it was not until lately I could get the better of my usual custom of ruminating as soon as I awoke in the morning, on the business of the ensuing day; and of my surprise at finding, after revolving many things in my mind, that I was no longer a public man, or had any thing to do with public transactions."] Guided by these lights, and influenced by an honest and good heart, he was imperceptibly led to decisions which were wise and judicious.

Perhaps no man ever lived who was so often called upon to form a judgment in cases of real difficulty, and who so often formed a right one. Engaged in the busy scenes of life, he knew human nature, and the most proper methods of accomplishing proposed objects. Of a thousand propositions he knew to distinguish the best, and to select among a thousand the individual most fitted for his purpose.

As a military man, he possessed personal courage, and a firmness which neither danger nor difficulties could shake. His perseverance overcame every obstacle; his moderation conciliated all opposition; his genius supplied every resource. He knew how to conquer by delay, and deserved true praise by despising unmerited censure. Inferior to his

Reflections on Washington's life and death

adversary in the numbers, the equipment, and discipline of his troops, no great advantage was ever obtained over him, and no opportunity to strike an important blow was ever neglected. In the most ardent moments of the contest, his prudent firmness proved the salvation of his country.

The whole range of history does not present a character on which we can dwell with such entire unmixed admiration. His qualities were so happily blended, and so nicely harmonized, that the result was a great and perfect whole.

The integrity of Washington was incorruptible. His principles were free from the contamination of selfish and unworthy passions. His real and avowed motives were the same. His ends were always upright, and his means pure. He was a statesman without guile, and his professions, both to his fellow-citizens and to foreign nations, were always sincere. No circumstances ever induced him to use duplicity. He was an example of the distinction which exists between wisdom and cunning; and his manly, open conduct, was an illustration of the soundness of the maxim—"that honesty is the best policy."

The learning of Washington was of a particular kind. He overstepped the tedious forms of the schools, and by the force of a correct taste and sound judgment, seized on the great ends of learning, without the assistance of those means which have been contrived to prepare less active minds for public business. By a careful study of the English language; by reading good models of fine writing, and above all, by the aid of a vigorous mind; he made himself master of a pure, elegant, and classical style. His composition was all nerve; full of correct and manly ideas, which were expressed in precise and forcible language. His answer to the innumerable addresses which on all public occasions poured in upon him, were promptly made, handsomely expressed, and always contained something appropriate. His letters to Congress; his addresses to that body on the acceptance and resignation of his commission; his general orders as Commander in Chief; his messages and speeches as President; and above all, his two farewell addresses to the people of the United States, will remain lasting monuments of the goodness of his heart, of the wisdom of his head, and of the eloquence of his pen.

The powers of his mind were in some respects peculiar. He was a great, practical, self-taught genius; with a head to devise, and a hand to execute, projects of the first magnitude and greatest utility.

There are few men of any kind, and still fewer the world calls great, who have not some of their virtues eclipsed by corresponding vices. But this was not the case of Gen. Washington. He had religion without austerity, dignity without pride, modesty without diffidence, courage without rashness, politeness without affectation, affability without familiarity. His private character, as well as his public one, will bear the strictest scrutiny. He was punctual in all his engagements; upright and honest in his dealings; temperate in his enjoyments; liberal and hospitable to an eminent degree; a lover of order; systematical and methodical in all his arrangements. He was the friend of morality and religion; steadily attended on public worship; encouraged and strengthened the hands of the clergy. In all his public acts, he made the most respectful mention of Providence; and, in a word, carried the spirit of piety with him both in his private life and public administration.

Washington had to form soldiers of freemen, many of whom had extravagant ideas of their personal rights. He had often to mediate between a starving army, and a high-spirited yeomanry. So great were the necessities of the soldiers under his immediate command, that he was obliged to send out detachments to seize on the property of the farmers at the point of the bayonet. The language of the soldier was—"Give me clothing, give me food, or I cannot fight, I cannot live." The language of the farmer was—"Protect my property." In this choice of difficulties, Gen. Washington not only kept his army together, but conducted with so much prudence as to command the approbation both of the army and of the citizens. He was also dependent for much of his support on the concurrence of thirteen distinct, unconnected legislatures. Animosities prevailed between his southern and northern troops, and there were strong jealousies between the states from which they respectively came. To harmonize these clashing interests, to make uniform arrangements from such discordant sources and materials, required no common share of address. Yet so great was the effect of the modest unassuming manners of Gen. Washington, that he retained the affection of all his troops, and of all the states.

He also possessed equanimity in an eminent degree. One even tenour marked the greatness of his mind, in all the variety of scenes through which he passed. In the most trying situations he never despaired, nor was he ever depressed. He was the same when retreating through Jersey from before a victorious enemy with the remains of his broken army, as when marching in triumph into Yorktown, over its demolished fortifications. The honours and applause he received from his grateful countrymen, would have made almost any other man giddy; but on him they had no mischievous effect. He exacted none of those attentions; but when forced upon him, he received them as favours, with the politeness of a well-bred man. He was great in deserving them, but much greater in not being elated with them.

The patriotism of Washington was of the most ardent kind, and without alloy. He was very different from those noisy patriots, who, with love of country in their mouths, and hell in their hearts, lay their schemes for aggrandizing themselves at every hazard; but he was one of those who love their country in sincerity, and who hold themselves bound to consecrate all their talents to its service. Numerous were the difficulties with which he had to contend—Great were the dangers he had to encounter—Various were the toils and services in which he had to share; but to all difficulties and dangers he rose superior. To all toils and services he cheerfully submitted for his country's good.

In principle, Washington was a federal-republican, and a republican-federalist. Liberty and law, the rights of man, and the control of government were equally dear to him; and in his opinion, equally necessary to political happiness. He was devoted to that system of equal political rights on which the constitution of his country was founded; but thought that real liberty could only be maintained by preserving the authority of the laws, and giving tone and energy to government. He conceived there was an immense difference between a balanced republic and a tumultuous democracy, or a faction calling themselves the people; and a still greater between a patriot and a demagogue. He highly respected the deliberate sentiments of the people, but their sudden ebullitions made no impression on his well balanced mind. Trusting for support to the sober second thoughts of the nation, he had the magnanimity to pursue its real interests, in opposition to prevailing prejudices. He placed a proper value on popular favour, but could never stoop to gain it by sacrifice of duty, by artifice, or flattery. In critical times he committed his well earned popularity to hazard, and steadily pursued the line of conduct which was dictated by a sense of duty, against an opposing popular torrent.

While war raged in Europe, the hostile nations would scarce endure a neutral. America was in great danger of being drawn by force or intrigue into the vortex. Strong parties in the United States rendered the danger more imminent; and it required a temperate, but inflexible government, to prevent the evil. In this trying state of things, Washington was not be moved from the true interests of his country. His object was America, and her interest was to remain in peace.

Faction at home, and intrigue and menace from abroad, endeavoured to shake him, but in vain; he remained firm and immoveable in the storm that surrounded him. Foreign intrigue was defeated, and foreign insolence was repressed by his address and vigour; while domestic faction, dashing against him, broke itself to pieces. He met the injustice both of Britain and France by negociation, rather than by war, but maintained towards both, that firm attitude which was proper for the magistrate of a free state. He commanded their respect, and preserved the tranquillity of his country. In his public character, he knew no nation but as friends in peace, as enemies in war. Towards one he forgot ancient animosities, when the recollection of them opposed the interests of his country. Towards another, he renounced a fantastic gratitude, when it was claimed only to involve his nation in war.

With Washington it was an invariable maxim of policy, to secure his country against the injustice of foreign nations, by being in a position to command their respect, and punish their aggressions. The defence of our commerce, the fortification of the ports, and the organization of a military force, were objects to which he paid particular attention. To the gradual formation of an American army, he was friendly; and also to military institutions, which are calculated to qualify the youth of the country for its defence. War he deprecated as a great evil, inferior only to the loss of honour and character; but thought it was most easily avoided by being ready for it, while, by the practice of universal justice, none could have any real ground of complaint.

In foreign transactions, his usual policy was to cultivate peace with all the world; to observe treaties with pure and absolute faith; to check every deviation from the line of impartiality; to explain what was misapprehended, and to correct what was injurious; and then to insist upon justice being done to the nation over which he presided. In controversies with foreign nations, it was his favourite maxim so to conduct towards them, "as to put them in the wrong."

In his transactions with the Indian tribes, Washington was guided by justice, humanity, and benevolence. His authority and influence were exerted to restrain the licentious white contiguous settlers, from injuring their red neighbors. To supply their wants, and prevent impositions, he strongly urged the erection of trading houses in their settlements, from which they were furnished by government with goods at first cost. The unprincipled were restrained from preying on their ignorance, by excluding all but licensed persons, with good characters, from trading with them. All this was done to pave the way for their civilization.

When Washington commenced his civil administration, the United States were without any efficient government. After they had adopted one of their choice, and placed him at its head, he determined that it should be respected. By his firmness order soon took place. There was one exception. The western counties of Pennsylvania rose in arms to resist the law for raising a revenue, by an excise on domestic distilled ardent spirits.

Reflections on Washington's life and death

On this occasion, the fixed resolution of Washington was, that whatever expense it might cost, whatever inconvenience it might occasion, the people must be taught obedience, and the authority of the laws re-established. To secure this object, peculiarly important in the infancy of the new government, he ordered out, and put himself at the head, of an ample force, calculated to render resistance desperate, and thereby to save the lives of his fellow-citizens.

In consequence of such decided measures, the insurgents dispersed, and peace and order were restored without bloodshed. The necessity of subordination was impressed on the citizens, and the firmness of Washington's personal character was communicated to the government.

Having accomplished every object for which he re-entered public life, he gave for the second time, the rare example of voluntarily descending from the first station in the Universe—the head of a free people, placed there by their unanimous suffrage. To the pride of resigning his soul was superior. To its labours he submitted only for his country.

Rulers of the world! Learn from Washington wherein true glory consists—Restrain your ambition—Consider your power as an obligation to do good—Let the world have peace, and prepare for yourselves, the enjoyment of that ecstatic pleasure which will result from devoting all your energies to the advancement of human happiness.

Citizens of the United States! While with grateful hearts you recollect the virtues of your Washington, carry your thoughts one step farther. On a review of his life, and of all the circumstances of the times in which he lived, you must be convinced, that a kind of Providence in its beneficence raised him, and endowed him with extraordinary virtues, to be to you an instrument of great good. None but such a man could have carried you successfully through the revolutionary times which tried men's souls, and ended in the establishment of your independence. None but such a man could have braced up your government after it had become so contemptible, from the imbecility of the federal system. None but such a man could have saved your country from being plunged into war, either with the greatest naval power in Europe, or with that which is most formidable by land, in consequence of your animosity against the one, and your partiality in favour of the other.

Youths of the United States! Learn from Washington what may be done by an industrious improvement of your talents, and the cultivation of your moral powers. Without any extraordinary advantages from birth, fortune, patronage, or even of education, he, by virtue and industry, attained the highest seat in the temple of fame. You cannot all be commanders of armies, or chief magistrates; but you may all resemble him in the virtues of private and domestic life, in which he excelled, and in which he most delighted. Equally industrious with his plough as his sword, he esteemed idleness and inutility as the greatest disgrace of man, whose powers attain perfection only by constant and vigorous action.

Washington, in private life, was as amiable as virtuous; and as great as he appeared sublime, on the public theatre of the world. He lived in the discharge of all the civil, social, and domestic offices of life. He was temperate in his desires, and faithful to his duties. For more than forty years of happy wedded love, his high example strengthened the tone of public manners. He had more real enjoyment in the bosom of his family, than in the pride of military command, or in the pomp of sovereign power.

On the whole, his life affords the brightest model for imitation, not only to warriors and statesmen, but to private citizens; for his character was a constellation of all the talents and virtues which dignify or adorn human nature.

> "He was a man, take him for all in all,
> "We ne'er shall look upon his like again."—Shakespeare

CPSIA information can be obtained at www.ICGtesting.com
Printed in the USA
LVOW060246130312

272802LV00001B/171/P